FOOL'S HILL

FOOL'S HILL

A Kid's Life
in an Oregon Coastal Town

by John Quick

Oregon State University Press
Corvallis, Oregon

The paper in this book meets the guidelines for permanence and dura-
bility of the Committee on Production Guidelines for Book Longevity
of the Council on Library Resources and the minimum requirements of
the American National Standard for Permanence of Paper for Printed
Library Materials Z39.48-1984.

Library of Congress Cataloging-in-Publication Data

Quick, John, 1931-
    Fool's hill : childhood days and dreams in an Oregon coastal town /
by John Quick.
    p. cm.
    ISBN 0-87071-385-X
    1. Quick, John, 1931- —Childhood and youth. 2. Port Orford (Or.)—
Biography. I. Title.
    F884.P7Q53 1995
979.5'21-dc20
[B]   95-15839
                                               CIP

Text of Typewritten Letter

October 25, 1937
Port Orford Elementary School
Port Orford, Oregon

Dear Mr. & Mrs. A. L. Quick

    I have spoken to Mrs. Grant about your son, John, and his inability to participate fully in her first grade class. In addition to problems with reading and writing, he interrupts the class and does not seem to differentiate between the truth and make-believe.

    I must endorse Mrs. Grant's recommendation that John be held back for at least one year. In the intervening months it may be possible for him to become a more responsible, attentive, and truthful young person.

Yours very truly

Mr. Arnold D. Watko
Principal

Preface

I decided to look back at my early life for clues that I might have missed when I was little—clues that were either: (1) too complicated for me and most other people to understand; or (2) so obvious that everybody in the world saw them except me.

This has been hard for me to unravel because of the fact that I come from a long line of chameleons, loudmouths, and the intellectual equivalent of Three-Card Monte dealers. There has been little substance among my family members for several generations. They are a bunch of fibbers, opportunists, and sex-coaxers who knew how to dress up convincingly and that was about it. I've known lots of dumb blue-collar workers who were proud to say: "I never made a dime wearing a suit." My old man was dumber than any of them, but it occurred to him very early in his life that people who wore suits had money and so he'd better by God wear suits.

That last sentence, by the way, pretty accurately summarizes my outlook, i.e., the appearance of something is equivalent to, or is just about the same as, the thing itself. Verisimilitude. My father was handsome and my mother was beautiful and what they did was just one big game of Dress Up and make-believe. They often worked very hard, don't get me wrong, and generally meant well. But they didn't have a clue.

In telling my childhood stories, and sometimes diverging to tell the stories of my ancestors, I have sometimes fallen into the waters of murky days when life and dreams were much the same; when truth and make-believe were blurred and indistinguishable.

I promise to tell you the truth, at least the truth as I remember it. (All historians work this way. They can't tell you what they've forgotten and they're bound to put a spin on what they remember. Historians become infallible only when the only other people who *really* remembered are dead.) But, honest to God, if a guy jumped off the cliff at Fort Point and fell 285 feet to his death, I'll report it faithfully. If somebody is decapitated in a wreck, I'll reveal it. And if I think something is particularly lucky or charmed, I'll divulge the information.

This book will tell you the year nylon got invented, and what "Coming On Like Gang Busters!" really means. You'll learn about human bones, Parker's Solid Gold Meteor, double homers, "Turd" McCormick's wagon, chicken massacres, the Prum-Yay Automobile, falling out of trees, lost or hidden or damaged submarines, sexual matters, trying to hang onto friends that are about to kick the bucket, and a cannibal pot. This is not something you should miss. It could be a very lucky book for you.

Table of Contents

Sentimental Crap

" Dad," my mom said to my Grandfather Frank. "You have to write down some of the stories about this town."

"No," he said. He didn't look up from his soup.

"But you have to," she insisted.

"No, I don't have to," he said.

"Nobody else will do it," she said.

"Louie Knapp will do it," he said. "Louie Knapp is *doing* it."

"No," my mom argued. "He's only talking about it. He tells stories in the barber shop and that's it. If you're not a man in need of a haircut or that awful "Lou" person, you won't hear the stories. Not at all. The stories evaporate into thin air."

"Or thin hair," my Grandfather joked.

Mom ignored him.

"Somebody's got to write them down," she said. "And you're the only writer in town. You're the only writer in the county."

We were having lunch in the breakfast nook. They don't build breakfast nooks any more. Ours was an indentation in the kitchen with a table and two benches on either side. It had a window and it seated four. However, there were five people sitting in ours during the conversation I'm trying to tell you about. My sister sat on a stool at the end of the table. My father sat next to the window and read *The Oregonian*. It was a morning paper published in Portland that got down to our town on the bus and was distributed about lunch time. My father wasn't in the conversation because it was my mom talking to her father and he knew better than to get involved in anything that might look like taking sides. My sister was in a big rush to go someplace with her friend, Louita.

We were having baloney sandwiches and alphabet vegetable soup. I was the only family member who required mayonnaise, mustard, and ketchup on a baloney sandwich.

(I like writing the word "baloney" because it was a popular word used by adults in mixed company when I was a kid—mixed meaning a combination of people, some of whom said bullshit most of the time and the others who said baloney all the time *instead* of bullshit. There is no place in my life for the spelling "bologna," this being pretentious, I believe.)

I was interested in the conversation because it involved my grandfather, who was a sort of hero to me about that time because he was giving me marching instructions with his Spanish-American War rifle.

"I've heard," Frank said, "that June Knapp has talked to the typing teacher at the high school and that the teacher will come out on Saturday mornings and write down some of Louie's stories."

"That story is about two years old," my mother said energetically. "It didn't happen. It isn't happening. It won't happen."

Grandpa Frank was stirring his soup very slowly and systematically as if looking for something.

"There are a variety of reasons for my not trying to write the history of this town," he said. "I'm too busy. And I'm too tired."

"That's not a variety of reasons. That's only two reasons. And they're no good. You're not too busy."

"I'm Justice of the Peace," he said.

"Phooey," my mother said. "This town is peaceful and everybody knows about justice. All you have to do is marry people now and then."

"And sentence transgressors," he added.

He was looking for something in his soup and I suddenly realized what he was doing. He was fishing individual letters out and arranging them on his bread plate. I was across the table from him and couldn't see exactly what he was up to.

"And as for being too tired," my mother continued, "you're not too tired to walk for miles on the beach and build bonfires that are almost as big as houses."

"An exaggeration," he said.

"I must remind you that more than one ship over the horizon has radioed the Coast Guard to ask if the whole town was on fire!"

"A fluke," my grandfather said.

This was before America got involved in World War Two and we got the coastal blackouts that made bonfires illegal.

"Here's what I think," my mother said, ever prepared to tell people what she thought. "I think it's your duty to sit down and write some of the stories about the history and the people and the funny incidents that you remember."

"My duty," Frank repeated.

"Yes, your duty."

It was about this time that Alida, my sister, hurriedly washed her dishes and put them in the dish drainer and rushed upstairs to her room for something. Alida was eight years older than me. (Is eight years older, and has maintained this lead over the years. It meant more then, of course, because I was in a lower grade and she was way up in high school. Little boys and budding young women didn't have a lot to talk about. Except maybe to fight over the Sunday funnies.)

Frank was silent. He was putting words together from the letters he'd carefully spooned out of his soup.

The word "duty" had a galvanizing effect on my father, it appeared, because he excused himself and left, saying that he had to re-open the store.

He took the paper with him.

I ate the last bite of my baloney sandwich.

"It is your duty because you are the grandson of the founder of the town."

"I'm not the only grandson of the founder of this town," he reminded her.

"To be sure," my mother said. "But you're the only one who lives here. Except Leslie of course. And you're the only one who gives a damn."

Everybody was using the word "damn" a lot that year since it had been legitimized by Clark Gable in *Gone With the Wind*. They tried to work in the whole sentence and start it with "Frankly, my dear, . . ."

Except Crawford Smith, the fisherman with the deepest, loudest, and foulest mouth in the county, who was much more apt to say: "Frankly, my dear, I don't give a shit!" Or worse. I heard him yell this up to the crane operator on the dock—that guy who lifted boats completely out of the water and put them on boat trailers on the dock.

"Why must I be the one who eternally gives a damn?" Frank asked.

"It's part of your job," my mother said. "It's part of your responsibility."

"No Bless O Bleege," Alida said, who had just come back downstairs and who then sped across the room and exited through the kitchen door.

I didn't know what she was talking about. I thought it was something she made up to mean "good-bye" or "so long."

"Here's what I think," Frank said, looking up from his typographical efforts. "I believe that I don't know as much history as you think I do. I don't believe that I remember as many anecdotes as you think I do."

I remember that I didn't know what an anecdote was, but presumed it to be a relative of some kind.

"And, " Frank continued, "I think that just about anything I wrote would be a lot of hooey."

"But you know a lot of beautiful stories, Dad!"

"Junk," he said. "Trash. Sentimental crap."

My mother was silent. She was trying to think of another approach.

It would never have occurred to her to be direct. Direct and simple. I think that if she'd said "Please write some stories as a favor to me," he would have cheerfully done so. But what can you expect from a family in which no member was ever known to have uttered aloud (or even whispered) the words, "'I love you"?

"Besides," Frank continued, "who cares? Who will ever care in the future? The words would only be words. Nobody would understand them. They would simply be my observations and reflections about unimportant matters."

"It would be important," my mother said but, as she said it, she knew that she couldn't prove it. Not in a million years. In my family you had to have proof. Absolute proof. Otherwise your ideas would never fly. They wouldn't get off the ground for even a second. And she couldn't even begin to prove her point about importance. Her conviction slackened. She would have to think of an angle. She was about angles. Side roads. Getting things done indirectly. She was a beautiful woman and I don't believe beautiful women ever learn how to be direct. Maybe they don't need to. They get what they want with hints. Artifice.

"Here you go," my grandfather announced. "Take a look at this!"

He pushed his bread plate around so that we could see it.

He had spelled NON COMPOS MENTIS with the alphabets from his soup.

It seemed an extraordinary accomplishment to me at the time.

"What's that?" I asked.

"It is a Latin term," Frank said. "A legal expression. It means *not of sound mind.*"

"Like nuts?" I asked.

"Like nuts." he said. "Exactly."

He scooted his large frame off the breakfast-nook bench.

"I've got to be going," he said. "I've got to go for my walk."

This reminded him to look out a kitchen window to the distant mountain down the coast.

"Cap on Humbug!" he said. (It may have been my grandfather's grandfather who first noticed that if there was a patch of cloud on the very top of Humbug Mountain then showers could be expected within an hour or so.)

"Don't stop thinking about the idea of writing some stories," my mother urged, needing to have the last word. I knew that she would spend a lot of time reflecting about an angle during the coming days.

"Do you want to come for a walk with me, Ellen?" he asked my mother.

"No, thanks," she said. "I've got to get back to the store."

"How about you, Johnny?" he asked me.

"I'll go part way with you," I explained. "Maybe to the tunnel through Battle Rock. I told Barnie Winslow I'd meet him around 1:30. We're going to play Commandos or something."

"Okay," he said. "Let's go."

"I've got to do my dishes," I said. Having had it hammered into me to both say so and do so.

"I'll take care of them," my mother said, uncharacteristically. I could tell she was thinking. "You two go ahead."

Which we did.

It was a Saturday. I'm sure of that. We didn't have lunch together on week days. And grandfather insisted on a big dinner at his house late on Sundays. So it was a Saturday, to be sure.

The two words, sentimental crap, have always stuck with me. They were a deterrent, for a long time, to writing things down. Especially stories that were not epics. Stories that were little. Unimportant in the great cosmic scheme of things. But, as somebody explained, "They're the only stories you have—so write 'em down. What is sentimental crap to some people may have some meaning to others. And the fact that you care ought to mean something."

And I do. I don't have Rhett Butler's attitude at the end of *Gone With the Wind*. I do give a damn, or at least sort of a damn. Enough of one.

Point Number Two: I should do it while I'm still COMPOS MENTIS.

Finally, I'd better do it while there's time. My grandfather was finally persuaded to start writing his stories, his recollections, but—of course—you can imagine what happened. He ran out of time.

He capitalized on the intention, nevertheless. At the instant he decided to try, he announced to everybody that he was "working on a history." And that was before the first word was written. Nobody ever found any notes or pieces of manuscript from this history so, presumably, it was all bullshit. It was like the character in *The Mikado* who keeps saying: "It's as good as done!" After a while, he mesmerizes himself into believing that "If it's as good as done, then there is no need to actually *do* it!"

Mind Movies

Among my thoughts are a great many vivid recollections.

The ones in picture form I call "Mind Movies."

I'll try to project one or two for you so that you can get a better view of Port Orford in the old days. Not the *old* old days, mind you, but the 1930s.

First I want you to get yourself up in the air about a thousand feet. Can you try that? Gain altitude and slowly fly like a seagull or an eagle. We'll start a few miles north of town. Look down and see a rugged coastline with rocky cliffs rising two hundred feet above a broad beach. Big waves from the blue-green ocean crash onto this beach. Okay?

The cliffs stop and there is a lake. Freshwater Garrison Lake and the ocean are separated by a wide beach named Agate Beach. The lake goes along for a mile or so. But keep flying south. Maintain altitude.

More big cliffs stick out. They curve around to a natural harbor where there is a dock. A road has been cut into the bluff and it runs down to the harbor. There are a lot of small fishing boats down there and a cannery where they pack crabs and salmon. The blue pickup is Crawford Smith's.

Up above, on the bluff, is the town. It has 500 people in it; 750 in Boom Times.

You can land now.

We'll walk around.

Over here is a tiny movie theater that's open only on the weekends; and next to it is Doyle's store with notions (whatever "notions" are), a soda fountain, and some tables to sit at while you have a sandwich. Doyle's is the Greyhound bus stop for the two buses a day that go through—one northbound up from San Francisco and Crescent City, one southbound from Portland.

There are five gas stations in town.

At the time I first started remembering, there were three food stores in town: two grocery stores and a meat market. My dad owned the meat market. Then he expanded. Not once, but twice.

There was Charley Long's general store. There was Lou Monescu's garage. Lou was not a guy; Lou was short for "Louise." She loved to hug and kiss me. Or maybe she hugged and kissed me because she loved me. Whatever it was, it wasn't the town norm. Not for me, at least.

There was a shoe store run by a guy named Herzog and the drug store and dental office operated by the Pughs.

There were three taverns: Red's, the Pastime, and T.J.'s Bar & Grill.

A woman named Studley owned a dress shop. A few yards away was Bennett's old grocery store.

There were four places to eat, including Margie's Cafe and Doyle's if you only wanted a sandwich. Then there were the Orford, and T.J. Collins' Bar & Grill.

Margie, by the way, had a coffee-cup fortune-telling system that she half believed in. She said that if the bubbles in your coffee floated toward you it meant money to come. If they moved away from you, money would be lost.

There was a hotel at the south end of town, a grade school on the north end, and a high school and a brand-new gymnasium on a hill in the middle.

The Knapp Hotel was white and was two or three stories tall, I can't remember which—I've had a little processing problem with this particular Mind Movie. Maybe only two. It was famous locally because Jack London had stayed there and written a couple of chapters of one of his novels. Most people couldn't remember which one. No one could recall exactly when Jack had stayed there. So historical detail was lacking altogether. It was torn down and for years afterward any resident who happened to be at that end of town talking to tourists would make a broad gesture toward where the hotel had once been and say:

"Jack London stayed over there. Maybe in 1910. Can't say for sure. Wrote part of a book there, we think. But we're not sure which one."

And the resident would point to nothing. The foundations of the hotel were, by this time, covered by grass and there were no chimneys standing, so the tourists would look where the person indicated and see nothing but the side of a hill. They were too polite to ask questions such as:

"Jack London stayed in what? A tent? A hole in the ground? I don't see anything over there. Are you sure you know what you're talking about? Are you *drunk* by any chance?"

Or they would treat the speaker like he was the town loony (one of which we had briefly, by the way, but she moved south, T.J. said, to Brookings).

In the middle of town was the house where my friend Pat Masterson lived, a place about fifty feet off the main street. It was a two-and-a-half-story yellow house with Victorian wooden curlicue decorations under the eaves. It had an attic. Pat lived in that house with his school-teacher mother and one of the interesting things he did as a kid was to climb out the attic window and leap into the air with a bed-sheet parachute that he rigged up with twine. This parachute did not deploy as planned and he nearly broke his leg. Or maybe he did break his leg, I'm not clear on this point. I'll have to check.

Dr. Baird was the doctor. Doc Pugh was the dentist. Doc Pugh's wife was the town's pharmacist.

Lou Monescu owned a roller-skating rink that was open only when Lou felt like roller-skating. So this wasn't anything to try to schedule well in advance and like say to your friends, Barney Winslow or Perk McCormick:

"Let's plan on going roller-skating next Saturday, what do you say?"

About the only thing a person could do was walk up the hill toward the reservoir (on the east side of town where the densely forested hills started) and see if the door was unlocked at the skating rink.

It was closed one time and I remember standing around with Perk trying to figure out where the word "rink" came from. As you know, you can drive yourself nuts by repeating a word so many times that it becomes senseless and stupid. Kids *and* adults, it turns out. Rink. Rink. RINK. You try it.

That reminds me of something else. There was a low gray building next to the road that led down the cliff to the dock. There was ice-making machinery in the building and on one of the rare times I remember the compressor running it made the noise of:

"Topeka, Topeka, Topeka, Topeka."

There was an exhaust pipe running from the side of the building and, at the sound of the *pee* in "Topeka," a perfect little smoke ring would blow out of the pipe.

Now the sound I'm talking about was not merely *sort of like* the sound of "Topeka." It was exactly the sound. A person from Kansas would have recognized it from four blocks away and dropped his pop bottle on the ground in amazement.

Say this word eight or nine times out loud as fast as you can (in your lowest voice) and you'll know what that compressor motor sounded like the last time I heard it which was probably when I was a really little kid in 1936.

(This word has magic power. When repeated several times, it can actually save your life. If you've had a few drinks and can't say "Topeka" four times in a row real fast, you probably shouldn't drive your truck or ask somebody to move in with you.)

Charley Long's hardware store was a high-ceilinged, poorly lighted museum of things, many forgotten on the higher shelves. It was cluttered with everything in the world. Many of the so-called "new" items looked used, merely because they'd been sitting around so long. My father bought me a pair of shoes there one time. They were so ancient and dried out that when I took the first few steps, the sole on one of them broke right across with a big snap. Charley laughed and gave my dad his money back.

Charley couldn't throw anything out. He sold hardware and clothing and shoes, ammunition and a few canned goods, fishing tackle, ropes and padlocks, toys, candy in jars, handles for axes and hammers, corsets, rifles, soap, and nails. A little of everything. Charley had a mechanical grabber on the end of a stick that he used for getting things off high shelves. He grabbed Lou's butt with it one time and she threatened to jam it down his throat if he ever did it again. He didn't.

Gene White was the constable. He drove a green pickup that rattled so loud that you could hear him coming from a mile away. It also backfired to beat the band. He had a loud voice and didn't carry a gun. He would yell at people and they would behave. Older people who got yelled at (like over at the Pastime when they got rowdy) would become silent and get red in the face. Children, such as myself, would turn white and run home to our rooms and hide out for an hour or so.

The mention of Gene's name suggested justice. His presence meant law and order. His other trick was to be every place. He appeared to be everywhere at once. Obviously, if he stayed at home or followed some semblance of a schedule he would have appeared to be normal or mortal. As it was, he was so omnipresent it was eerie. If you even thought something bad, he was right there, ready to nail you before you even started. There wasn't a day in my life that I didn't see him at one end of the town or the other, down at the dock, on the highway through town, shouting at a boat on the lake or some guy at the lumber mill, or merely driving energetically and noisily from one place to another in the green pickup—neither too fast nor too slow but always with a look on his face that a calamity was imminent.

Gene spoke with a strange dialect. When I got shouted at, I was sometimes not sure of what I was doing wrong or what I should be doing right. With the notable exception, of course, of when I was in the second grade and persuaded Gene's first-grade daughter, Annette, to take off all her clothes in an abandoned chicken coop behind their house. Gene showed up (naturally—what could I have been thinking of?) and bellowed: "FOR SHAME! *FOR SHAME!*"

Talk about terrified. I can still hear his voice.

I stayed in my room for the rest of the day waiting for my parents to beat the literal shit out of me but, by some miracle, Gene must not have told them. His words still echo in my head, decades later. Any other kid might have been turned queer on the spot, but I was trying to work another deal with Annette within two or three weeks, talking her out of her clothes.

Rain

Here's a brief story about rain, which can fall for days at a time during the winter on the coast of Oregon. Since lunch time was a busy period for the store, I'd usually eat alone in the kitchen with the comic page from the daily *Oregonian* propped up in front of me on an aluminum newspaper holder. One particular day I came home, took off my boots, my "slicker" and sou'wester rain hat and was prepared to eat. I stopped. My sister and mother were both sitting on the couch in the living room. My sister was crying. My mother was sniffling.

"What's the matter?" I asked them. It scares kids a lot to see older people upset.

"Oh, . . . it's the rain," lamented my sister.

"The rain," echoed my mother.

I looked out the window at the sky and verified to myself, yes, it was indeed drizzling a little bit. So? So what?

"What about it?" I asked.

"It never stops," one or the other of them said. Maybe both.

"It keeps raining and raining and raining," my sister sobbed.

"It's been raining for weeks," said my mother. "We haven't seen the sun."

Funny thing, but when you grow up in a place you don't have unreasonable expectations about it. If it rains, it rains. Obviously. If it keeps raining, it keeps raining. So what if it drizzles a couple of weeks at a time? One shouldn't expect to see the sun very much.

I couldn't understand it. It wasn't reasonable. There was a logic about Port Orford and rain was a part of this logic.

My sister tried to talk about it.

"I grew up in California," she snuffled. "It never rains like this in California."

She is my half-sister, you see. She spent some time in California growing up. I never did.

Grandfather Frank, by the way, was known to hate Californians. He didn't want them buying property in Oregon. As far as I knew, he didn't hate my sister (who was his full granddaughter and he regarded my mother being married to that California guy long enough to have Alida was a fluke, not unlike the two-headed lamb fetus that some dumb-cluck farmer sought to display in my father's grocery store, where people came expecting to buy food, for crying out loud, not to see a monster!).

They continued to whine and lament about the gray weather. I calmly ate my soup and read the comics.

Bottle Caps & Life in General

Picture this. It will set the tone for how my mind worked as a kid. Four people and a small dog are going someplace. Specifically, it was my great-uncle John Tichenor, my mother, my father, me, and Skippy. We were walking to Doyle's one summer afternoon so that Uncle John could get a chocolate soda, his favorite. Uncle John said (from completely out of nowhere):

"You don't pay attention."

He referred, of course, to me.

"That is correct," my mother agreed.

"Yes," my father said.

Uncle John continued.

"Take right this minute for example."

Everybody looked at me.

I looked back at everybody else.

"What?" I asked. "What do you mean, right this minute?"

"Instead of paying attention," Uncle John said, "You are picking up pop-bottle caps."

This was true. I had spotted a purple grape-soda pop-bottle cap, picked it up, and was evaluating it. The cap was in brand-new condition and hadn't been run over by a bus or anything and I was trying to decide whether to start a pop-bottle cap collection. I was constantly starting, but never continuing, collections. A "collection," as my grandfather had frequently observed, by definition ought to consist of more than one or two items. He only sulked when I pointed out that maybe somebody (like me) could find the Only One of a particular thing and collect It and be able to truthfully say:

"Here it is. See? The one thing of its kind; the only one in the world; and I've got it. It is a Collection of One. I collected it. I am the collector. I deem this collection to be complete. It is quite wonderful."

He would have none of it. I was lazy. It was a grownup perception that laziness and lack of attention were linked attributes. What they were voicing, of course, was their observation that kids didn't pay attention to what they, the adults, wanted the kid to pay attention to.

I put the purple pop-bottle cap in my pocket and remember very clearly saying to Uncle John:

"I found the pop-bottle cap, didn't I? That's Paying Attention, isn't it?"

There was a pause. I knew what was coming next.

"Don't be a smart-aleck," my mother said.

I paid attention in roughly the same way that Skippy paid attention. Did I mention that Skippy always appeared to be smiling? Well, she did. She was always agreeable and happy and seemed to be smiling. Ear to ear. Strangers, California tourists who came to town and stopped at the store, would notice this and comment about it.

"This little brown dog is smiling!" they would say. "Look."

As if we had never noticed.

When we went on walks around town Skippy always stayed nearby, but zigged and zagged and paused and examined things, smelled them and tasted them, picked them up, or stared at them in a kind of dog wonder.

On that particular purple grape-soda pop-bottle day with Uncle John I consciously reaffirmed my belief that it was okay to have a Skippylike approach to life and look at everything that came along. This was much more satisfying than having to bore straight down the line like my Uncle John and be grumpy as the dickens because things didn't fall into place. As if Life was supposed to make Sense. Or as if Life could be made to shape up by yelling at it loud enough.

Let me tell you something that will be hard for you to believe but which is gospel truth. Uncle John would wear his Portland, Oregon, police captain's uniform to Port Orford on vacation. The whole outfit! Would you dream of doing something like this? I doubt it. Swaggering around talking tough and trying to be in charge whether he had any jurisdiction or not. He and his brother, my grandfather Frank, would occasionally stroll around town smoking cigars and acting like big shots.

Just to be funny one time, he slapped handcuffs on my sister, Alida. He was constantly doing things like this "just for laughs" as he said, "just for the fun of it." Well, my sister didn't think it was very funny at all. As a matter of fact, the experience really frightened and humiliated her but she never told anybody until just lately.

"You've got to learn how to take a joke," John intoned.

He was good, he thought, at giving advice to young people. Advice they would remember.

But don't get me wrong.

I thought life was pretty good.

Somebody told me one time that he had been very unhappy as a kid and then he asked me if I had been unhappy, too. I said no, that I had not been unhappy. It is true that I had my dark moments. There were times when I was frightened and hid in my room with the blinds drawn. Like the time when the constable bellowed at me for trying to monkey around with his daughter. I was sometimes angry with my parents because I couldn't understand them and they couldn't understand me. But I don't think it was their fault. They were simple people who wanted things to go their way. They were busy and frustrated and didn't have a clue about raising a kid. One of the qualities they talked about all the time was obedience. I didn't possess this quality. I was constantly having orders repeated to me. I was forever being yelled at to do my chores. In my parents' view, disobedience was right next door to laziness. And being lazy about not doing what you were told led very smoothly and seamlessly into lying—as in:

"I know that you told me twice to bring in the kindling, but a seagull flew into my face and I sprained my ankle."

They wanted obedience, industry, cheerfulness, loyalty, honesty, speed, rote memorization, punctuality, and trustworthiness.

They had the wrong kid.

The things they disliked in me, such as being a smart-ass and a storyteller, were the very qualities that endeared me to my adult friends. They didn't think I was a snot at all. They saw me as a novice Baron Münchhausen and loved my mixed-up helter-skelter stories.

The only point to this was that if I was ever unhappy, it didn't last very long. I can't remember many problems that weren't erased with one night's sleep. I would greet each morning with fresh enthusiasm and a renewed interest in defeating that day or at least steering it around to my direction and set of purposes.

I was never bored and seldom sulked. It was a great life. That is to say, it was a life you could make for yourself if you put your mind to it. It had possibilities.

Very First Memories

Port Orford recollections begin with a word soup of impressions and memories. Everything runs together in a moosh of early recollections about my first weeks and months in Portland. Diesel smell and WAH—I can't sleep. The beautiful park lights incandescent glowing in the trees and Grandma's lavender smell, and the green and white sailboat that I was told I didn't remember when in fact I knew that Uncle Floyd gave it to me and sailed it in a circular pond in the park, and just as clearly I recall the bluish glare from a streetlight that fell through the slats in my crib and made weird shadows. Cigarette smoke curled gray up beams of sun. There was a step down into the living room and, if you looked up, there were clouds and sky above painted on the domed ceiling.

And more than once I rolled down a flight of carpeted stairs without getting killed. Another time I was hiding very quietly under the dining room table and my grandmother turned the place upside-down looking for me and decided that I had been kidnapped like the Lindbergh baby! There was a musical top that hummed and hummed until it finally tipped over.

If my sister dressed me as a girl and put lipstick on me I don't remember, but she says she did and that all the neighbors thought I was her baby sister and was really, really cute. Whatever took place, it didn't make me weird. That was in Portland.

There was an apartment house with a tiny balcony where we stayed until my dad packed a pickup and away we went.

South. Down the coast.

To Port Orford.

> *"Evening red and morning gray*
> *Will speed a traveler on his way.*
> *Evening gray and morning red*
> *Will bring the rain upon his head."*

It rained all the way down.

I remember that my sister and I thought it was fun to ride in the back of the pickup under a tarp.

I was, when we arrived, a small bright-white boy with blond hair and dark blue eyes, perhaps three feet tall. A sand hopper popped up from some kelp one day and landed on my head. My mother and her family were very fair and wouldn't tan. My father was dark and had a "farmer's" tan, that is to say he was tanned on his arms and face but nowhere else. It was soon discovered that I could tan very darkly at which time a small non-pigmented symbol of a tiny king in his crown would appear just above my right knee. This effect was pleasing and magical to me, a little snowy blaze. And my hair would bleach even further to a platinum white. I added weight slowly and was thin. But I was wiry and could run like nobody's business or, as Crawford Smith said, "like greased lightning."

I very early learned to cope with my name and the big joke from adults who would always ask: "Are you really Quick?" My earliest response was a demonstration in which I would run away as fast as I could, going, in Margie's words, "like a bat out of hell," or, better yet, in T.J.'s opinion, "like a streak of shit."

Genealogy

I got interested in my own family history in a sort of backwards fashion. I didn't care a bit about genealogy, partly because I was so enthusiastically encouraged to do so by my grandfather, Frank Tichenor. The more people wanted me to do something, the more apt I was to resist. Frank was crazy to trace his origins back to important people. He lied, in fact, about the Tichenor line. I didn't know that at the time. As I said, it didn't matter to me.

The thing that finally got me interested, through the back door you might say, was something that happened during a visit by my Aunt Katherine and Uncle Bill Belcher. I couldn't believe that I had the good fortune to know anybody with such a funny last name. Since Katherine was my father's sister, it was possible (and sometimes necessary) for Katherine to sign her name Katherine Quick Belcher. To a six- or seven-year old, this is too hysterical to be believed. All you have to do is imagine a quick belcher, one who could do a loud burp after a single swallow of root beer.

The Belchers were freeloaders of a highly developed sort. They loved to take vacations. They were the cheapest people in North America and they had visiting down to a science. Bill met a lot of people in the matchbook-collecting world, since he was one of Washington State's leading matchbook collectors. So he would visit fellow matchbook collectors where, one would suppose, they would drink beer and compare their latest matchbooks. Bill and Katherine also had lots of relatives all over the country. Like us. So they would visit family and friends according to a very careful schedule. They would arrive at night, spend two days and three nights, and then leave early in the morning of the third day having sweet-talked you into loading their picnic basket full of fruit, sandwiches, cold chicken, and anything else you had lying around. This way they wouldn't have to pay for food on their way to their next target which had, of course, to be within a few hours' driving distance from your house.

On one such visit, Katherine surprised everybody by talking about something new. Usually she told old stories about growing up on the farm in Kansas, matchbooks, or the Cootie Auxiliary of which she was a member because Bill was a World War One veteran who had served in France and had earned the title of Cootie (apparently the hard way). She had, she reported, been admitted to the D.A.R., the Daughters of the

American Revolution. She mentioned this in my dad's store in front of several other people. My mother and father registered no interest because they didn't know what Katherine was talking about. The Mayor's wife, however, exclaimed that she, too, was a D.A.R. member and warmly shook Katherine's hand. This immediately captured my mother's attention since she was a society wannabe and had never had her hand earnestly shaken by the Mayor's wife or anybody else of importance.

My mother got on the phone and called Grandpa Frank Tichenor. He came over and inspected the genealogical record that Katherine had put together to prove her eligibility to become a member. That's when I saw the copy of the letter in which she had written Katherine Quick Belcher, which made me choke and which I still think is wildly funny.

Something about the Quick family genealogy irritated my grandfather. It upset him. I could tell. I had seen him act the same way when the driftwood on the beach was too wet for him to start a bonfire. He wasn't getting his way, I could see it in his eyes. I figured that anything that bothered him that much was probably worth looking into.

I eavesdropped on a conversation that he had with my mother in the kitchen.

My mother wanted to know that if her marriage to Al qualified her to become a D.A.R. member.

The answer was no, it did not.

Well then, she said:

"There must have been plenty of Tichenors in the Revolutionary War because you have said many times we can trace our ancestors all the way back to Plymouth Rock and therefore surely we can find somebody in our family that served in the Revolutionary War."

His answer was a short "Humph."

My mother glared at him.

"Well, *do* something, Dad," she insisted.

Frank did something all right. He left in a hurry.

I knew in a flash that I should pay attention to history, if only to agitate Frank Tichenor and become at least a part-time player in the genealogy game.

I can summarize things very, very briefly, partly from the very records Katherine Quick Belcher presented to the D.A.R.

The Quicks

My father's name was Al. You already know this.

My father's father was Francis Quick. He was born in Normal, Indiana, in 1874. But Francis wasn't called Francis, he was called Frank. He was a farmer. He had two daughters (Katherine and Alta) and three sons (my dad, Al, my Uncle Floyd, and my Uncle Harvey). Since neither of my uncles had any children that meant that I was the last Quick in that particular line.

I visited Grandpa Frank Quick in the summer of 1942 and he was a grim man if there ever was one, a humorless, hard-working farmer. My mother and I went for a visit on our way to the East Coast and I were assigned a "few little chores" which I will describe later.

Grandpa Frank Quick took time off from work one day to show me the piles of stones in the corners of distant fields where my father had killed snakes 30 years earlier.

Al was scared to death of snakes and wasn't content to merely kill them. That didn't get them dead enough, I guess. So he would continue to toss stones on the dead snakes (from a safe distance) so they could not come back to life and attack him in the night or from behind when he was doing chores. There are ways to describe little stone monuments like these, but I don't know the right words. To me they were tiny Kansas pyramids. They were not in memory of fallen kings or heroes, but to the revolting slithery enemies of Al. Grandpa Frank Quick died in 1946.

Frank's father was Cornelius Quick (1850-1935). Cornelius' father was John S. Quick who was born in 1813 and died God knows when. John's father was named James. They were farmers and therefore characters not usually found in stories of voyages and legends. But they were not, on the other hand, bullshit artists.

Here is the first part of a little picture.

James Quick (Great-Great-Great-Grandfather)
John Quick (Great-Great-Grandfather)
Cornelius Quick (Great-Grandfather)
Francis Quick (Grandfather)
Al Quick (Father)

The Tichenors

Captain William Tichenor was my great-great-grandfather. He was born in 1813. He died in 1887.

Jacob Tichenor was my great-grandfather (1843-1889).

Frank Tichenor was my grandfather (1872-1943).

Frank Tichenor had four daughters. The oldest one was my mother, Ellen. I talked to my Grandfather Frank Tichenor a lot as I grew up and, therefore, knew him.

Here is the composite picture.

James Quick (G.-G.-G.-Grandfather)	James Tichenor (G.-G.-G.-Grandfather)
John Quick (G.-G.-Grandfather)	William Tichenor (G.-G.-Grandfather)
Cornelius Quick (G.-Grandfather)	Jacob Tichenor (G.-Grandfather)
Frank Quick (Grandfather)	Frank Tichenor (Grandfather)
Al Quick (Father)	Ellen Tichenor Quick (Mother)
	John Quick (Me)

It is interesting, don't you think (TV newscasters would call it "ironic") that I have two great-great-great-grandfathers named James and two grandfathers named Frank?

I will tell you quite a bit about my grandfather (Frank) and a little about his grandfather (William). About Jacob, my grandfather's father, I can tell you everything I know in about two paragraphs.

He was born on March 2, 1843, near Newark, New Jersey. At the age of nine he came to Port Orford in 1852 via the Isthmus of Panama with his mother and two sisters. Jacob and his sisters were the first white children on the southern coast of the Oregon Territory (Port Orford). He studied in the East and returned to Oregon in 1861 when he finished his formal education at Willamette University. During the Civil War he enlisted in Company K, First Oregon Volunteers, and was discharged as a corporal. He taught school for several years, and was the first teacher in Port Orford.

In 1885 he moved his family to Roseburg, Oregon, where he took over the operation of a thousand-acre ranch. He then moved to Salem, Oregon, where he served as secretary of the Prohibition Party campaign. All told, he had 11 children. Shortly thereafter he went into business with Hendricks and Saubert, real estate agents, a position he held until his untimely death at 46.

He died March 20, 1889, and was buried in the Tichenor Cemetery.

John's mother Ellen and her mother Mary, taken about 1910 in Spokane

Some of Jacob's children died in infancy, and others lived in Port Orford or Portland and were known to me. I talked to them and drank soda pop with them. The following were my Grandfather Frank Tichenor's brothers and sisters (my great-uncles and my great-aunt). We will start with Anna Ellen. She married Tom Guerin and they managed the Guerin Hotel in Myrtle Point, Oregon. Both were charming and interesting and treated children as actual persons (briefly trapped in tiny bodies as if by a witch's spell) instead of morons. Grover Cleveland Tichenor was for many years a deputy sheriff of Multnomah County, Oregon. Carol was a streetcar motorman in Portland for 46 years. John, my namesake, was the police captain I told you about from Portland. Leslie was deaf (and so was his wife). They both lived in Port Orford and "talked" to you with pencils on little scraps of paper. Since I couldn't read their writing, I treated them as wraiths and always took the long way around their yard. For sheer interest of another sort, my vote has to go to Herbert Elmer Tichenor who changed his last name from Tichenor to Irish, moved to Cedar Rapids, Iowa and, I quote from the genealogical history, "was for many years an advance agent for a traveling carnival."

In general, all the Tichenors I ever met liked to wear uniforms or otherwise get dressed up. They loved titles. They simply couldn't wait to be invited to talk somewhere. They were crazy about initials after their names.

(P.S. My mother never got into the D.A.R. The Tichenors couldn't pull it off.)

Captain William Tichenor

I don't remember people reading me bedtime stories, except for my grandfather, Frank, that is, and I wonder if it wasn't nap-time stories back at a time when I was still supposed to take naps; or maybe he told me stories a couple of times when I was sick and was lying on a couch in the living room looking out the window instead of resting and getting well. The point is, it was my grandfather who told me stories about *his* grandfather, Captain William Tichenor, the man who founded the town of Port Orford. It was really something to be lying on the couch looking out at the identical same town that your grandfather's grandfather founded. My grandfather thought it was a very big deal and it always sounded as if he was a little envious of his grandfather and Captain William's relative fame. My grandfather had a small share of publicity and fame, but it wasn't on the scale of William.

Here is basically the story of William, my great-great-grandfather on my mother's side. He was born in Newark in 1813 and first went to sea when he was 12 years old, sailing to Europe as a cabin boy. He went back to school, studied navigation, and decided to become a sailor. At fifteen he crossed again to Europe, returned to America, and worked as a mate on a steamer in the New Orleans trade. When he was 20 he married Elizabeth Brinkerhoff in New York City, changed his mind about seafaring and moved first to Indiana and then to Edgar County, Illinois. He took an active part in public affairs, studied law, and passed the Illinois Bar. He was well acquainted with Abraham Lincoln. In 1845 he recruited troops for the Mexican War, taking part in raising two companies. Early in 1849, at the age of 36, he decided to head for the California gold fields.

He started overland with a wagon train but soon became dissatisfied with their slow rate of progress. (I don't know, but this may be the origin of the famous "Hurry up! Let's get going!" trait of all the Tichenors I've ever known.)

He spoke to the Captain of the wagon train about his concern that they should increase their speed while the cattle were in good condition and there was plenty of feed.

The Captain disagreed. William then decided to leave the train and said if anyone wished to accompany him they were welcome. Since many were eager to join him, he was appointed Captain of the new company and the two trains separated. Tichenor pushed ahead as fast as he could.

He reached "Hangtown" (now Placerville, California) on the 3rd of August, 1849, without loss of life. The original, slower, party met with many mishaps as feed became scarce and many of the cattle had to be left behind. Many members of the party died on the plains and others perished while crossing the Sierras.

Having reached the gold fields, William determined to be a prospector and, working alone, set out with one horse and one mule to do some looking around. After a good deal of hardship he struck rich diggings in a place which still bears the name of "Tichenor's Gulch."

By October 1849, he had panned 70 pounds of gold, journeyed to San Francisco, and purchased the schooner *Jacob M. Ryerson*. After a voyage to the Gulf of California he returned in March of 1850 with a load of fresh green turtles which he sold at a handsome profit. He was then made Captain of a fast brig called the *Emily Farnham* and made trips to the Columbia River in Oregon. In a couple of brushes with corrupt officials he offered to: (a) blow the brains of a customs collector "masthead high"; and (b) throw overboard the Doctor of the Port of San Francisco.

My grandfather embellished the last two stories in considerable detail.

My Folks

My father was born at the end of the last century. He was not very well educated (he only went to the eighth grade, he said) but became one of those typically American rags-to-riches stories. Through hard work, luck, and long hours, he created a substantial amount of success for himself. By the end of the twenties, he had a big house, a store building, two big cars, and a motor launch on the Columbia River (with its own big boat house). That was in Portland, Oregon. Then the Great Depression came along like a big fog bank and everything disappeared.

He vowed to start over, only this time with a new rule: "If it can't be purchased for cash, it can't be purchased." He was determined to own everything outright. He no longer trusted banks and he disapproved of time payments. Success, for him, would always be measured in what he truly owned.

So that was it: the New Rule said that you didn't really own anything if you were still making payments on it. Everything had to be cash.

We left Portland on that rainy day when I was three or four and moved to Port Orford. Since my mother's ancestors had founded the town, there were memories there for her. It's where she grew up. For my father, it was just another place to start over. He opened a meat market scarcely bigger than a one-car garage. It had a butcher block and cases to put meat in. He expanded at the back, and then to one side. He added canned goods. He built another store. It had fresh fruits and vegetables. Then he built a third store—twice the size of the second.

He was determined to be successful and believed that sheer effort was substitutable for brilliance. The store was open six days a week and most evenings. If people wanted something on Sunday they would walk up the hill and rap on the door, and my father would open the store and sell them what they needed. He became a prisoner of the store. But a willing prisoner. It meant that he didn't have to take vacations. We never did. Imagine that.

My father was a handsome sturdy fellow about 5' 9". He had black bushy eyebrows and always wore a dress hat when he went outside. He thought it was gentlemanly to wear a hat and to tip it (actually bend the brim of it slightly) when a woman approached. He always had time to talk to his customers and was regarded as friendly and generous.

In the first of his stores, the tiny one, he was always very busy with his two brand new, double-sized meat cases. When he wasn't cutting meat, he would rearrange the trays on a regular basis.

"Why do you do that?" I asked him one day.

"For two reasons," he said. "First of all, I don't want the cheap cuts in one case and the high-priced cuts in another. I mix them up so that people are sure to see what they didn't think they wanted when they came in. Second, if I keep the same cheap stuff in the same place all the time, people with almost no money might be embarrassed to stand in front of it. So I always put the hamburger, the cheapest stuff, next to the filets, the most expensive stuff. Do you understand?"

I said that I guessed so.

As I said, our family never went on a vacation. To anywhere. To do anything. Sunday picnics were the closest thing to it. And these were rarely any farther than the State Park at Humbug Mountain, seven miles away.

My dad did not play baseball with me because he was too busy or didn't feel like it and because he probably didn't know how to play baseball. He did not do anything with me, now that you mention it, any outdoor stuff unless you count shooting off fireworks on the 4th. But Doc Pugh didn't do anything with Richard, either. Mr. McCormick worked so hard at the mill that he'd come home and collapse on the couch and demand total quiet from anybody within shouting distance. When I grew up, fathers worked and kids dorked around. My old man talked to me, don't get me wrong, but it was always about practical matters relating to business and industry—how to buy produce and how to dicker with the regional Heinz salesman, a guy named Oscar. He talked about how to feed and when to kill chickens. He described how cars were greased and the way different cuts of meat came from a cow. It was very boring.

Let me tell you something about the way he dressed.

All he owned were suits. Cheap suits that came with two pairs of pants. One pair he'd designate as the Store pants, or the behind-the-counter pants. The other was for Show. Only he seldom went anywhere for Show so, naturally, when the Store pants got ripped or slashed, the Show pants were promoted to Store and the damaged Store pants were demoted to "Work," such as carpentry and really dirty plumbing repair.

That was my old man. Always in a white shirt with a tie. Store suit pants. A white apron. Dress shoes. The dress shoes followed roughly the same course as the suit pants. When finally ruined with animal blood and other spilled substances, they took their place in the Work category. So my father's appearance never seemed to me to change because the costumes certainly didn't. He looked about the same when he crawled underneath the house to fix a pipe as he did behind the counter of the store. On his daily trip to the bank, he put on a hat and a suit coat that more or less matched the pants. All of his suits were about the same shade of dark brownish-gray. That's where he went in his complete outfit, his uniform. To the bank.

– 25–

We didn't go to church. Had we gone to church, he would have worn a suit. He wore it when we went up the coast to the movie theater in Bandon or, infrequently, to the chop suey joint in Coquille. Chinese restaurants in those days were universally called "chop suey joints." Sunday mornings my father would read *The Oregonian* in a pair of intermediate suit pants, in other words, Show pants rapidly on the way to becoming Store pants suit pants, a white shirt without a tie, and dress shoes.

I recall three or four picnics we went on in my entire early life and that was the costume he wore to each. It was also his walk-on-the-beach outfit. In the only photograph of me and my father, with just the two of us, we are standing on a rock that an ocean wave has just washed around. On this tiny island in the Pacific we are both barefoot. Both of our pantlegs are rolled up to just below our knees. I am in kid's clothes. My father is in a suit, a tie, a hat, and a topcoat. The picture is in the front of this book.

I knew from the movies, newsreels, and magazines of the Thirties that men wore other kinds of outfits. They appeared to have hunting clothes, golf clothes, evening clothes (especially two or three kinds of tuxedos), special clothes to wear to the race track, tennis clothes, and swimming suits. So it made apparent sense at the time that since we didn't have hunting, golf, night clubs, race tracks, or tennis courts (and that my father never went swimming), then he would not logically own any of those clothes.

There were a limited number of uniforms to be seen in our town and all of them were instantly distinguishable: fisherman outfits, lumber mill overalls, farmer costumes, and merchant get-ups like my old man's.

Doc Pugh wore a tie over at the dental office/drug store. Charley Long wore a tie at the general store. Don Doyle wore a tie over at his bus-stop cafe and notions store. Officials like the guy at the Post Office wore ties and so did the principal and the mayor. The constable did, too.

The Greyhound Bus drivers had uniforms and so did the State Patrol guys with their big hats. Uniforms with ties.

My grandfather, Frank, wore dark blue three-piece suits with a gold chain that went between two pockets of the vest and from which hung a hideous yellow tooth.

But I'm wandering off. Let's get to my mother.

My mother worked in the store as well. And she shared the same dream as my father. To work themselves back up and achieve the relative luxury they'd once enjoyed. With ambition comes a certain restlessness and an almost total lack of patience. What they needed was a sturdy little son with ambition. A tough little volunteer who wanted desperately to be down at the store unloading vegetables off trucks and stacking canned goods on shelves. Somebody with a desire to learn the business and understand about profit margins. They yearned for a kid who was first in his class and won spelling bees, and who received little metal statues for reading the most books. A kid they could smile about when they saw him coming a block away.

Instead they got me.

"Lazy" was a word that I heard about once a day.

"Stupid" was used perhaps weekly.

"Fool" was a word used by my mother in one of her frequent bitchy moods when nothing was working out or was ever apt to work out. The word was generally accompanied by a slap on the face. Since she was right-handed, I'd get it on the left cheek.

"Scrawny" could have been another one. It fit.

My father was stocky, had a square, resolute jaw, and black hair. I was the opposite: skinny, blond, and frail-looking.

I worked at the store only reluctantly; under duress. I had household chores but had to be forced and threatened to do them. I dabbled around at school after I concluded that the teachers didn't seem to know anything or care about anything.

I hung around with my grandfather Frank because he would set aside time for me. Frank had an all-consuming interest. It was in himself and his own happiness. But that was not discernible to me. All I knew—about all I had learned by the time I was seven or eight—was that people who were truly *interested* in something were also interesting.

Therefore I was attracted to such people, most of whom were older than me. The Frenchman was a fisherman who liked to fish. His life was about boats and being on the water. Smitty liked to swear real loud. Herzog could calmly convince me not to use expressions like "Jew him down," and to say Brazil nuts instead of nigger-tocs. Mr. Fletcher's life was in his workshop silently making bows and arrows. The town's young minister and his wife were clearly maniacal about God and Jesus, and I cared less about their stories than about their zeal. I loved their intensity. I was not selective in my appreciation of anybody's true interest. I liked a couple of drunks, "Zoom" Zumquist being one of them, because their lives were earnestly centered on drinking and joking. They had as much fun drinking as the Frenchman had fishing or the minister and his wife had religioning. Gene White loved being the constable. Why else would he be driving around town alone in his pickup, smiling like that? One day I overheard the guy who ran the lighthouse up the coast say to my father about his work:

"I have the greatest goddamn job in the world!"

It reminded me of an *Oregonian* one-page ad for Ringling Brothers. But my folks? Especially my mom? Did they have any of this enthusiasm? No, not really. They were pleasant enough with customers but quiet most of the rest of the time. They were quiet and undemonstrative with each other and impatient with me. It was like living with prisoners who were doing their time. My father was a handsome man who felt that he was simply reliving an earlier start-up phase of his life. My mother, tall, blonde, and attractive, felt that she belonged in another world, not just another town—another world with style and expensive clothes; and places to go such as night clubs with orchestras and palm trees in the corners.

It was as if both of them were just waiting to get out. Waiting to be free.

That was it! Crawford was free. Nels Anderson, the lighthouse keeper, was free. Nels could stand at the top of the tower and look out at the ocean and be excited about being there—truly interested. He wanted to be there. The people in Woodbine were free. They were free to go anywhere else and do anything else in the world, but they chose to be with one another playing cards, eating potato salad, and laughing. They chose their way of life and picked a handful of little cottages clustered two miles out of town to live in. "Bohemians!" my frowning parents called them. "People who refuse to work any more and just want to play."

My mother and father didn't know what they wanted, but whatever it was wasn't in Port Orford. It seemed odd that they were reluctant prisoners while a few other people in town were doing pretty much what they wanted to. At their own pace. Free. Not cooped up.

Being unfree made my mother eccentric and sort of nuts. She was especially quirky when it came to certain words. For example, dinner was dinner, not supper. And it was forbidden to say pancakes. They were hotcakes. She would blow up about things like this. Later, when there was a war on and people were being bombed to pieces and ships were being sunk under our very noses, and news about concentration camps was coming in—there was my mother, with no perspective at all, becoming completely enraged and shrieking when my dad accidentally said *pancakes*. Poland could fall and London could be bombed flat but our house was not the place to learn about perspective or priorities. My mother was nuts when it came to certain tiny, trivial things—I mean zoo-noise crazy.

My father would say *chimbley* and she would bellow like a water buffalo. She would squawk like rare parrot when he said *breffcuss* instead of *breakfast*. It never did a bit of good. Not one bit. The word *extra* most often came out as *ex-tree*.

And people would ask my mother if she wanted to go to the Show. They meant movies, but everybody called it the Show. My mother would get all haughty and say:

"The Show? What show? I was not aware that we had a theater in these parts."

She was a real snot on this subject, let me tell you. Many people didn't appreciate it.

My mother had mostly work dresses and one or two Dressed-to-the-Hilt dresses but there was never anyplace to wear them. Except, once in a while, over to Don and Eve Doyle's place for dinner. Eve was the other beautiful lady in town (beautiful *respectable* lady, that is, because there were several others over at Red's, mind you, who were not). Eve, too, had a couple of extravagantly fashionable dresses that could be worn nowhere except at dinner with my mother. Don and my dad would wear their best Show suits and my mother and Eve would wear their *Vogue* imitation dresses. I would be polished up and dressed in whatever clothes of mine that were the newest and least ruined. Baby-sitters were unheard of at the time. I was expected to eat dinner in silence and then read books in whatever room was farthest away from the adults.

The Doyles tried very hard to be sophisticates. I mean real ones. Not chameleon ones like my mother. Don, after all, was the only guy in town besides the principal who had graduated from college. (Well, that's not true. Many of the teachers had, not to mention both of the Pughs—you can't be a pharmacist or a dentist without going to college.)

You know what the Doyles did? They built a two-story, two-unit apartment house, just so they could live in an apartment on the top floor instead of a house like everybody else in the world. So the dress-up dinners I just mentioned were always at the Doyle's apartment, not in the living quarters we had later behind the new store, where a goofy little bay window looked at the slab side of the little movie theater. There was nothing fashionable about our place. It was nothing to compare with a top-floor apartment on the side of a hill where you could look out at the town.

My folks and the Doyles would start with cocktails, like in the movies, except that my father would drink ginger ale because if he drank even a little bit of whiskey he'd go nuts. He certainly wasn't a drinker of the collosal stature of our California cousin, Ed Rowland. At any rate, they'd start with "drinks" and then there would be dinner at which I was supposed to be quiet, and this would be followed by card games with just the adults at which time I would be dispatched with Rico, their dog, to a corner room to read in a chair or listen to a turned-down radio until I fell asleep.

Was Rico an Agent of Darkness?

Rico. Almost all dogs are fond of humans in an across-the-board, all-out, I-really-love-you fashion. Dogs won't differentiate on account of anybody's size or weight, or their color, national origin, or profession. You can be a grocery-store sacker or a Nobel Prize winner and it doesn't make any difference to the average dog. But Rico was different. Rico never wagged his tail. He was a shit-ass little dog, all black, like his heart. He growled at Eve and Don and actually nipped at everybody else. He had bitten every kid I knew. He would never come when called and he hated to be touched. He had to be bribed with food. He was a worthless, neurotic, and untalented little dog who disliked everybody and tolerated me. That was the very most that could be said about his powers of affection. He tolerated me and, now and then, even showed a slight curiosity. When I was sent away to be quiet during card games, Rico would accompany me. He would come along and sit down across the room from me. He would watch me. He would watch me turn pages. He would listen to mystery shows on the radio. He would fall asleep after I fell asleep. So my memory is of him always watching me.

"Rico likes Johnny," the four of the adults would chant. It was like a ritual the church people had. The perverse little dog's choosing to join me was interpreted as "Rico's Affection For Johnny." If I'd ever dared to pet him he would have bitten me as hard as he could. I knew this. Rico knew that I knew this.

All of my life, as I've told you, I have searched for signals from God or Clues About the Meaning of the Universe, and maybe there was one right there in memory all along. About a little black dog who hated people, a fact stark enough to be intelligible even to a kid like me. All dogs love all people. Rico hated everybody, including his owners. Yet Rico tolerated me. What was the lesson there? Was Rico the embodiment of Evil? No. He did not bite out people's eyes or curdle their will to live. Rico may have been merely a living symbol of Un-Love. Or disaffection. A portent of value to all of my later life, had I only seen it in time. "Beware of me because I am Black Life. Don't expect anything. Nothing is safe. Nothing is going to be easy. Nothing is simple. It is dark and unfathomable and you can be bitten suddenly and without provocation, even when you think you're safe and have everything figured out. There is no king's ex."

So there it was: the Anomaly Dog, Rico, in the tiny town's Anomaly Manhattan Apartment. I hear my parents' voices now: "Don't wear those good shoes to school. Save those shoes. We're going over to the Doyles on Sunday."

Even before I left town in the sixth grade I knew that Don treated Eve like shit and that Eve had her own bedroom and Don had his. And, I suspect, Don had secured Rico because Rico treated everybody like shit. And that Don and Rico deserved one another and Eve deserved neither. It was kind of an early-life pre-seminar entitled: *Intro to Shit.*

The best time Eve had was when the war broke out and Don was so leery of getting drafted that he went down to Oakland and got a job in a shipyard so he'd be exempt. I heard T.J. Collins tell a guy that Don was a two-bit little chicken shit, a piece of news that didn't go over well when I passed it along to the family at dinner that night.

So it was Show Clothes and Show Nights in the immaculate Show Apartment.

What a fool I was for not seeing the signals. They were as obvious as mile-high Technicolor messages in the sky. It was as if somebody had screamed: "Johnny, for Christ's sake pay *attention* to this stuff! Your life can be easy and all downhill from here on in. You will be safe. The signs are all here. Don't be blind."

I should have made notes.

Rico hates me least. Lou Monescu loves me most. Indifference doesn't matter. Furtiveness gains little.

Millions of young people have died in wars in this century without a scintilla of this knowledge, all mine by a very early age.

Critical Observation

Being a kid was wonderful and largely free from mental illness because of our short attention spans. Mysteries without answers would cause us to become deranged and flop on our beds or on the ground in frustration. I actually raised a cloud of dust one morning in the gravel road in front of my dad's first meat market, about exactly what problem I don't remember. It could have been about who made God.

A few days ago a friend of mine said that his four-and-a-half-year-old son was getting ready for bed last week and, out of nowhere, raised the question: "Who made Mother Nature?" While my friend and his wife thought about an answer, the kid interrupted and answered the question himself: "Oh! I bet *she* did!"

I can remember flapping in the gravel back in the 1930s and having a little kid this smart, and at least a year younger and a lot shorter, walk up to me and say:

"Get up, Johnny! Stop it! *God* made God! Don't be an asshole!"

As you've noticed, children threaten to throw up or even die if they don't get a satisfactory answer immediately. If the solution to a puzzle can't be found they will throw tantrums, turn blue, and promise to nurse a particular grudge for 80 years and then kick the bucket, still cursing.

My deepest and most permanent psychotic rage could be cured in two or three minutes by 7-Up-float therapy, or in as little as 10 seconds by a telephone call from another kid with a play-related subject to talk about.

Severe episodes would pass like clouds. The lunatic of 11:00 a.m. was transformed back to Dr. Jekyll in time for baloney sandwiches at noon. I remember a massive Pat Masterson Derangement, a particularly high fury at the apogee of which he threatened to kill all us other kids who were present, and most of the grownups in town, with a tiny blunt penknife. Then he found an unopened Tootsie Roll on the boardwalk in front of Mrs. Studley's dress shop and did a complete Presto-Change-O.

Lunatic behavior disappeared with new experience. It went away, without treatment, almost instantaneously. I think it is why Moran, later on, kept insisting that people retain as much of their childness as they could. I don't know if he meant "optimism" or what. He would say: "If you do not use your rubber band, you will lose your capacity to snap back."

We need to preserve our elasticity and flexibility, and also encourage instant amnesia about trivial annoyances.

My old man was beside himself for nearly 60 years—on and off—in his anger about being swindled out of two bucks for a system that *Absolutely Guaranteed the Eradication of Flies Without Harmful Chemicals!* He read a small ad in the newspaper and seized on this as an alternative to fly paper and the ugly sticky strips that would hang from the ceiling in various parts of the store and attract sickening collections of flies that would land and then never take off again. You couldn't use fly spray in a place with fresh fruit and vegetables. He ordered the device, waited, and then picked up a tiny package at the post office and unwrapped it on the counter next to the cash register in front of a whole bunch of us. It contained two small blocks of wood and full instructions which I reproduce here in their entirety:

"Place fly on one block. Crush fly with the other."

My father went crazy with rage. He threw a fit and turned colors. My mother and I hurried through the door next to the meat locker and into the living quarters behind. We ran through the living room, then the kitchen, and off the back porch. We ran behind the garage. We laughed until my mother fell into a bush.

My father, however, never once saw the humor in this. Not for one second. He demanded that my grandfather, the Justice of the Peace, bring a law suit. Everybody in town tried to help him through this crisis, but he wouldn't be helped. He didn't think it was funny at all and thought the lying, cheating sons of bitches should be shot.

Descriptions of People

Gene White was a tall, rangy guy who looked quite a bit like Gary Cooper until you got real close and saw that his teeth were yellow from smoking cigars.

Charlie Long? Fat guy. His belly drooped over the top of his pants and his face was so puffy that you had to look carefully to see his eyes. He had hair the color of plug tobacco, dark brown, almost black, and a graying walrus-type moustache that collected food fragments of various colors. Charlie moved slowly. He always seemed to be carrying a seven-foot-long weird stick with a pistol grip at the bottom and a sinister looking metal grabber (like a guy with an amputated hand might have) at the other. He would use this tool to get dusty stuff off the top shelves in his store and also to grab the asses of little kids and—just the one time—Lou Monescu. He'd sneak up and let you have it. He thought this was very funny but I didn't. He called me a Little Whippersnapper one time, laughed heartily, and thought it was hysterical. I did not.

Don Doyle was on the short side, maybe 5' 7", and had small white teeth. His complexion was dark and his hair was black. His eyes looked black. Don had a lot in common with his dog, Rico. I wasn't the only one in town who noticed this. They were both dark and unforgiving. The dog whined and snarled at people and so did Don. Nobody could understand why Don Doyle, a person who worked so much with the public, would behave this way—especially toward the hired help. He would bitch at them incessantly, and then turn around and be unctuous and mealy-mouthed to customers. He put something in his hair to make it shiny. He was an oily little man.

Eve Doyle was at least three inches taller than Don and had brown wavy hair and brown eyes. She had a marvelous figure and was as beautiful as a movie star. Once again, I wasn't the only person in town who felt that Don and Eve shouldn't be together. I always secretly thought she should leave Don and Rico to live with one another while she went to Hollywood and married somebody nice like Ronald Coleman who would dance close, act nuts about her even in public, and buy her valentines in July and November.

Crawford "Smitty" Smith was red. He had the kind of complexion that goes along with reddish-brown hair. You know people like that, I'm sure. They never tan. They just get red. Smitty had a hawk nose and fiery blue eyes. He was one of my dock friends. I would walk down there in the afternoons when he and the Frenchman would come back in their fishing boats and drink beer, the empties of which they would give me to sell for a penny apiece. Crawford was a kind of anchor for me. Perhaps I can explain that later.

Dr. Baird, it seemed to me, was actually baird colored and drove a baird-colored car. He could as well have been called Dr. Beige. You've seen tan bricks. That was his color. Skin, hair, eyebrows. Beige. If you added just a little yellow you would have a very sick-looking man. But he

Aunty Marnie

looked okay. He needed a little bit more red-brick color to look healthy, however. He was a worried-looking gaunt man with small brown eyes made smaller by round silver eyeglasses. His face was thin and his hands were very long and delicate. Moran called them "surgeon's" hands.

Aunt Margaret (Aunty Marnie) was dark. She tanned. The other Tichenor girls were blonde and didn't tan. Marnie, as a young woman, had dark brown hair. She worked as a waitress, a soda jerk, and a lifeguard. There is a newspaper picture of Marnie saving a guy's life; she looks like an angel of mercy in the picture taken at the scene on the Columbia River—the guy's name was Al Heib and she gave him artificial respiration. During World War Two she also worked as a taxicab driver, a crane operator, and an optical technician. And she fabricated boxes in an ammo factory. She was, to me, a female Captain Marvel. Margaret's middle initial is "B" and it stands for Brinkerhoff, which, if you remember from the genealogy story, was Captain William Tichenor's wife's maiden name.

My mother and father were comedians and named me John B. Quick, but my middle initial stands for "Barton." I'm told that my mother read this name in a magazine and liked it. I think it stinks. I like Brinkerhoff a lot better. Or Tichenor.

Yeah, I know, why don't I change it? (It would only cost fifty bucks.)

You Want to Hear More About Eve Doyle?

Once in awhile, especially when things don't seem to be going too well, I'll step on an elevator with a couple of women and suddenly everything will be okay. Happy. It's the perfume. One of the women will be wearing a perfume that was like Eve Doyle's.

My mother's perfumes were hard. Glassy. Maybe it was her physical makeup; it was certainly her personality. She could put on an expensive perfume and turn it into a warning, not an invitation. There was nothing alluring about the way she smelled. Perfumes became repellents. She drove people away.

Eve's perfumes were soft. She would make anything smell good. She put on a little of the dime store junk I bought her one Christmas and she made it smell just fine. My mother was scandalized.

"Don't do that!" she squealed at Eve, like one of the Three Little Pigs. But it was too late. Eve gave me a hug of thanks. She added some elegance to the perfume. Presence.

When the elevator events take place I close my eyes and there is a deep feeling of security and tranquillity even after the women passengers get off at their floor. The scent and the idea linger.

Most of the time when I went anyplace with my mother and Eve (and they were both were dressed up and wearing perfume) it was to go Christmas shopping in the town that used to be called Marshfield. It had the only department store in miles. Three or four stories. Really tall. As we drove, the car would fill up with perfume and fur smell. It was a rare occasion for them to get dolled up. Shopping in Marshfield, which is now called Coos Bay. Off we'd go. North on Highway 101 through the woods and the rain. High anticipation.

Then it was Christmas decorations in the store. And some old fat-guy Santa Claus imitation, by then past my interest. There was the Toy Department to drool over stuff until I got dragged away to "hurry over here" and take a look at some goofy sweater or something else practical. I would be coerced into modelling things and walk back and forth. It would have been intolerable had it not been for other kids being forced to do the same things. We gave sad, embarrassed looks to one another and never spoke.

So the fact is this: I smell a sweet perfume and suddenly the world is small and perfect and I'm in the back seat of Eve Doyle's Buick serenely gliding northward half asleep dreaming of presents and holly and Christmas tree lights and a nice lunch in a chop suey joint later on, walking down the street under the awnings to keep out of the rain and smelling Eve's perfume which was accentuated in the cool air blown in from the bay.

Not mom's. But hers; Eve's. Because Eve's perfume clung to the neighborhood and lingered on passersby whom, I imagined, probably smiled and felt a bit as I do now as an adult.

My mother's perfume dissipated skyward into the scud or lurked briefly as a warning to the people who tormented and irritated her. Maybe that was it. Her impatience and irritation with just about everybody—certainly me—wrecked the best perfumes, ruined their compounds, hardened their effect, gave them a metallic edge like an Arabian Nights dagger in the mural in the lobby of the Aladdin Theater in Portland. (Where, now that I think about it, some of the movies were enhanced by sitting between Uncle Harvey and Aunt Hester who was another person that always smelled just terrific from a perfume that smelled like big rare flowers and who had no trouble loving people. Yeah, that was it. Popcorn and mints and the dark perfume and not minding one bit that Hester clutched my hand in the scary parts.)

Do you suppose that some people's ability to love other people enhances their perfumes? Their willingness? Their vulnerability? Does it cause the fragrances to hover and keep and stay intact instead of blinking out?

Uncle Harvey and Aunt Hester

Evening in Paris. That was it. In a cheesy little blue bottle. Sold only in dime stores. But Eve gave it heart and substance. It was Christmas Day over at the Doyles' apartment and there were fresh-coffee and breakfast aromas and pine scent and the fragrance of new clothes in opened boxes under the tree.

"Don't do that!" said my mother with a to-a-kid note of irritation and command even to her best friend Eve, who ignored her and deflected her with one of her big perfect smiles and undid the little cap on the Evening in Paris and rubbed some of it on her wrists and then put her wrists on her neck and then gave me a big satisfying hug of thanks and her long brown hair swirled around my head like magic.

Looking back as an adult I see now that she was hot. Kid-warm to a then-kid but now-man hot. She was like a bright neon *Open* sign—that's what the smile conveyed. My mother, on the other hand, was like a handsome store the people and contents of which had been emptied and the electricity turned off. Later in life she was completely boarded up.

I think the ultimate in the perfume experience was one time in Marshfield when we got stuck in the crowd trying to get into the department store and I was maybe eight and not tall and got sandwiched between Eve and my mom who were wearing their big fur coats and I was blinded and lost in the fur between them and my mother suddenly asked: "Where's Johnny?"

I didn't want to answer because my face was in Eve's fur coat and I was perfectly content to be squeezed and almost breathless and lost in that kind of dark.

Mid-Thirties

No, not the age of anybody—the years of the decade.

In the mid 1930s I was about four and had major memories of a bloody massacre, animals acting weird, drinking creek water, and the fire that nearly killed everybody. And I'm not bullshitting about this for one second. We went to Port Orford where a first memory was that of the Port Orford High School Yell which went like this: "P. O. R! . . . T. O .R! . . . F. O. R! . . . D! . . . That's the way you spell it! Here's the way you yell it! Pooooort *ORFORD!*"

When one is very little and doesn't understand about thermals or winds that rush up the sides of cliffs it comes as a terrible shock to see seagulls rise from the ocean without flapping, and soar upward from shadows into the morning sun. Not only that, but to suddenly and unexpectedly appear about ten feet away from you when they hit the light. Right in your face.

"They're just as afraid of you as you are of them," was some adult comment at the time. Phooey! The gulls weren't half as startled. Not a tenth.

The Goat. My memories of our goat are just about as short as the word itself. I try to remember it and all I can bring up is GOAT, and it's gone. It was a white goat, I'm pretty sure. It was my sister's and my goat. It was tied to a stake by a rope in the field next to the chicken coop. You would think that somebody would remember something as big and important as a goat, but I simply don't. It might have had horns, but I could be imagining things. It may have butted me with its horns but it may not have. Some days I think it did. Other days I'm not sure. Maybe it bumped me. It must not have been very important if all I can get is the flicker of GOAT and the memory zips right past. Maybe we didn't have a goat at all.

The Seagull. I (think I) am sure that we had the goat at the very same time that a seagull got caught in a wind gust and slammed against the side of the house and practically killed itself. It was lying there helpless. I can remember it exactly. Lying there with its white breast and gray wings tucked in. Looking up. My father made a nest for it from some excelsior he took from a banana crate and put in a Campbell's Soup box. He put the box in the corner of the chicken coop and would go in at the end of the day and feed the seagull by hand. (So here's an example of memory: I can't remember the goat standing out there, two hundred times bigger than a seagull, but I can remember the shredded paper, the Campbell's Soup box, and which corner of the chicken coop the seagull's nest was in.) And the final thing I remember—bright as daylight—was the particular morning we were all assembled to watch the seagull set free. It had gotten well enough to hop around with the chickens and fly up to their roosts. The wind was blowing, but not hard. It was sunny. My father opened the door of the chicken coop and tried to shoo the seagull out. He cornered it and the seagull slashed my father's hand with its beak. Badly. There was blood all over everything. I could see how angry my father was when he came out with the bird, obviously torn between letting it free and wringing its neck. But he pushed it into the air where it took wing and flew away—at first toward town, where it quickly realized it didn't belong, and then toward the ocean, home. It glided swiftly downward toward the dock.

My grandfather was there in his usual navy blue suit with vest and gold key chain looped across the front—the one with the dreaded weird tooth on it. My father was wearing his customary white shirt (which got blood splattered on it). My mother was standing on the chicken-coop side of my grandfather and my sister, in a print dress similar to my mother's, was standing on the other (the Gene White's-house side). I was slightly behind everybody, I remember, because of the possibility that the seagull might fly directly in my face and put my eyes out. I was looking west, toward the ice house (*Topeka-Topeka*) almost straight ahead and the administration building—just then under construction because I remember the raw lumber framework. Perfect picture. But do you think I can see a goat in the picture? Something as big as a goat? I still can't.

You're probably sitting there right now thinking: "The kid wanted a goat real bad but they wouldn't give him one. So he dreamed up a goat that was never there. And that's why he can't see it. Because the goat never existed. That's what really happened. Nobody can remember a non-goat!"

I honestly believe that somebody gave my father the goat in lieu of paying an overdue bill—a farmer or somebody who was pulling up stakes and leaving town. And that person said: "Here, Al. Take this goat. I don't have the money I owe you, but you can sell this perfectly good goat to somebody and then you'll have the money. Good-bye."

So the goat was there, I'm sure of it. But it wasn't a pet goat that we'd always wanted. It was merely a Sudden Goat that was tied up in the field until my father could get rid of it. Maybe the reason I can't visualize it very well was because I didn't care about it much.

The upshot is this: everything was personal and local—like getting drowned in the tunnel under Battle Rock when the tide came in. There was no national or international news worth my remembering. Wait a minute, that's not true! A hotshot criminal named Dutch Schultz was gunned down by G-Men. And my grandfather said that night baseball started in Cincinnati. "Night baseball, for Christ's sake!" he said. The game of Monopoly was invented and we bought it. A moron young cat of ours chewed up the red hotels. One of the first songs I remember was "Moon Over Miami." I tried to think of some others and so I asked my sister, Alida, who is eight years older than me.

"Popular songs of 1935?" I asked. She rattled off a bunch as if she'd been there yesterday. "Red Sails in the Sunset." "The Music Goes Round & Round." "I'm In the Mood for Love." "I'm Gonna Sit Right Down and Write Myself a Letter." "I Won't Dance." Son of a gun. She just rattled them off like a Tommy Gun (so nicknamed from the Thompson Submachine Gun that was everybody's favorite, cops and bad guys alike).

"What else happened that I would remember if you told me?" I asked her. It was kind of a yo-yo question, but she knew what I meant and she said: "Fibber McGee & Molly started on the radio. Remember Fibber's closet with all the junk falling out of it?" It worked. She told me and I remembered.

"They lived on Wistful Vista Avenue," she added. "And Gang Busters started on radio in the same year, along with Your Hit Parade, sponsored by Lucky Strike cigarettes." We wouldn't miss the weekly Hit Parade show for anything.

At the very beginning of the radio program Gang Busters there were police whistles, sirens, police cars chasing somebody, machine-gun fire, and tires squealing. And scary music. What an opening. It came on like Gang Busters. (Gang Busters is what you might call a Fossil Expression. It's been buried so long that nobody knows the original meaning any more.)

"And remember," Alida asked, "When Lucky Strike Green Went to War?"

"Yeah, yeah," I said. "But that was eons later."

I got lost at a picnic. They said for only 15 minutes. This was a lie, it had to be. It seemed more like a week.

I had a nightmare in which Technicolor water rose in my room nearly to the top of my bed and my parents said it couldn't have happened. Another lie. Even though I was having a high fever, I know it happened. I woke up and it was still there, green and purple water.

Then there was something that was not a lie, but a disappointment. They got a Saint Bernard "puppy" named Prince that grew up fast and got its leash—a length of chain—caught around my ankle and dragged me halfway across town through the gravel next to the highway. T.J. Collins came out of his Bar & Grill and saved me. I have one picture of

Johnny with the Wrong Dog, wearing the Wrong Shoes and the Wrong Pants.

me and Prince. Prince looks stupid and so do I. My pants are practically under my armpits. Let me tell you a little something else about this picture. The shed in the background shows the chicken coop. The sloping field next to it was where the Maybe Goat was tethered. The building on the left was a garage in which Frenchie kept a car called the Dooz-Yem.

The messages anybody could derive from this photo are these: Do not attempt to control animals larger than yourself, especially ones which are chained. Pay attention. If the animal has an interest in going north then abandon your intention of going eastward. Wear sensible shoes. Do not let your mother choose your pants.

Which leads me to wonder if my mother utilized me as a sort of sight gag, a comic figure to take her mind off the drudgery of the store.

They gave Prince to a farmer out on Elk River and then got Skippy. One of the first things that happened was that Skippy, a pointy-nosed little brown dog, ran after the car clear over to the Doyles one Sunday when we went for Dress-Up Dinner at the apartment. Rico charged out and tried to terrify Skippy, but Skippy simply sat down and looked at him. This really annoyed Rico, but all he could do was sit down and also pretend that it didn't matter. I think Skippy absorbed some of my magic power with respect to Rico because Rico thenceforth tolerated us both, boy and dog.

Every single one of the kittens we ever owned grew up to about half size and got killed by lumber carriers passing the front of the store on their way to the dock. The bodies had to be buried in soup-can coffins behind the chicken coop. Skippy was about 50 times smarter than cats and never got run over and killed.

I saw a newsreel of a kid in an Iron Lung and it gave me nightmares for almost a month.

"The kid wouldn't eat his spinach," my mother said. "And that's why he will always have to live in a machine with only his head sticking out!"

Popeye had nothing on me after that, let me tell you.

"Put vinegar on it," was my grandfather's advice about spinach. Right, as usual.

What else?

In 1936 the Spanish Civil War started. I got confused because my grandfather had served in the Spanish-American War which wasn't the same thing at all. The first Sit-Down Strikes started in Detroit and I thought this was a pretty funny picture in my head with adults saying: "Stand up! Sit down! Stand up! Sit Down!" like playing "Simon Says" at birthday parties.

Kodachrome came along from Eastman Kodak, and Ford V-8s were popular. On my own I remember the movie *Captain January* with Shirley Temple and two particular songs: "Pennies from Heaven" and "I'm an Old Cowhand From the Rio Grande." My sister helped me remember "Poinciana," "I Gotta Feelin' You're Foolin'," "Boo Hoo," " It's a Sin to Tell a Lie," and "I've got You Under My Skin."

At about this period of history, little chrome sailboats were popular; little chrome sailboats afloat on a circular blue mirror the size of a large plate. Mom bought one and I loved it. I could look at it a long time and imagine a perfect blue lagoon.

Ways to Get Memories That Last

I guess I don't remember any of the peaceful stuff, the calm things that went on from day to day in my early life.

I think we all forget security and normalcy and tend to remember, as I did, the three classes of experience that make for lasting memories. All were characterized by one element: they were usually sudden and unexpected. But the three classes, for me, were these:

1. Condition #1: General Horror—events or circumstances that generated fear, dread, and panic. These caused instant screaming or speechlessness, it all depended.

2. Condition #2: Amazement—experiences that could astonish and astound; that would leave any normal person instantly dazzled and flabbergasted.

3. Condition #3: Mystery—episodes or incidents characterized by secrets, puzzles, and enigmas—the unknowable and the unfathomable.

The younger you are, the more likely that all of these conditions happen simultaneously.

After six years of age, they can happen one or two at a time.

Here's an excellent example from when I was five or so.

My father went to a cattle farm on Elk River to pick up a side of beef for his butcher shop. I went along in the pickup. This was fun because they had just put a new metal surface on the Elk River bridge which made a marvelous noise when you drove on it, plus it vibrated your bottom something terrific.

While my father negotiated with the farmer in the barn, I was left outside by a wooden fence. I saw a pig in a sty. I recognized it.

A cow was standing under a tree. It had something which dangled under it with knobs.

Another cow rushed from behind the barn with something really big sticking out from under it.

It jumped on the first cow and stuck the thing into it!

An attack!

CONDITION ONE! Horror! (Sub-Variety: Speechless.)

The second cow was obviously trying to kill the first cow!

The second cow humped and struggled and moved that thing in and out of the first cow, but without killing it!

This triggered (you guessed it): CONDITION TWO! Amazement! I was stunned and bamboozled by this performance.

The second cow finally stopped doing it, pulled the thing out, and ran back behind the barn.

The first cow went back to eating grass! Just like nothing in the world had happened!

CONDITION THREE! MYSTERY. What was it? What caused it? Why did it happen? It was totally beyond my imagination.

My father and the farmer came out of the barn. I didn't say anything, mostly because the first cow seemed to be okay and I wouldn't have known how to get the conversation started anyway.

The farmer said to me:

"How's it going?"

I then realized that I was still mute from Condition One. So I couldn't say anything. I could not. It was impossible. My father commented on this in the pickup on the way back to town.

"You ought to have said hello to Mr. Blake. That was not very polite. He was just trying to be nice."

Later in the summer I saw the McCormick's dog, Jerry, sneak up and try to do something similar to another dog, but the effort was on a much smaller and more intellectually manageable scale.

Furthermore, the cow experience helped me to handle the incident in which I dropped in unexpectedly on Nadine and Howard Spence over at their Motor Court one afternoon and found them on their hands and knees in the living room, undressed, doing precisely the same thing!

I was mystified for weeks afterward.

It was about this time that my father completed the chicken coop behind the garage—a big chicken coop with a fenced-in area where the birds could peck around when they weren't in the chicken house laying eggs in their nests. Later, I gained the courage to go into this coop and take eggs right out from under the hens, eggs that were still warm, but occasionally with chicken dump on them. But that's another story.

There were white chickens and red chickens, and one special chicken that was bigger than the others and had extra stuff on his head and was called a Rooster. It didn't take long for me to observe that the rooster was doing something very much like the cows, Jerry, and Mr. & Mrs. Spence. I was beginning to see a pattern.

I waited until my father happened to be present one time when the rooster jumped on one of the chickens.

"Say?" I asked him. "What's going on there?"

"Where?" my father asked, looking right straight at the chickens.

"There," I pointed.

My father looked at them and said: "Nothing."

I checked to make sure they were still doing it.

"What do you mean, nothing?" I asked him. "Look at them."

He thought about it.

"They are playing," he said and hurriedly disappeared into the garage.

Playing.

I thought about this. But it didn't figure. It didn't add up. I had been an eyewitness to this several times. I had observed that the creature on the bottom was usually minding its own business, eating or just looking at something, when along comes the other one who suddenly, for no reason, jumps on top! It certainly wasn't the kind of playing I did with my friends. I didn't buy it.

I discovered that this subject was not discussed by any older person in the entire town. And was not to be discussed. It was off limits. Just like the taboo against conversing with (or even being near) the women who worked at Red's Tavern and against talking to strange men, especially the sailors off ships that docked to pick up lumber. All of this stuff was a mystery.

And remained so until Moran came to town and put it all straight. Usually in one of his calm, unfrightening, and unflabbergasting stories about the true nature of things. Stories which unraveled mysteries and revealed the codes. Moran was the best cryptographer I ever met. If I could go back in time I would tell everybody to mind their own business and I'd just hang around with Moran. He made my first-grade teacher, Mrs. Grant, look like a moron. As a matter of fact, I would have learned more just by sitting on a revolving stool at T.J. Collins Bar & Grill talking to the customers and the help.

Other combinations of the Three Conditions were present in some of the following stories. You talk about *fear*. Jeez.

First is a short recollection about Battle Rock. This big rock, just south of town, has a natural tunnel going through it. When the tide goes out (all the way out) you can walk through from one side to the other in comfort and complete safety. This would be my advice for somebody with a small boy maybe four or five years old. Do not wait as my parents waited until the tide is coming in and big waves crash through the tunnel and make everybody scream as if they are about to get killed. I certainly gained the impression that I was going to get killed. Little kids can't tell the difference between HELP screaming and ROLLER-COASTER screaming. The two sound exactly the same. Remember that if you ever have a kid.

Next were the white chickens.

What's scary about white chickens? I'll tell you. Four- or five-year-old people should be sat down and carefully talked to in daylight about what it's going to be like later on that night when a big fire is set at the edge of a field near the chicken coop and a huge pot of water is brought to a boil (which is pretty eerie just by itself, with the big flames flickering through the steam coming up from the water) and chickens are assassinated. Add the chopping block and a razor-sharp hatchet and the sudden massacre of a lot of the white chickens (plural), and you have the fine beginnings of an absolute living wide-awake nightmare! The daylight talk must surely emphasize the gruesome news that chickens can have their heads chopped off and *still run around like crazy!*

A child should also be warned that this bloody business may stimulate people to begin shouting such things as:

"Over there! Over there! He's heading for the corner of the field!"

Or: "STOP HIM! STEP ON HIM! GETHIM!"

Or: "OH MY GAWD! THAT ONE'S GOING CLEAR ACROSS THE STREET TO GENE WHITE'S PLACE!"

These were my parents and that's what they screamed in the night. Not overly swift to begin with, now they had suddenly gone crazy! And the chickens were darting erratically around in circles with their hearts pumping blood out their necks! My mother was chasing madly all over the place. My sister was doing the same in another direction and my genius father, having forgotten that I've never seen anything killed before, much less a lunatic FLAP-FLAP-FLAPPING chicken that refuses to die, instructed little me to:

"GO GET HIM. GRAB HIS FEET! *GRAB HIS FEET!*"

Up to that moment I was too frantic to cry or scream or speak: too stunned. It tied Conditions One, Two, and Three into a tight bundle. There it was: on a moonless night, in the Halloween flickering firelight, I was supposed to go into the black shadows of the grass in pursuit of a ghost-white chicken without a head.

An adult plunged into this situation for the first time would simply have said: "No. This won't work, Al. I can't handle this. I'm going over to Red's for a beer. Give me a holler when this thing is over, will you?"

As a matter of fact, my Aunt Anna, who swore better than just about everybody, including Smitty and Lou Monescu, was invited to participate in this drill one night and summed it up when she told my dad: "Fuck it, Al."

I ran into the house but was yelled at to come back out and help. I hid out in the corner of the field but unfortunately a headless chicken ran right at me. This was followed by the stinking part when the dead chickens were plunged into the boiling water and their feathers were plucked out and thrown every which way.

What a frenzied, ghastly thing to witness for the first time. Primitive natives don't scare the crap out of their primitive children in such a witless and heartless fashion.

The red chickens, I soon recognized, laid eggs and were safe. The white chickens were doomed. Advice for Life: either be a red chicken, or at least learn how to look like one long enough to escape. If you can't do that, then try something extraordinary and unexpected. Herzog said later on that everybody in Denmark told the Nazi invaders that they were all White Chickens, all Jews, in a heroic trick that worked.

But let's get back to experience in the field. The second time this slaughter happened I caught on; I suddenly understood. I noticed the resemblance to the chicken parts on my plate. That was it: those white chickens became the stuff in the meat case in the store! Some of the stuff in the meat case made it to our kitchen where it went in the oven or the frying pan. I ate those chickens. And they were good.

By the third Blood Rite, I was a full participant, chasing down chickens with the best of them. Nothing to it. This was part of life. If drumsticks were your favorite, along with your mashed potatoes and chicken gravy, then this was a necessary activity. It was another year, however, before I realized that a side of beef was the major part of an actual cow! Possibly even the very one who had stuck his thing into the cow under the tree.

Finally—*Bones!*

My father would be cutting away at his butcher block and throwing bones into a box—free bones for customers to give to their dogs. The McCormicks were over a lot for bones, and not just for their dog, Jerry, I realized later, but sometimes for soup for their family of seven.

I asked about the bones.

"They come out of the cows," claimed my old man.

"Why? What are bones doing in cows?"

"Holding them up so the cows don't fall down," he explained.

"How does it work?"

"Cows have skeletons."

I didn't like the sound of this.

"What are skeletons?"

"All the bones. The bones are all hooked together. Remember the administration building when there was just the framework and you could see through it? Before the walls and the roof were put up?"

"Yes." I also remembered the day the stupid seagull slashed my dad's hand, but thought I'd better not bring it up.

"That was the building's skeleton," he said. "Now do you get it?"

"No."

My sister walked past.

"Are you going anywhere near the library?" he asked her.

She said she was.

"Would you take Johnny with you and show him a picture of a skeleton?"

"Of a person?" she asked.

He said yes.

A person, I thought to myself. Holy Smokes!

She took me over there and showed me a picture in the encyclopedia.

"That's the Halloween Thing!" I noted, only slightly relieved.

"Yes. It's a human skeleton," she said. "It shows all the bones. Everybody has that many bones inside."

"They do not," I said, because it was just too horrible.

"They do, too." she argued.

"They don't," I said. "I don't have a skeleton."

I wouldn't have been caught dead with such a gruesome thing inside me.

"Here," she said. "Feel this." And she held out her wrist for a medical inspection.

"No, I won't."

I am very lucky that my sister is such a kind person and always has been. She could very well have shown me some other pictures in the encyclopedia that would have caused me to die on the spot—like the colored pictures of all the muscles and guts inside people. That would have done it. I would have either died instantly from terror or would not have slept for several weeks.

A few days later my mother handed me a key and told me to give it to my father.

"What is it?" I asked.

"A skeleton key."

I dropped it like it was poison and refused to pick it up. How could anybody touch such a thing? I ran from the house into the wood shed.

Everybody laughed about it at dinner. Some joke.

Order in the Universe

There is order in the universe when you grow up in a grocery store and meat market. There is plenty of order because everything has a right and proper place. I had restocking duties starting when I was four and five. It was in those years that I learned about onions and the fact that they were not supposed to cohabit with potatoes in the potato bin. Onions stayed with other onions. Not only that, but white onions and yellow onions were further segregated from one another.

I developed a theory of organization in which vegetables and fruits of the same color ought to be displayed next to one another, in other words oranges, carrots, and pumpkins (when pumpkins were in season) were meant to be adjacent. This system was rejected by my parents. There was the citrus family to think about, they said—with regard to lemons and grapefruit—and there was a need to separate fruits and vegetables for some reason lost in ancient history.

Everything made sense in the store. Canned goods were on shelves at the north end of the store. Powdered soaps and cleaning supplies were at the other end of the store from the canned goods. Ammonia was not near the sugar. The salt was over by the pickles and the olives.

I would restock the shelves according to the shapes and colors and sizes of things. That is how illiterate people operate. I remember very well. And illiterates, by and large, can do a pretty good job. They remember the patterns. Breakfast cereals were easy. Rice Krispies had three little guys on the front: Snap, Crackle, and Pop. Wheaties boxes were a distinctive orange color. Pep boxes had a characteristic pattern.

The biggest joy was the canned goods because most of them carried the picture of the things that were in the cans. There were colored pictures of the carrots, peas, and corn. They were all right there on the label. Also, one could easily tell what was in a jar by looking through the glass at the product inside. Like prunes, for example. Or beets.

I was more than 90 percent perfect at restocking bottles, boxes, jars, and cans. But there was one area in which I fell short. The Campbell's Soup section.

I loved canned soup. And my mother loved the fact that I loved canned soup. It was the easiest thing in the world to fix soup for my lunch. She would let me choose the kind of Campbell's Soup I wanted and then she would open it up, add either milk or water, and put it on the stove. When it bubbled I could eat it. I would eat my soup with soda crackers. My mother thought it was bad manners to crumble soda crackers in soup. But I had heard President Roosevelt in an informal interview on the radio say that he crumbled his crackers in his soup and I used this as an argument with my mother. It was one of the rare times when evidence I attempted to introduce in a case was actually accepted. I may have become a Democrat because of this and because of the President's radio voice. My parents hated him and said he would cause the downfall of the country. I partly liked Roosevelt because it irritated my parents to hear me say that I liked him.

But let's get back to the soup. (Excuse me; but I sometimes wander off like Skippy.)

I knew from my daily eating experiences that there were many, many kinds of Campbell's Soup. But they all looked the same on the shelves. All of the cans were identical. They were uniformly red and white with a little gold seal and had squiggles on them. There was no way to differentiate these cans from one another. None.

They had the letters of the alphabet on them. But letters and alphabet have no meaning to an illiterate. Let me give you some examples about reason and logic. Shoe laces have a reason that is obvious. You would run right out of your Keds if it weren't for the shoe laces. The cherry on the top of a chocolate sundae at Doyle's had a reason. It was both beautiful and tasty and you saved it for the last bite. The chunks of smelly fish in a crab-pot had a reason because the chunks were used as bait to lure the crabs into the trap.

There was order in Port Orford and I knew about it. The sun rose from the eastern hills and set in the ocean. Always. Water from a pure spring filled the reservoir. The northbound Greyhound bus went to Portland where my relatives lived. The southbound bus went to California where Shirley Temple lived and where they made movies. People swam in the lake in the summer because the water was fairly warm then. In the middle of winter was Christmas. Easter was about eggs and chocolate bunnies. Everything made perfect sense except Campbell's Soup and something called the Future. My sister tried to explain both of them but to no avail.

She would take me to the mysterious soup section of the shelves.

"Look here," my sister would insist, pointing at a can: "TOMATO."

I would run down the aisle to the canned tomatoes and pick up a can to show that I wasn't totally stupid.

"Come back," she would say. "See the difference here? Look: GREEN PEA."

There was no difference, of course. None. There wasn't any difference. But I would go to the pea section of the canned goods and point to a can of Del Monte Fancy Green Peas. It had a picture of lovely green peas in a white bowl.

It was hopeless. She couldn't get anywhere. It was as futile as the time I had come across some Buck Rogers comic books and was asking about the pictures. I wanted to know where the action was taking place. She explained that it wasn't as much where as when and that Buck Rogers and his girl friend were in the distant future. In her attempts to explain the future, she asked me to think about the past. This was easy because I knew about the past. I could remember Christmas for not just one, but for two years back. I remembered the summer before. The upshot was that I believed that the future was a special part of the past. I couldn't get it to fit anyplace else. It was a fork in the road somewhere in the past that was different from dinosaurs and broken Greek temples. I remember trying to do research in the blue Books of Knowledge trying to find pictures of space ships and women in pointy metal brassieres, but I couldn't find anything. I was disturbed, but I got over it.

A young person seeks balance as much as order. Balance is crucial. If the things you know and care about more than outweigh the things that are incomprehensible to you, then you're okay in your head. I knew what I needed to know to get most of the things done in my life and to do my work in the store. I didn't get spelling. But it wasn't imperative that I did so. I was mostly functional. I could dependably get toilet paper and string beans to their proper destinations. I could stack lemons properly and build pyramids out of cans of coffee. I could read the "5" and the "10" on the scales and could, therefore, bag five- and ten-pound bags of potatoes. I could not read a clock, however, but what difference did it make? There were plenty of people around who could read clocks. I would not look at the shelves of Campbell's Soup cans when I walked past them. I could not stock those shelves and that was all there was to it. Somebody who could read had to do it. Again, there were plenty of people who knew how to read. More than enough people. Certainly, my learning how to do it had no great priority.

As there was order in the store, there was likewise order in the town and the woods outside of town. Hailstones melted on the stove and the powerful light of the lighthouse was useless in the fog. The foghorn worked in the fog, however. Like a charm. Things that you could not see you could hear. A person didn't have to know how to read in order to listen to I Love a Mystery on the radio. I could walk around the store with my eyes closed, that's how well I knew the layout and the aisles. And I frequently knew where I was by the smells of the powdered soap, the bread, the cookies, and the fruit.

But a crisis loomed and I was greatly worried by it. Everybody of about my age was obliged to go to school. And one of the requirements in school seemed to be a preoccupation with reading and writing. Squiggle decipherment. So I was constantly having somebody thrust an *Oregonian* at me and pointing at a word in a headline.

"There! You see! See this word? It says: POLICE. "

My parents seemed always to use the Raised-Voice technique of teaching, the one in which if they yelled loud enough they thought they could force information directly into my brain.

On my computer is a character font called Zapf Dingbats. Here are some samples.

✈ ☞ ❁ ❦ ✳ ❖ ❧ †

That's approximately what I saw on the label when my sister thrust a can of Campbell's Cream of Mushroom Soup at me. And it was also exactly what I saw when she thrust a can of Campbell's Mock Turtle at me. Not only those two looked the same to me, but so did Vegetarian Vegetable, Green Pea, and Black Bean. The headlines of the *Oregonian* made the same kind of non-sense. There was nothing to go on. And no real reason to go in the first place.

Little did I know that there were evil people in the world, chiefly in the form of Mrs. Grant, who believed the opposite of what I did—who believed that the heart of all knowledge was an understanding of *reading*. My days were numbered.

Charms, Magic, In Cahoots With God

Charm bracelets were popular when my sister was of an age to be interested in them. She had one (but only because other girls did). She also had a Ouija Board that she said was faulty. It didn't work. It didn't give the correct mystic answers that she and her friend, Louita, wanted. On some other days, it didn't work at all, period. They put more trust in pulling petals off daisies and saying: "He loves me; he loves me not." There's a word to describe this kind of divination. It's called cleromancy. It was one of the MANCIES that a guy named Moran later told me about. *Eenie meenie miney moe* is another example.

I didn't understand the true meaning of charm bracelets until well into adulthood. I thought they were merely charming or cute, and that's where the name "charm" came from. I wasn't aware of amulets; of small ornaments owned or worn to confer good luck or ward off evil. Charms are magic. If you find enough of the right ones you get to be in cahoots with God (or many different gods) and you will enjoy the benefits of a secret partnership. You have known a lot of people, I'm sure, who failed for the lack of the right charms. They had every other advantage: they had looks, connections, family, money, but all failed. Utterly. In the meantime, total idiots succeed at things they have no right to succeed at. Dumb Luck is what it is, the right charms.

As far as I was concerned, Japanese glass floats were pure magic. Japanese fishermen wove glass floats into their fishing nets. Then they'd lose the nets, the floats would become free, and the transparent glass globes would drift across the Pacific to the Oregon coast. Many were the size of oranges or grapefruits. I never found any of these as a kid. Others did, including the huge yellow one—two feet across—that Dr. Pugh picked up on Agate Beach. I returned to Port Orford in my twenties during a big storm. I was the first person on the beach at dawn of the day after the storm and found nine glass floats, one of which was blue. The others were the more customary green. Some shades of blue are very lucky.

Many times as a child I would stand on the beach looking west-ward trying to imagine just how far away Japan was and what it was like if you ever got there. Was it as if Oregon and Japan were once part of the same continent and got broken apart and that Japan and Oregon had the same rugged coastline and cedar trees? Did they have roller-skating rinks like Lou's? Did children wear Keds and have balloons blow up in their faces at birthday parties? Why weren't the Japanese fishermen a little more clever about protecting their glass floats? How well did their nets work anyway? Crawford didn't use nets. Frenchie didn't use nets. Nobody I'd ever heard about used nets. What was the deal?

Older people would stare at the stars at night and get themselves very perplexed and even frightened trying to figure out the true depth of the universe and where did it finally end and how long had time been going on and was God really out there and, if so, where? I did the very same thing, but on such a smaller, more manageable scale. I could do it without getting scared.

All the water I could see from the beach or from a higher vantage point was the ocean. True fact. There it was. The ocean had a name; it was the Pacific. On one side of the Pacific—the Oregon Side—was us. On the other side was Japan. I suppose I knew that Australia was in that general direction, too, and certainly China, but the thing that made Japan truly exist were the artifacts that would wash up on our beaches. The floats. There were no Chinese floats, just Japanese ones. They were a constant reminder that Japan was over there. Japan was real. I asked Crawford if any of our stuff washed across to Japan and he said no, it didn't work that way, that the currents were one-way only from them to us. So that was it. We got messages from them. Presents, you might say. – 55–

I don't remember how many times I stood there wondering. What were they like? The Japanese? How would they treat me if I suddenly appeared across the ocean?

There is something in this book called Fossil Words. The expression "works like a charm" is a phrase that has lost its original meaning. Nobody knows what a charm is. When my father painted signs for his store windows they were like hexes. They were charms. He had first painted them when he had to compete aggressively against others. When the need passed, he continued to paint his signs because they had been lucky for him and if he stopped his luck might diminish or go away. You keep doing the things that you think are good for you. Early magic.

All of your favorite memories are charms, they are experiences the memory of which confers more good luck and blessing.

Eddie Baker once broke a broken mirror, saying each time: "Seven years. Seven years. Seven years." He smashed the fragments with a hammer and the bits glittered on the ground near his house for years. He sought to prove something. I didn't understand it at the time. I think he busted his own bad luck to smithereens.

Smithereens, by the way, is a swell word and a nice concept.

Aunty Marnie said that in the Old Days carnivals would come to town and set up their tents and their rides in the place where Battle Rock State Park now stands. One time the carnival had a lion in a cage. A Port Orford kid stuck his arm in the cage and the lion bit it off at the shoulder. If you don't think this doesn't create an Instant Legend, you're mistaken. The kid didn't die, Marnie said, and was still a strong swimmer in Garrison Lake. Magic memory of the Lucky Boy.

There was a another carnival I remember only vaguely. It was up in Coquille. They had actual freaks in Freak Shows in those days, and these were the first ones I'd ever seen. They including a pinheaded woman with her hair pulled back in a knot to make her look even freakier and more pinheaded. She touched my hand and smiled at me with an ancient, distant look which I have never forgotten. A stunningly beautiful woman who had been born with no arms wrote calligraphically with her feet. I had a little card for a long time with my name footwritten on it. Assuredly magic. The India Rubber Man farted during one of his contortions and I don't know whether it was part of the act or not but it was very funny and everybody laughed. For a nickel, people could rub the hump of a hunchback for luck and, to my surprise, there was a long line of people waiting to do it. My dad wanted to but my mother talked him out of it. Maybe our family luck would have changed if he had. It started to rain and we drove back home.

Speaking of luck, some old guy in town made a comment about our house on the hill when it was being finished. He said. "For luck, enter a new house for the first time through the back door." Everybody looked at him and realized in that moment that my father had designed a house with two front doors. Now what?

The truly great mysteries were commonplace ones, information that could throw you into a funk for days. I can remember that grapefruit was an example. Does a grapefruit grow on a vine? No. Is it purple? No. Is it little? No. Then what was the connection? Who was on duty the day that particular fruit was named? Was he or she crazy?

I was next perplexed by the role of "chance" in life. It began when one of my parents declared that some undertaking, whatever it was, seemed to be "Chancy."

"Who is Chancy?" I asked. "What is Chancy?"

I think I had a vision of a person like an Uncle or maybe a new dog. They said that Chancy was dangerous and that didn't help much at all. My confusion was deepened by the expression: "Don't leave it to chance."

Other references were made to "a Chinaman's" chance, even though there were no Chinese people probably in the whole county.

There was an identical condition called A Snowball's Chance in Hell. Then therere was "not half a chance," which was supposed to mean the same thing as no chance whatsoever. This kind of logic can induce headaches in small children. It makes them wrinkle their faces in confusion. Once, while I was standing around in my father's store I heard two people speak simultaneously in response to somebody's unlikely or stupid proposition:

"Fat chance!"

"Slim chance!"

I asked if I was supposed to believe that fat chance, no chance, half a chance, and slim chance meant approximately the same thing. The answer was yes. Maybe my grandfather had been right when he said that everybody should learn to speak Latin. Maybe Latin was less confusing. Who knew. I sure as hell didn't.

Along with confused, I also got scared when somebody mentioned "Ghost of a Chance!"

Come on, guys, give a kid a break.

Garrison Lake– Swimming

Swimming memories start with my mother and my aunts, all qualified Life Savers and Swimming Instructors. I attended my mother's lessons at the inland end of Garrison Lake with other kids. There was a dock there which was 60 feet long with a diving board at the end.

The depth fell off quickly. You were up to your (6-year-old) waist by the time you were 10 feet from the shore. Then it fell off to beat the band. It must have been 20 feet deep at the end of the dock. The water was very clear. The lake had waterdogs in it. That's what they called them. They were salamanders that were brown on top and orange on the bottom. Elusive. Hard to catch. And nothing to do with them after you caught them. Daryll Sauers, Ted's cousin, blew one up with a firecracker once, but that was about it.

Garrison Lake is a freshwater lake separated from the Pacific Ocean by a quarter mile of sand. You flew over it when you were a bird, remember? The white beach serves both the ocean and the lake. The winds on the lake were from the north in the summer, so if you were at the south end you could have ocean-like waves. There were dunes down there as well. Big ones. So it was our favorite place to swim. You could catch the waves. You could race to the leeward side of the dunes for protection from the wind. It was warm there and you could lie, facing uphill, and cover yourself with sand that had been heated by the sun. It was great. Since there wasn't anybody around within miles, we'd swim nude. So that was fun, too. White summer clouds, blue ocean, bluegreen lake. The waves and froth. Hot sand. Terrific.

There was also the minor wonder at the size of a visiting kid's dick. Our dinks were the size of our thumbs. He was the same age but his was enormous by comparison. Amazing. This lanky little kid with the big dick. (Word was he stuck it in Peggy, a next-door-neighbor kid. This fact was later confirmed by Peggy herself, during one of our anatomical comparisons and discussions in the deep woods way beyond the place where my submarine was later lost in the murky water tank.)

Magic recollections about other waters.

Aunty Marnie, who lived in Portland, took me north across the Columbia River into Washington State one time to a place called Battleground Lake. It was strange because it had a wooden swimming pool sunk in the lake next to the beach. ("What's this?" some jerk little city kid said. "Is this to protect us from sharks?" "No, you jerk," I wish I'd had the capacity to say, "it's to keep you from drowning your stupid little ass!") A walkway went all the way around and boards kept you in the "pool." That's where kids and the elderly were supposed to swim. Adults could rent boats and row them to the middle of the lake, then swim wherever they wanted. The lake was good because it was still. There was no wind. And the water was warmer than Garrison Lake because it wasn't cooled by winds off the ocean. I'm told that much farther north, in British Columbia, the ocean is warmed by the Japanese Current and you can swim in it. But not in Port Orford, where you'd freeze your gonads off by going in the surf. Kids were also warned of the Demon UNDERTOW, which killed everybody no matter what. With the exception, of course, of Doc Pugh. Every year on the 4th of July, the elderly, gray-haired, fragile-looking Doc Pugh in his baggy swimming trunks would plunge into the surf and swim around Battle Rock! Just like it was nothing! Talk about cheering and clapping! Wow.

I loved Battleground Lake. The whole place smelled like ferns and moss and it was still. This was in contrast to the wind that always seemed to be blowing in Port Orford. And the other thing I liked about it was the fact that Margaret and Tom took me there and they really loved each other and I was glad to be with them. My parents didn't act that way. They were always too busy working in the store. They were always tired. They were frequently short-tempered. Margaret and Tom smiled at each other and had fun. And they cut me in on the fun. I felt part of a special group, not some kid being tolerated. They had a little cabin down the Columbia and when I visited them in Portland they would take me there to spend the night. It was high above the river and I remember one of Roosevelt's Great White Fleet exercises, with battleships and cruisers going up the Columbia toward Portland. White ships quietly going up the narrow river on a mostly foggy day.

This would have been before the War, maybe 1938 or 1939. That's when I saw the dirigible *Los Angeles* drumming hollowly along overhead, as if its engines were in a deep barrel. Here's a fact for you. The *Graf Zeppelin* was LZ-127 (LZ meaning "Luftschiff Zeppelin"). The *Los Angeles* was LZ-128. And the *Hindenberg* was LZ-129. German passengers on the *Graf Zeppelin*, on its regular flights back and forth from Germany to South America, used to complain about not having a piano. Apparently they'd like to hoist a few beer steins and sing. So the *Hindenberg* set that right by having an aluminum baby grand piano that everybody could gather around at night. Please imagine gliding 400 feet above the Atlantic on a moonlit night, engine noise barely noticeable, and singing with your friends around an aluminum baby grand piano.

V-8 juice was introduced, I loved it, and Margaret bought cans and cans of it.

Margaret and Tom lived in an English-looking building on the fourth floor high up.

Also, about this time, it was Aunt Margaret who took me swimming at Jantzen Beach, a famous old amusement park north of Portland. It was the first time I'd ever been in a real swimming pool. And the pool was huge. Also, we'd gotten to the park early, so there was hardly anybody around. I couldn't get over it! All that sparkling clear and WARM water. If not warm, at least not goose-bump-raising cold water like Garrison Lake at the beginning of the summer.

I remember how much fun it was to swim alone in that pool. Margaret was sitting in the sun, half watching me, but with most of her attention focused on a magazine. Jantzen Beach—a magical and sort of surrealistic memory of a vast white concrete apron around the big expanse of aqua water. With a huge roller-coaster in the background where, every few minutes, screaming people rattled past in green and yellow and red cars.

Once, at Margaret & Tom's place, Margaret got into an old trunk and showed me some things that happened when she was born —especially having to do with her birth announcement and some people's responses to it. This will give you some further insight into my grandfather Frank Tichenor and his need to be a Big Shot.

Johnny with Aunty Marnie

Frank Tichenor's (Actually His Daughter Margaret's) Birth Announcement Sent Worldwide

In 1913, to celebrate the birth of his fourth child (a daughter like the other three of his children), my grandfather, Frank Tichenor, hired an artist friend of his from Gold Beach to create a birth announcement which told a story through its graphic elements alone. The card contained the following information:

The mantle of the fireplace says Seattle, Washington, and on the clock above it shows the time to be 1:50. Shadows thrown from a chandelier signify an early morning birth. A stork is holding scales which shows the baby's weight to be seven and a half pounds. A doctor's case has the name of Dr. E. M. Carney on it. A nurse leaving the room has the name J. Prince inscribed on the back of her apron. A calendar on the wall says Mimor Private Hospital, Thursday, April 17, 1913. My mother, Ellen, is seated in a chair reading a big book entitled *15,000 Selected Names for Boys*, while my twin aunts, Marianne and Anna, stand mischievously with little hammers held behind their pinafores, contemplating God knows what mischief. A trunk beneath the baby says Margaret Brinkerhoff Tichenor. On the parlor wall hangs a drawing of Battle Rock, the most distinguishing landmark of Port Orford where Frank himself was born.

According to a newspaper clipping, this announcement was accompanied by a genealogy prepared by Frank which purported to trace the family name back to Martin Tichenor who took the oath of fidelity in the New Haven Colony in 1644. (Bogus.) The newspaper story also noted that this announcement was "sent to Governors of every state in the Union, to the White House, to Oyster Bay, and to Buckingham Palace."

It also went to many other foreign countries and to lawyers, bankers, presidents of fraternal organizations, business people and nobody knows who else. An enormous scrapbook was created for Margaret which contained responses from all over the world. This maneuver was executed for the greater glory of Frank Tichenor, there's no question about that. My Aunt Margaret (Aunty Marnie) was merely a convenience; a good excuse. It must have been a big thrill for my grandfather to see that

"Frank B. Tichenor, Seattle, Washington," was enough of an address to insure prompt delivery.

Frank was, in most respects, a blatant bullshit artist, an adumbration specialist who created a sketchy idea about himself, a vague outline that suggested reality on a monumental scale. He did a few things that were real and true. The rest was sham. The genealogy was contrived by him. In later life, he admitted he was wrong. The Tichenors of whom he was a part could only be traced back to his great-grandfather, James Tichenor.

But it didn't bother him. He wanted to be associated with greatness, with being related to Pilgrims and founding fathers. It was the same with the correspondence itself. He placed himself in a league with governors, presidents, and kings. Even the most remote association counted. He made the great philosophical mistake of trying to graft quality from one thing onto another, in this case himself. He must have believed that a person who consorts with the powerful, however slightly, gains power.

Some Startling Things

I would call the first ones "Unexpected Smells and the Failure to Be Able to See."

The town would all of a sudden smell like lumber and sawdust and wood smoke. Try to figure that one out when you're little. Try to explain wind to somebody three or four years old, much less a change of wind direction and woody smells from the mill. Direction? What's direction?

When a cloud comes down, some people said, it's called fog. At least so they tried to persuade me. I went blind out there once, one of the first times I walked back to the store from the barber shop by myself. The fog suddenly rolled in and was so dense that I could barely see my feet. I could see absolutely nothing around me. The trucks and cars stopped and the drivers turned off their engines. It was spooky silent. Simply white. I knew I was pointed in the right direction, but I was stopped dead in my tracks. I thought about crying, but I didn't. The amazement and mystery of such a thing (Conditions Two and Three) overcame the fright at being "lost" (Condition One). I just stood there. Soon, I heard voices—beacons—that called to the lost.

"Over here, I'm over here at the Associated Gas Station!" Or: "Here, come this way. I'm at the Post Office!" We lost ones would call out: "Where are you? Say something again. Keep talking, will you?" Then, like airplanes, we homed on the beacons.

"Johnny!" I could hear my distant father calling from the front of the store. "Johnny! Over this way!" And his location was clearly different from the gas station or the post office, either of which was closer.

Mystery won out. I decided to go for the store. I stumbled a few times in the loose gravel by the side of the highway, but I finally made it. I requested a baloney sandwich to regain my strength from this episode, even though it wasn't lunch time. I got it, along with a cup of cocoa, which I consumed while I looked out the window waiting for the fog to lift. It was the longest and thickest in anybody's memory, including Mrs. Leneive's, who was the oldest person in town. And I had made it through.

There was one other startling thing I should mention. It's about Bruno. "Bruno the Terrible" ought be the title of this one.

I was given a bear that scared the shit out of me. That was not the intention, of course, because my parents thought it was possibly the best bear in the world. Presents like the bear were supposed to make up for any other deficiencies my mother and father had as parents. A big hug would have been far superior to an entire bear, but they weren't aware of this fact. Looking back on it, I don't remember them even hugging one another, let alone me or my sister. They didn't.

Anyway, suddenly there's this bear.

I suspect that right now you're sitting there thinking about Teddy Bears that you have owned or seen—soft, floppy things that can be made to sit up and look like they're reading a book. Or a bear that you could take to bed with you or to go for a ride with in the back seat of a car.

But this is nothing like Bruno!

Bruno was the bear's name. That's what they named him.

Bruno was a riding bear!

I have never seen one like it since.

Bruno stood on all fours and was solid and hard, not soft or flexible. He stood on all fours and looked straight ahead with angry brown eyes made of glass. His ears were three and a half feet from the floor and the entire bear was maybe four feet long. Bruno stood on an iron frame with an axle between the two front feet and an axle between the two back feet. At the end of the axles were sturdy iron wheels, perhaps six inches across. Bruno was made to roll.

He may have been a German bear. I think this is so. I think he was made by German engineers who gave no thought to children, but considered only true bears and how they looked and the noise they made. Bruno was lifelike and ferocious looking and had a ring on his right side that you could pull. When you pulled the ring (which was hooked to a sturdy chain) it would activate a roaring mechanism deep inside Bruno. It was much more than a growl; it was the sound of a grizzly bear about to charge. It was the sound of a bear that was pissed off about having stepped on a thorn. Or a bear that suddenly hated somebody's looks badly enough to attack the person. I hated that sound. It was horrible and unpleasant. I hated the bear and the people who made him.

I was three or four when Bruno arrived on a birthday or Christmas. I couldn't get on Bruno. You needed to be at least 10 or 11 years old to get on Bruno and have your legs long enough to push yourself around on the wheels. By the time you were this age you would be too old for such silliness. Also, the bear didn't have a saddle or a bridle, so there was nothing to sit on or hang onto. I would slip off. Bruno was covered in short brown fur which was slippery. So grown-ups would put me on the bear to see how I'd look. I would no doubt look just swell—the little kid on the bear. But there was nothing to *do* on the bear. Nowhere to go. Merely sit there until you slid off and banged your feet or your knees on the iron frame at the bottom.

"Let's put Johnny on Bruno," was my cue to sneak away.

It was not a bad bear to observe. Germans frequently build things that don't do very much but create a wonderful appearance. This was Bruno. He looked like a great toy and made a noise that satisfied all the adults, I suppose because it would scare them half to death and cause them to exclaim: "Jesus! That sounds *exactly* like a bear!"

Bruno was at once terrifying, satisfying to look at, and boring. I could not use the toy in any way. I could try to get on it by standing on a footstool or a box. But, once aboard, there was nothing to do except look around and wait to fall on the floor. I was not about to pull the ring and make it roar. What was the point? To frighten myself in an empty room? No, thanks.

Over the next two years my parents would say things like:

"Why don't you play with Bruno?"

"Why is other stuff stacked on top of Bruno? Don't you like your bear?"

"I never notice you riding Bruno."

"Do you realize how much that bear cost?"

They would speak about him with great solicitude as if the bear had feelings and I did not. They would chastise me for not liking the bear and then walk over and give him a nice pat and say, "Good Bruno." Then—as likely as not—they would give the chain a big pull and make him roar like a demented dragon or an animal that had been kicked in the nuts.

My Aunt Anna's little son, Charles, visited one time and expressed a great deal of interest in the bear. He didn't even seem to mind the roaring. So I decided that he was a goof-ball.

"If you are not careful," I was solemnly advised by both my mother and my father, "we will give Bruno to Charles."

I said swell. By all means. Give the bear to Charles. Give the bear to Charles *today!* I would be happy to get the bear out of my room. It took up an entire corner. It did nothing but stand there and continue to startle me. I wasn't even allowed to throw my clothes on it. So I instead threw them on the floor where my genetic code—and the instinct of all boys—directed they be thrown.

The bear was worth a fortune to my parents and zero to me. Less than zero.

"What's your problem?" I would be asked. And this was a question, by the way, that was likely to be raised two or three times a day in connection with other issues usually having to do with my lack of performance or judgment, or my faulty reasoning abilities.

"Don't you recognize quality when you see it? What's your problem?"

I figured it was not *my* problem, it was Bruno's problem. I tried to explain that Bruno would work better if he had a seat you could sit on and if he had rubber tires instead of stupid iron wheels. Also, he would be vastly improved if the front wheels were steerable, then you could ride down hills or something. Best yet was my advice about having bears with motors in them— bears that you could drive like cars.

"There you go again!" I would be scolded. "You should be ashamed about how lazy you are! A motor indeed!"

They were terrific at encouraging creativity. (Not.)

At any rate, to teach me a lesson, they gave the bear to Charles.

I don't have any pictures of me on Bruno. Apparently none were ever taken. But I still have a picture of Charles on Bruno. He is sitting there with a glum look and I know precisely what he's thinking. He is thinking: "What am I doing on this stupid bear? And how can I get off without hurting myself?" Or: "Oh, oh, I'm starting to slip off! Oh, my God!"

Teach *me* a lesson, will they!

Well, maybe it did. Maybe the experience taught me that anytime somebody gives me a horrible present that I turn right around and give it to somebody else—I give it to the first person who admires it and then later, when the original presenter looks around the room for it, I explain that it exploded or was stolen or that I developed an allergic reaction to it and had to give it to somebody who lives on a farm and has plenty of room and fresh air. Something plausible like that.

Like one of my stories to my parents to explain how I'd broken a bottle of medicine I'd picked up at Pugh's. I told them the accident was actually caused by an old, blind seagull which had suddenly flown into my face and caused me to wreck my bicycle.

After I grew up, I met a German guy who said he was on the Russian Front during World War Two and what a catastrophe it was to be in battle during sub-zero weather, in conditions so cold that equipment wouldn't work. He described some brand-new sophisticated German tanks that would not run when the temperature was under 20 below zero because the hydraulic systems would freeze up. However, he said, you could hear the Russian tanks coming across distant fields—Russian tanks that, by comparison, were buckets of bolts, that wheezed and clanked and back-fired, but that came relentlessly on. Russian tanks whose guns could be cranked around by hand. He said it would make you weep to stand there next to your superior tank (whose gun couldn't be pointed) that was about to be blown to ratshit by a technically inferior tank that worked!

I told him that I bet I knew who designed those German tanks. It was the same guys who dreamed up Bruno before the war.

Goose-Drownders

When a big winter storm would blow in from the south, the harbor would be closed and all the boats would be lifted out of the water and placed on trailers on the dock. A large crane would swing out and pick them up like toys, then place them safely out of the water. A true whopper of a storm would pick up froth from the water and the heavy winds would blow these suds all the way up the cliffs into town. Patches and piles of this white foam would be all over everything. If you picked some up and tasted it, it was as salty as sea water, which, of course, it was.

Fishermen would sit in people's kitchens and drink coffee during storms. Crawford Smith's was a favorite, Smitty's. His kitchen had paths worn down through the linoleum from all the people who would enter the room through the back door to sit down at the big table and drink coffee from the enameled pot on the big range and smell Lottie's pastry baking inside. In a short time they would eat hot cookies straight from the pan.

Crawford was one of my heroes, and not just as a kid, but later when I was grown.

Eve Doyle used to be a Catholic and told my mother that Saint Barbara can be invoked to abate storms. She knew a lot about protective saints, ones I've never heard of. She believed in angels. She said one time during a lull in a conversation at dinner at her and Don's apartment that, if there is a sudden pause in the conversation when the room is full of people, it's because angels are passing overhead.

During a storm, a group might also congregate in the back end of Red's Saloon, which was really a Tavern, but everybody called it a Saloon. There was a pool table in the back but only a few people could play on it. There were several places on the table's edges where the cushion had no spring at all. Also, there was a bad dip at one end and a sort of a slant on the other. Playing pool on it required a thorough knowledge of the table's peculiarities, and the various techniques and tricks to overcome them. There were card tables back there, too, with green-shaded lights over them. The cards would click as the rain streamed down the windows and rumbled in the gutters overhead.

"A Goose–Drownder," somebody would inevitably say.

Way up the hill at the Coast Guard Station the rescue men would drink coffee in rooms where they waited for the S.O.S. from ships in distress or from actual shipwrecks. Some were "up above" where officers and men lived in either a barracks-like building or little houses. "Up above" meant on the top of the cliffs. "Down below" meant at the building where rescue lifeboats were launched. This building was on the beach in a cove below and could be reached only by descending several hundred wooden steps that snaked down the steep hill. They were painted white. Men would try to set new records in running down those steps but I don't know what the best time was.

When I was small I had to be helped more than once when high winds caught me outside and forced me to stand behind a tree and wait for a grownup to come and get me. I couldn't walk against it by myself and the wind was always in my face when I would try to walk home from school. In weather like that you could lick the rain off your lips and realize that it, like the white foam, was sea water that had blown ashore; it wasn't regular rain at all. Seagulls would sit in the rocks and bitch at the storm as if saying "If you won't let us fly, then we'll sit here and squawk! We'll show you!"

These would be good days to play with toy soldiers or hook my train together and watch the warm lights of the cars as they hummed around the tracks. It was usually a day like that when I'd be crouching on the floor or sitting next to the wood stove when somebody would come in and report that another one of my part-grown cats had just gotten run over, and that we needed to form a Burial Party.

I favored only two kinds of cats (which, luckily, were born thereabouts in abundance): orange-and-white striped or mostly black. I stopped being creative in naming them when I realized the awful mortality facts. So these cats were named either "Tiger" or "Blackie." My grandfather took on the responsibility of creating various Roman numerals to put behind their names. We got at least to "Tiger IV" and "Blackie III." Then, as I said, I shifted my affections to Skippy, the dog, who appeared to have a greater appreciation for the odds of being able to run under a lumber carrier and live to tell about it.

(Why did I just say Skippy, the dog? I'll tell you. At about this time the little goof-ball, Charles, was given the nickname "Skippy." I thought that was terrifically funny when I first heard about it. My mother said I was a miserable little brat.)

We would walk on the beach after big storms because, as I've said, it was a good time to find glass floats from faraway Japan. I remember the beach south of Battle Rock after goose-drowners—with tight groups of seagulls scurrying along looking like foreign refugees in the news-reels, leaving their footprints in the wet sand and not disturbing the black cormorants who stood at attention, sentry-like, eyeing the "civilians" but then looking straight at the breakers as if wondering whether it was time to eat—standing there in twos and threes looking at one another questioningly, figuring out what to do, or maybe waiting for an officer's orders.

Farther down toward Hubbard Creek, giant old boilers from ship-wrecked ships kept rusting away and long ropes of kelp washed up, green-brown in color and tapered like lion-tamer's whips. There were iodine smells and transparent jellyfish, new driftwood and broken boxes, bottles, and those big dead creatures such as sharks or seal lions lying on their sides with mouths hanging open and their teeth showing. They stunk and had to be approached from upwind.

Then probably another black night would follow with thunder all over, now and then with lightning interrupting everything. A bell buoy sounded near a distant reef, a bronze song if you listened—it was out there waiting for first light like the rest of us. Then it would be sunrise with clouds racing through it, soon to be smeared over with another part of the storm and more rain hammering on the tin roof of the storeroom and coating the windows. Then the wind would go at it again—gale force.

In such weather a ship once went aground a few hundred yards south of Battle Rock. The storm, practically a typhoon, had been very strong during the day, with foam hurled up to the town and shingles blowing off here and there. But it receded at nightfall and the night was quiet except for the waves, the combers, rolling into the beach. I have a black-and-white memory of this event, no grays. The Coast Guard was shooting white flares to illuminate the scene, so it was either silver light or black shadows.

The outline of the ship was huge and close, alarmingly so—as if a big building had suddenly parked itself on the edge of the beach. It didn't have any business there. A breeches buoy had been strung from the boat to the shore and men were shuttling across to safety, almost in the fash-ion of my Flash Gordon rocket ship that would ride down a long piece of string. A bonfire was built from driftwood in order to throw more light. This made my grandfather ecstatic because he loved flames, and he be-came the fire's superintendent. I remember the smell of the kerosene used to start the wet wood. The rescued men sat around the fire, sorting through whatever possessions they had managed to bring with them.

Later, some salvagers tried to get what they could and then the ship was dynamited to break it up and the remains were set on fire. We watched it burn for several days—the orange flickering out there in the green ocean and the white overcast. The ship was named the *Cotteneva*.

Speaking of fires. Let me tell you something else before I forget it.

Forest Fire

The hugest forest fire of the time came along and burned miles of trees. Not only that, it burned the town of Bandon right to the ground! It burned for days and came real close to our town. It could not be put out by the firefighters. I remember the orange light on the horizon to the north—that's how close it got. The fire chased animals in front of it, deer and chipmunks—and also people. They ran before it. I recall people in cars coming down from the north, only the cars didn't look like cars at all, they looked like lumps because they were covered with all the things that people could load up and take with them. Mattresses and chairs and bundles of clothes were tied up in sheets and then lashed on the tops of the cars with clothesline. People drove slowly through the thick, smelly smoke and the headlights of the cars were orangey in the dark. (It was the very same color, now that I remember, as the dial on our Philco radio that we'd listen to in the dark and the rain.) It got so bad that the Navy sent down a ship and everybody in town was told they could pack one suitcase and get on the ship. That there was going to be a disaster—just like Bandon—and everybody had to leave. My sister cried in frustration about what to take. I figured it out pretty easily. As long as I didn't take any clothes I was okay. So, while my mother and father were dashing around, I unpacked the clothes my mother had prepared for me and put them back in the drawers. I refilled the bag with toys and games. Heavy rains came but they didn't put out the fires. T.J. said the raindrops turned to steam. The wind changed, though, and it helped a lot, blowing the fire back on itself and away from the town. We were saved.

I went up to Bandon a few days later with my dad in the pickup. It was leveled. I remember all the basements. Block after block of nothing but concrete basements filled with charred wood and debris. The fire had burned away the wharves and left nothing but charred pilings for the gulls to sit on.

History Assignment

I was asked to do a writing assignment in some early grade. I was supposed to interview my father about his life but he claimed he was too busy. I had a whole week. But he kept being busy. As if he were trying to keep a secret. But he wasn't. It was painful to talk about, he said. Because he had once been a bigger man. By which he meant a more important man with a big boat in the river and clouds painted on the living room ceiling. Time was running out and so, the weekend before the paper was due, he sat down with a pencil stub and wrote some stuff in one of my Big Chief notebooks. I then rewrote it as a history-collecting interview.

Here is what my dad said:

"I will give a few of the places I have been. On the west coast from San Diego to Seattle, Wash. and through a few states from Portland to as far east as Davenport, Iowa. I have been to Reno and Carson City, Nevada.

"Here are a few places where I had businesses. In 1923 I worked in a market on 348 Belmont Street in Portland. I worked there about six months and the owner leased it to me for 3 years at $135.00 a month. I did pretty well. I always remembered I made over $5,000.00 the first year but not quite so well the next 2 years. Then I went back to Kansas to see the folks.

"Then I leased another market on Williams Avenue. I had it about three months that would be in 1927 then I was operated on for a ruptured appendix. When I got out of the hospital the business had gone to pot. As I was not very strong I got out of it. I took it easy for a few months. Then I bought a market on 42nd and Belmont Street. In a short time the owner of the Belmont Market came to see me about leasing the market again so I took another lease for three years. After that then I went and bought a big market that had been closed for two years. I cleaned and painted it up and opened it up and ran it for two years then I leased it to your Uncle Harvey for a year. That was April 1932. You were about six months old. I had a new Graham car so we went to California and visited Ed Rowland and his folks, and then to Los Angeles to visit some more of your mother's folks. It was then off to Kansas for four months to visit the Quick family.

"Those markets I had on Williams Avenue I don't remember the numbers. There was a shopping area around the corner of Williams Avenue and Russell Street. I had another market about three blocks from that nice home we had in Portland.

"Anyway the depression got real bad and I was pretty near broke and just had the restaurant left. Your grandfather Frank Tichenor came to Portland to see us and said they were building a breakwater for shipping and a saw mill so we sold out and moved to Port Orford and started over from scratch. I realize what the number was on Williams Avenue. It was 530. I have an old flyer from years ago that gave SPECIALS FOR THIS WEEKEND. It's from my Quick's Quality Market, 530 Williams Avenue, Second Door North of Russell, East Side of Street. There were three specials good between 8 and 10 a.m. Saturday: (1) Tender Sirloin Steaks: 10¢ per pound; (2) Pork Steaks: 3 pounds for 25¢; and (3) Fresh Ground Hamburger or Sausage: 3-lbs for 20¢. Other all-day Saturday specials included Fancy Leg of Spring Lamb (12½¢ a pound); Top Sirloin or Rib Steaks (12½¢ per pound); Fresh Salmon (5½¢ per pound); Breast of Veal (7¢ per pound); and Lean Sliced Bacon (15¢ per pound)."

The day before I took the paper to school, my dad asked me:

"Maybe you'd like to take this to school to show your friends."

He pointed at a badly chipped salt cellar under the cash register. He kept old coins in it. He dumped out the coins and showed me the salt cellar. It was the size of an adult's cupped hands. It was transparent glass, solid and heavy.

"I found this," he said with pride. "I was walking along when I was a kid and saw a little piece of it buried in a dirt road. Do you know what it looked like? It looked like a diamond."

I tried to imagine the junky piece of glass looking like a diamond and couldn't do it. Maybe the sun had hit it just right.

"I found a stick and dug it up," my father continued. "I was late for school it took so long."

I didn't say anything. I had nothing to say.

"I took it home and washed it off. I really had to scrub in these cracks and corners. It cleaned up real pretty. Don't you think?"

I confessed that I thought so, even though I hadn't known what it looked like when it was dirty.

"I've always kept this. I've kept it with me for luck."

I stared at it.

"It is something important that I found myself."

I said nothing. I could appreciate his feelings because I was a collector myself. But not of old glass salt cellars.

"Your friends might be interested to see it. I guess you could say that it's a part of my history. It kind of goes with the story."

I didn't agree with him but I was diplomatic enough not to say so.

I was also savvy enough not to lodge a complaint about having to take it to school. I had learned duplicity by this time. I had learned that if you make a convincing enough *beginning* it will appear that you are bound accomplish the entire job.

I took the proffered salt cellar.

I wrapped it like a piece of meat, first in a piece of waxed paper. Then I wrapped it in white butcher paper and tied it with string just as my father had taught me to. He watched enthusiastically.

I put the wrapped package in a brown paper bag, said thanks, and walked to my room.

I had conveyed the idea that I was going to take the salt cellar to school and concluded that I might even do so, only that I wouldn't open the package. That way, if I was asked if I'd taken the thing to school, I could honestly say that yes I had—I had taken it to school.

That's what happened. I took it to school and put it in my desk.

But the teacher saw me. The teacher knew that I didn't bring my lunch. I went home for lunch. So I was asked what was in the paper bag.

I revealed the contents and told everybody the story about my father finding it when he was a kid. The salt cellar was carefully passed around and generated mild interest. The other kids were mostly being polite.

At the end of the day I told my dad that it had been a big hit and he was extremely pleased.

Tonsils and Adenoids

Dr. Baird was the gray-haired Scotsman who had served in World War One and didn't smile very much and kept to himself. He never ate in a restaurant. A woman cooked for him and he ate at the kitchen table in his house by himself.

He was craggy and seemed to be humorless, but he was accessible. People could talk to him on the street and raise questions about their ailments or complaints. He would always listen and the most frequent diagnosis was apt to be: "It's nothing for you to worry about."

It was free. If anything really did seem out of the ordinary, he would book an office visit right on the spot and address the problem. Over the years he pulled people out of wrecked cars, managed difficult births, and set fractures. He operated when he had to.

Dr. Baird accepted cash for payment, of course, but was also known to take I.O.U.s, gasoline, canned goods of all kinds, and, at least one time, a pig.

There is still a scar on the top of my left index finger where Dr. Baird sewed the end of it back on.

Anyway, the story goes this way:

My throat was sore and I could hardly talk.

Dr. Baird was walking past the plate-glass windows of the store. My dad ran out. Dr. Baird listened to an explanation and I watched him nod his head. Dr. Baird came in. He looked at my face. He asked for a spoon.

Using the spoon as a tongue depressor he peered into my throat. I gagged. I hoped for the remark about "it's nothing to worry about," but Dr. Baird frowned instead.

"Tonsils," he said. "They have to come out."

I was horrified, but I hoped he would do it on the spot. That way it would be over with.

He then explained something to the effect that bad tonsils can't be taken out when they're bad, they have to be taken out when they're good. You have to wait for unhealthy tonsils to become healthy in order to remove them. This didn't make a lot of sense to me.

Dr. Baird was asked when he could take them out and he said that he wouldn't personally take them out and that I'd have to have my tonsils and adenoids removed in the hospital in Bandon. (This was after the big fire and when Bandon had been rebuilt.) Going to the Bandon hospital was not good news. It was, in fact, a terrible shocker because the Bandon hospital was where people died. I had not heard a single report of anybody going to the Bandon hospital and coming out alive. The Bandon hospital was where victims of car wrecks went to die the same night or, at the very latest, the next day. A man named Carter from way up Elk River became prematurely aged and skeletal but was afraid to come to town and admit that he was sick. He was diagnosed with a huge tumor and Dr. Baird drove him up to Bandon in his baird-colored car. Carter died within hours after surgery. I had the idea that the moment you went through the doors of the Bandon hospital you probably died. It didn't occur to me to wonder why the doctors and nurses didn't die in the infernal place. Patients died, that's all I knew or cared about.

I was given three or four weeks to contemplate the fact that not just my tonsils were going to be removed, but also my adenoids. I didn't know what either one of these things were. I remain cloudy to this day about the purpose of adenoids and what they might do for me (or against me) if I still had them.

The next three or four weeks were spent worrying. Each night in bed I would fret about the Bandon hospital. I was afraid. I told myself: "You will never forget this. You will never forget this. If you do not die, that is. You will always remember this fear. Believe me when I tell you that you will always remember this. You will probably remember it even if you die. And you will probably die. Because everybody else who goes into the hospital in Bandon comes out dead."

How was I supposed to know that people were cured there? How was I supposed to know that people actually went back home and ate hotcakes covered with syrup from a tin made in the shape of a little house that had a screw-on lid where the chimney was supposed to be?

The paradox was, of course, that the very minute you were feeling just great was the time for you to get trundled off to the Bandon hospital. It was a sunny morning. We got up very early and drove to Bandon. I was white with fear. And I was put in a little room of the same white color and told to take all my clothes off. It was the first indignity before death and I knew this. I put on the stupid little gown and looked out the window at the river and the seagulls on pilings. Lucky bastards, I thought, to be ought there free and flying around. Seagulls probably didn't have tonsils, I reasoned, and they for sure didn't have Seagull Hospitals. I was in the hospital and they weren't. I could die and they weren't likely to. They were flapping around and squawking just as happy as you please.

Back in those days, pre-operative drugs were not administered. At least I don't remember anything that made me dopey and cooperative.

The last words were these: "When it's over, you can have all the ice cream you want."

This was from my mother. My father was safely back at the store, probably smoking a Camel and having a cup of coffee. Or painting a sign in red and blue tempera.

The other last words were from a nurse who put me on a wheeled cart and said: "This will be fun."

I was wheeled down a hallway and into an operating room with a big round light. None of it looked like fun.

They transfered me to an operating table and put a cloth and metal cage on my face and started to drip ether on it. I took one whiff and decided that this was the moment to resist. It was time to rise up and escape! My nights of worrying myself to sleep popped into perspective. "Fight!" a voice in my head called out. It also screamed: "*SAVE YOURSELF!*"

I thrashed about. I punched a nurse in the stomach so hard that she screamed. I kicked over a little wheely cart of instruments and they scattered all over the floor. I clutched the mask on my face, pulled it away, and threw it across the room.

I was winning.

But only for a matter of seconds. Many strong hands held me down. New instruments were fetched. The mask was again forced onto my face. The dripping stink of ether resumed. I continued to resist. But the fighting was useless. I grayed out. I looked briefly at the face of the person administering the anaesthetic and knew that it was the last face I would ever see. Reality ran out in an ever expanding dark hole that slipped upward and around me like a big black sock and I thought I died.

Nothing.

Nothing.

For a long time.

Then haze.

Something.

The outline of the white room.

I was lying in the bed.

I could glimpse the gulls. They were still okay.

I was not okay.

My throat hurt. Terribly.

My mother sat in a chair with a magazine.

She looked at me.

I looked back.

I had been betrayed and deliberately injured. I had been badly injured. I was in deep pain. My mother asked me if I wanted some 7-Up. I couldn't talk to say no so she thought I said yes. The 7-Up wouldn't go down. 7-Up had always gone down very well in the past. I then realized that the reason I hadn't died was because it wasn't time yet. There was more suffering to be done, this time of the physical sort. After a suitable period of suffering I would die in the Bandon hospital. This much became clear to me. There would be much more pain, a final glimpse of the sea gulls, and then death.

I fell asleep.

I awoke in the afternoon. 7-Up was tried again. It worked. It didn't work well, but it worked. Vanilla ice cream went down. There was a chance. It wasn't a very big chance, but I seized it. The doctor walked in, peered at my throat, and said Fine.

Fine? What was that supposed to mean?

My mother took my clothes from the top of a bureau.

It was only then, at that very moment, I was told that I wouldn't have to stay in the hospital for weeks! That had been my vision: I would either die or I would be in bed for weeks.

Somebody should have explained that it was possible to get out of the hospital the same day you went in. They didn't. They hadn't. The fools.

I was driven home.

I ate cream of tomato soup for two days and a hamburger on day three. Death, who had been first in the white room and then no further than the shrubs outside the hospital window, retreated to the Tichenor Cemetery on the afternoon of the second day. He was all the way to Japan on day four and, by the weekend, had been completely forgotten—a thing of the past.

Here is a tip. Two tips, actually. If you find yourself beginning to get skeletal, consult a physician. Two: If you are merely down in the dumps and start getting scared about being down in the dumps, take a big glass and fill it two-thirds of the way with ice-cold 7-Up and then add a big glop of vanilla ice cream. Eat it with a spoon and you'll feel better within a matter of minutes. I guarantee this.

Battle Rock

Captain William Tichenor, my great-great-grandfather, had made the trip from San Francisco to the Columbia River in Oregon several times and had seen the southern coast of Oregon from the sea. In the month of March 1850 he set sail in his schooner, the *Jacob M. Ryerson*, for the Trinity River in northern California and a big storm blew up near Cape Mendocino, about 90 miles south of Crescent City. When the gale subsided a week or so later, he found himself near Cape Blanco only seven miles on a bee line north of Port Orford. He went ashore in a whale boat and examined the cliffs, creeks, and rivers southward to the present location of Port Orford but didn't go ashore because of the hostile appearance of the natives.

In March of 1851 he took command of the 400-ton sidewheel steamer *Sea Gull* and made numerous trips between San Francisco and Portland. During the last of May he decided to establish a settlement at Port Orford. In Portland he met a man named John Kirkpatrick who was a veteran of the Mexican War and a pioneer who had crossed the Rockies with Kit Carson. He appointed Kirkpatrick head of a small expedition and Kirkpatrick recruited eight other men and they were tranported to Port Orford on the *Sea Gull* and put ashore on June 9th. Kirkpatrick didn't like the looks of things and persuaded the Captain to give them a small cannon that was aboard the ship.

13621- Battle Rock, at Port Orford, Scene of Indian Conflict, Oregon Coast Highway

Captain Tichenor promised to return in two weeks and then sailed away to San Francisco.

The next morning, about one hundred Indians of the California Siwash tribe attacked the nine men on Battle Rock but were repulsed. A truce was negotiated when Kirkpatrick and his men conveyed the idea that the ship would come back in 14 days and they would leave.

The 15th day came and, since the *Sea Gull* had not returned, the Indians attacked again with a larger force. They were again unsuccessful in dislodging the Americans from the rock, but Kirkpatrick resolved to lead his men to safety in the north. After much hardship all nine men made it safely to a white settlement some 75 miles to the north called Umpqua City on July 2, 1851. Umpqua City, some ten miles up the Umqua River from the coast is now called Scottsburg.

There were two points about this saga that I never forgot. One was the fact that the first Indian charge was led by a white man in a red shirt. He was said to have been a Russian sailor who had survived a shipwreck many years earlier. The second part of the story that I thought was wonderful was the fact that a friendly Indian who spoke some English helped the nine men and, in the course of their journey, they passed a 20-foot-high white pole standing in a large pile of rocks at the edge of the beach. The Indian explained that once they passed the pole they would be safe. The California Siwashes would not dare to come north of the white pole because the Coos Bay, Umpqua, Clickatats, and other tribes would make war against them and drive them back.

"Like a real king's ex!" I remember saying to my grandfather who often told me the story.

"Yes," he smiled. "Exactly."

And what happened to Captain William?

After promising to return in 14 days with additional men and supplies, the Captain returned to San Francisco and became involved in business matters. He asked Captain Knight of the *Columbia* to stop at Port Orford to drop off reinforcements. Knight arrived in Port Orford just one day after the nine men had begun their escape to the north. He found the body of the white man in the red shirt and the remains of a big fire in which were found bits of bone and teeth. Knight presumed that the nine men had been killed by the local Indians.

Captain Tichenor returned to Port Orford on July 15, 1851, with 67 men, several cannons, and plenty of rifles. He built a fortification of two blockhouses on Fort Point. Houses were built. Cattle, pigs, and horses were brought in.

In May of 1852, Captain Tichenor brought his family to Port Orford—his wife, Elizabeth, his daughters Anna (15), Sarah Ellen (4), and his son Jacob (9). They were the first white family on the west coast between Astoria and Humboldt Bay. My mother, Ellen, was named after her great-aunt in much the same way, it was said, I was named after my great-uncle but my father knew very well that his great-grandfather had been named "John." Eddie Baker told all of my second-grade classmates that I had been named after a toilet. A real joker.

Think Chrome

I keep saying that I never did anything fun with my dad, but I did. It wasn't greatly interactive. It wasn't like going fishing with somebody or even going on a hike. I went to the can dump with my dad. It was not called a "garbage" dump or, as people I've known in other places called it, simply: "The Dump." It was a place out of town and we went there often. Later a guy picked up the garbage and took it to the dump. It was his job. It was some years later, however.

My old man created a lot of trash, chicken guts, fat scraps, old vegetables, and other refuse from the store and had to go there a couple of times a week. When I felt like it, I'd go with him. And he must have reasoned that this was a perfect place for a lazy boy with destructive tendencies to go, so my dad would contrive to stall and smoke cigarettes while I broke glass. Grandpa Frank had his bonfires. I had bottles and jars. You could break glass all day long at the can dump. It was sublime. Nobody cared. So my father stood around and let me do it.

I remember that he shot a pistol in the dump one time. A .38 cal. automatic that somebody gave him instead of paying his bill. He shot it just once. It scared the shit out of him. He didn't pretend otherwise. Driving back down the hill into town, he admitted to me that it had frightened him. Badly. Call this: *Introduction to Firearms Safety.* I wouldn't have touched that .38 with a stick.

The can dump was in a ravine. It had always been in the ravine, I guess. It had started at one end decades earlier and was gradually working its way north. Except that it didn't look all dump. The old part had grown over, in some parts with actual trees. So there was actually a three-stage dump: (1) old dump with small trees; (2) intermediate dump with shrubs and vines growing up, and (3) new dump with fresh garbage. In the no-man's land between old and intermediate I made a discovery, a find based on a glint.

Among the ancient rotted posts, broken machinery, bits of lumber and wire, rusted pipe, and empty paint buckets was the back end of a pickup that somebody had tried to fashion into a two-wheeled trailer. The tires were flat and gray and the years and the elements had destroyed all the paint until it was all rust orange. Dirt had caked on the tail lights. Also, it was barely visible in a tangle of blackberry vines. The only thing that remained undamaged was the chrome bumper which looked like it had left the factory only the day before.

This discovery was very confusing to me. At an early age, I had a pretty good vocabulary for describing the things I came into contact with, but little intellectual experience in dealing with anomalies such as the bumper. I knew the words *chrome* and *bumper*, for example, and understood their place in the scheme of things. But one did not expect to see such an object hidden in the old part of the can dump. Everything was dead there. The chrome was alive. There was a terrible inconsistency here, but Boom, there it was—a perfect silver jewel of a thing.

From the very first I could see my distorted image in it. I waved my arms to signal my presence in the bumper, my entry into it. The green leaves were mirrored in it and the sky above was captured with every single one of its white clouds. I had seen millions of bumpers before and paid no attention to them. I hadn't studied them. I hadn't tried to dive into them. They were attached to clean blue cars and green cars and other colored cars. They were only natural. The bumper on the sawed-off piece of junk pickup, however, seemed a curious mutation. It should have died and corroded or rusted in time with, or to the cadence of, the decay in the rest of the dump. The bumper had resisted, however. Perfectly. It continued to display its beauty. It was eternal.

I cleared away the weeds and examined it carefully and didn't find a single nick or pit in it.

My dad said. "Come on, Johnny!"

I replied with my usual: "Wait a minute."

The back of the bumper was crumbling rust, as was the metal that connected it to the frame. The rust would scale off in small sheets with the pressure of a sharp stick. Like the stick my father might have used to dig up the salt cellar. But the rest: it was shining radiant chrome, gleaming there as a beacon. That's right, a beacon, a tiny glimpse of which had signaled me in the underbrush in the first place. In the first moment, I thought it might have been a fragment of mirror. But it turned out to be the perfect-appearing bumper.

I was made to leave.

But we returned, of course, in a matter of days.

I rushed back and nothing had changed, of course. There it was. I wondered if anybody else knew about this bumper and, more importantly, if they comprehended the greater meaning of chrome; its ability to resist death.

I wasn't ready to talk about this to anybody but speculated that I might be the discoverer of something important, the finder of a crucial fact which the original inventors of chrome hadn't even thought about. That chrome lives on. Chrome is permanent in a world of decay. If only dead people could have been imbued somehow with a bit of this chromeness they wouldn't have died when they did and gradually turned to dust and humus and, here and there, the odd yellowish bone. Or, if they did eventually die, then they'd leave a token like this chrome bumper behind, a shining talisman or signal of their having been. Something to wink at boys through the weeds and then reveal a bit of cenotaph that remained perfect, a faithful record of what had been one time.

Grandpa Frank said that he would leave me his watch when he "passed away" but I knew even then that it would likely remain in a box or a drawer because it was fragile and needed protecting and tending. It would not be left outdoors where it would remain radiant and glowing.

On about my third chrome bumper trip, I stood there thinking that, at the very least, I must immediately share my discovery about chrome with the people who made markers for graves. That they could immediately stop working with dead-colored rocks and instead fabricate fine chrome markers that would stay lustrous and alive for ten thousand years—forever.

"Here," one of them might very well say, "lies my own grandma and she once smiled this brightly. You could feel it a block away. You can still hear her singing if you look deeply enough into this chrome. You can smell her pies and her fruits at canning time."

Something of people's purity and clarity could be contained and reflected from it, I was pretty sure.

The bumper lodged in my mind as a peculiar symbol—an enduring icon or emblem of That-Which-Will-Persist despite a deadly world passing overhead with its atmosphere of continuing decay and destruction and small men in huge machines that crush everything and grind it out of sight and memory; the purveyors of cruelty. Despite all bombs, the bumper would always be a smile of hope hidden in the brambles of the can dump.

All my life, when faced with uncertainty or fear or discomfort, I have tried to remember Chrome or Think Chrome, or even *Become* Chrome in the small-child's belief that chrome was not merely a very thin surface plating, but solid like steel or gold. That people could have a huge block of real chrome and, if they had the equivalent of the hot knife that goes through butter, could slice off perfect mirrored slices of any thickness. Chrome chrome. Solid. Mirrors into infinite mirrors endlessly side to side and back to back. Chrome into which one could disappear into an eternity of pure reflection. Security.

It's calming to think of Chrome in this way. As a talisman against death. To Be Chrome is to resist it; to ignore it; to reflect death back onto itself and into itself.

Car Ghosts and Other Problems

My mother did things to scare me. She accomplished this by capitalizing on the things that terrified me in the first place, not ideas that she tried to dream up on her own.

There was a house up in Bandon that had a tall, thick hedge in front. A sinister archway had been cut in it and it was the entrance to a long scary walkway up to a Witch's-looking cottage that was such a dark color of gray that it looked black. It was also in shadow all the time because of three huge haunted trees. This place was the True Shits when it came to frightening.

I guess I discovered it one time as we walked past it. I made the supreme mistake of saying something about it. And from that moment forward it became part of the pantheon of threats to correct my behavior.

"Stop doing that! Or we'll take you up to that place in Bandon and leave you at the Witch's House!"

"We will give you to the Witch in Bandon."

Later, I learned the trick of not appearing to be frightened. So she substituted the threat of sending me away to a military academy near Portland.

There was also the matter of certain photographs, one of which had a ghost in it. It was a large photograph showing my Great-uncle Carroll, Grandma Holt (my grandfather Frank Tichenor's mother), Frank, and Leslie (Frank's deaf brother). Leslie alarmed me quite a bit because he never spoke and only wrote messages on slips of paper. Also, something had caused him to have an extraordinarily long face like a Modigliani painting only he was real.

These four people are standing in the woods in front of two automobiles. In one of the automobiles is a man sitting in the back, apparently smoking a cigarette. He is barely visible and is probably the Devil.

Why would anybody remain in a car when there was a picture to be taken? No right-thinking person would do that. This much was clear to me even as a small child. When somebody took out a camera, it was time to stand dutifully and have your picture taken.

Since the man in the car picture frightened me so, my mother started threatening me with it.

"Do you want me to get out the Picture?" she would say in her horror-movie tone of voice.

I remember talking to my sister about it: "That is a ghost," I told her. And I pointed it out in the picture.

"No," she replied. "It isn't. It's only a person. There are no ghosts."

"Then why does everybody in town talk about the Tichenor Ghost up on the hill, floating above the cemetery?"

"It's only fog or something, maybe marsh gas. I don't believe in ghosts. I am not superstitious."

Not superstitious? That came as a surprise.

Who taught me the following?

"Star light, star bright,
First star I see tonight,
I wish I may, I wish I might
Have the wish I wish tonight."

My sister.

And who taught me to make a wish before blowing out the candles on a birthday cake? My sister.

Who would get disgusted when I broke off the best part of the wishbone from a chicken or a turkey?

And who was it who told me that if you divulge your wish to anybody (the wish you make when seeing the first star, blowing out all the candles, or winning at wishbone) then it won't come true?

Who worried about the sinister power of black cats? Who would never, under any circumstances, kill a Ladybug? And who shuddered at the sight of the Ace of Spades?

You guessed it. The same person. My sister.

And, speaking of shuddering, you know how it is when you involuntarily shiver or shudder? You may not even be cold, but you'll suddenly quake and then be perfectly okay again? Well, I was visiting my kindly old grandma in Portland one time and did this exact thing in her kitchen. She noticed me do it and promptly announced:

"Ah! Somebody's walking over your grave."

Try to process that one when you're nine or ten years old and fairly confident that you're not dead yet. Had grandma suddenly turned into a Witch? Like the Bandon crone of my imagination?

How anybody ever grows up in this country to become a functioning adult is beyond me. Perhaps they don't. Maybe that's it. Maybe that's a fundamental point that I've been missing for so long.

Pyro— My Grandfather, Frank

Here are some little fragments that will help you understand my grandfather a little better.

Hubbard Creek. For some reason or other something happened to the water supply one time and we had to drive to a creek and get water in buckets. It was the same creek, Hubbard Creek, where my grandfather and I used to fish, but without ever catching anything. My grandfather referred to it, nevertheless, as "a splendid creek." We went fishing one time and stuck our lunch in the crotch of an apple tree in a deserted orchard nearby. When it was time for lunch we couldn't find the paper bag with our sandwiches in it. It also contained, by the way, a bottle of milk and my favorite mug which was made of transparent blue glass with a picture of Shirley Temple enameled on it in white. We searched the orchard for a couple of hours and couldn't find it. We went back the next day. Same result. No lunch bag. We never did find it. I wish I had the Shirley Temple mug today— not to sell it, mind you, but just to have it and look through the blue glass at the world.

Witness. Best Man.

Since my grandfather was Justice of the Peace, he frequently performed civil marriage ceremonies. Sometimes I would be recruited into the little white house to serve as a Witness. In these instances, the house-keeper, Mrs. Lacey, and I would flank the prospective bride and groom, she with a small bouquet of wild flowers, and I with the ring. At the appropriate moment I would hand the ring to the nervous groom. After the ceremony, my grandfather would accept his fee and stand all the adults present to a shot of "a little something" from a top cupboard in the kitchen. I was "best man," as he called it, a great number of times but only got soda pop as a reward, never a shot of the "little something."

Beach Fires.

My grandfather had pyromaniacal tendencies. No question about it.

We'd be walking along the beach south of Battle Rock and he'd suddenly be overtaken by the desire to start a fire. There was always tons of driftwood on the beach in those days. In the early stages of one of his bonfires, I was able to help. But, once he got going, the fires needed to be bigger and better. This meant larger pieces of wood. I was no longer able to help at this stage of the operation, and would just stand and watch. With tremendous exertion, he would drag veritable logs to the fire and struggle them onto it. These fires were frequently as big as houses, with flames churning 30 or 40 feet in the air. The omnipresent Gene White would appear on the cliffs above to find out what was going on. He would shout down to us. My grandfather, who hated distractions when he was doing something important, would scream back at Gene: "Go to Hell!" My grandfather was the only person in the county who could get away with such behavior. It always seemed remarkable to me that after he said this to Gene, Gene would disappear. For a long time I wondered if he had, indeed, gone to Hell. These huge fires would roar and whistle and Grandpa would shout right back at the inferno, sometimes waving a stick like a sword and shouting passages from Shakespeare. These fires would often last an hour after the very height of their magnificence. Then we would put them out with sand and go home, my grandfather often too hoarse to speak.

Lumber Ships.

Before the war, ships from a lot of different places would tie up at the dock and take on lumber. This was great business for my father's meat market and grocery store because the ships would take on stores— not so much canned goods, but fresh meat, vegetables, and fruit. The American ships were always respectable enough looking, but there were also rusty Chinese and British tramp steamers. I'd go aboard some of these ships when my father delivered provisions and get to see the galleys. I was glad I didn't have to eat food from some of them. I saw a rat in the galley of a Chinese ship.

The Japanese ships, however, were an entirely different matter. The men on the Japanese ships wore uniforms and the galley, the decks, the dining rooms, the holds even, were spotless and shipshape. "Ready for inspection," one of the guys from the Coast Guard Station said once after he had gone aboard one such ship on business. Also the officers of the ship were quite charming and always bowed and smiled. All of them had cameras and they spent a lot of time taking lots of pictures from the tops of the cliffs.

They would make my grandfather furious.

"Those are not merchant seamen!" he would proclaim to anybody who would listen. "They are regular Japanese Imperial Navy officers and men and they are here to spy!"

He tried to tell the publisher of *The Oregonian* this, but was dismissed as an alarmist.

"And I am positive they are finding military uses for the Port Orford Cedar that is being loaded aboard those ships!" he would lecture.

Later, he was proven correct. The wood was used in battery separators and for spars in lightweight Japanese fighter aircraft.

I can see those Japanese now. Smiling. Ready to jump on Pearl Harbor the same way that Blake's cow leapt on the other one. Or the way the rooster jumped on the hens.

"The dirty sons of bitches are up to no good," my grandfather would say, over and over again..

They may have been dirty sons of bitches, but they had the cleanest ships in the business. That much I remember for sure.

Blabbermouth— The Kindergarten Kid

What I am about to tell you happened to me just before the minister's wife decided that it was time to have a kindergarten. The town had never had one of these before. So she was going to start one: a church kindergarten, so children could "get off on the right foot," whatever that meant. I studied my right shoe but concluded nothing.

I was about five years old and, therefore, a candidate. A few other town kids were, too. Maybe a few from the Coast Guard Station. No. Wait a minute. That couldn't be true. The Coast Guard station didn't open until 1939.

The important thing that happened to me was this:

I liked to talk. I was encouraged by my parents in this so as not to be shy and to be sure to talk to people in the store. The grownups thought this was funny, this kid talking up a storm. But it got out of control.

So there was a big switcheroo. My parents tried to encourage me not to talk so much to the customers. They said I was getting too gabby. I was accused of being able to talk an arm and a leg off somebody. Which, naturally, I couldn't understand. One can't talk arms and legs off people even if you stood there and tried all day.

Gabby. Blabby. Blabbermouth. These were some of the things they were suddenly calling me. Plus Chatty and Chatterbox. It seemed to me that it went from "You've got to talk to people a lot more," to "You've got to stop talking to people so much," in the space of about a week. It was longer, obviously, but it seemed like a week.

So I took my act on the road.

Instead of talking to customers, I'd walk across the street and talk to the mechanic at the Texaco station while he was working on an engine. After him, I'd drop in at Margie's and talk to either Margie at the counter in front of the restaurant or to Cliff out back in the kitchen. This usually also netted me a couple of bites of pie or fried potatoes.

From Margie's I could walk the rest of the way into town on a route that took me past the workshop of the guy who made bows and arrows, to my grandfather's house, and thence to Pugh's Drugstore at the southernmost edge of the town. The guy who made the bows and arrows ("Championship Quality," it said on the engraved sign of his workshop door) didn't mind my stopping off and exchanging a few words.

I was about the only person in town who talked to him. He was a reclusive person. The first time I met him he was testing a bow next to his workshop. I asked if I could try it. He found a smaller bow and let me shoot an arrow into a tree. It was very satisfying and I remembered to say "thank you." He must have supposed that I was okay because I could always drop in to see what he was doing.

He could continue working on a bow or attaching feathers to an arrow while we talked. He sold his products to stores Back East. And I learned a lot. I learned that a special kind of war arrow shot from a longbow invented by the English would go through 20 enemies if they all happened to be standing in a row and weren't wearing armor. Zap! 20 dead men with a single arrow!

At any rate, I was not being the "pest" that my father thought I was being. Or, as my namesake, Great-uncle John, would have it: "a big pain in the ass." (John, being a Portland police captain, could get away with talk like that, partly on account of his great size and the fact that he always wore his uniform and carried handcuffs.)

The last name of the man who made bows and arrows was actually Fletcher. Which meant nothing at all to me until, in one of our conversations I was informed that a "fletcher" was a someone who made arrows! Honestly! And that the word came from *fleche*, the Old French word for arrow, and *flechier*, a guy who makes them. It was the most amazing coincidence I could have ever imagined.

I hopped right out and informed half the people in town. This also led me to investigate a bunch of other names to see if those people actually did what their names stood for. But the Smiths were fishermen, and the town didn't have any Cartwrights or, for that matter, any carts.

The Pughs didn't stink. The Bakers didn't bake.

There was a Pickel family at the Coast Guard station, but that didn't count because, as somebody tried to explain to me, the "Spelling" was wrong.

The whole concept of spelling, as you know, was entirely unknown to me. All large posted signs were merely a form of design or pattern. The neon ones didn't have to have meaning beyond their bright colors.

Speaking of the Pughs, Mrs. Pugh was usually my last stop. She could talk while she made up prescriptions. Doc Pugh would have a few words if he wasn't busy being a dentist and working in there with his special light over somebody's gaping mouth.

Lou Monescu was crazy about me and would have listened to me all day long. She was fat, talked dirty, and fixed broken trucks and heavy equipment. A highly competent welder—people said—an unheard-of thing for a woman. They called her "mannish" and worse.

Charley Long was a pretty good talker, especially in the afternoon after lunch when he'd had three or four beers.

Moran was one of the best talkers around, but he didn't show up until quite a while later.

Then, just before Moran, was a guy off a ship who was, according to my father, "just a little too god-damned friendly." The exact menace of grown men talking to little boys was never explained to me in any detail. I was simply warned that something bad could happen. Something really awful.

Who else did I visit?

Knapp when the Knapp Hotel was still there. Before it was torn down.

I visited Herzog before his shoe store went away. Herzog showed me how to hold a sugar cube in my mouth and suck tea through it. He said it was a European custom where he came from.

Mrs. Bennett was on the Tour, but only if we would discuss her three canaries—how they felt and what they'd been doing by way of new "tricks." I remember that one jammed his neck into the cage wires one day and just hung there dead. That was quite a trick. Mrs. Bennett was in bed for days with her distress over this hideous circumstance.

A couple of doors over from the Bennett's was T.J.'s place. T.J. thought I was the funniest thing around and would sneak me in the side door of his Bar & Grill to talk to me for a few minutes. One of the Sacred Rules was that no kid was Ever to Go Into Taverns—Red's, the Pastime, or T.J.'s—under any circumstances. It was a rule right up there with Do Not Climb a Dead Tree.

(Why must you not climb Dead Trees? Because if you ever fell from the top of one, the limbs would just bust off under you all the way down. Pat Masterson fell out of a dead tree one time trying to prove to us that the Rule About Climbing Dead Trees was Bullshit. He must have broken 75 tree limbs on the way down, each of which popped like a firecracker and made brown dust. We picked him out of the kindling at the bottom and then knew for an absolute fact that the Rule About Climbing Dead Trees was *not* Bullshit. We had seen Masterson plunge to his death, at least that's what we thought at the moment.)

T.J. made no effort to either clean up his language or be selective about subject matter and would talk to me in exactly the same way he would talk to truck drivers. He would also let me drink things out of beer mugs. T.J. and Moran were two perfect people in my book. There was nothing anybody could have done to make them any more perfect. I learned all the finer points of swearing from T.J. "Piss poor" was one of the first things I learned—especially as a modifier of "job" or "idea."

Then there was Old Lady Beck, who could talk about gardening until you practically fell asleep.

Finally there was the Minister Jenkins and his wife, if you could put up with enough Jesus Talk to earn yourself a cup of hot cocoa. They were a challenge, even for a blatherskite (Dr. Baird's term for me) because they were constantly maneuvering to get people, even little kids, to give themselves up to the Lord. I never said that I would or wouldn't when I was sitting at their kitchen table, mostly because I didn't understand what they were talking about. Criminals gave themselves up to the police, I knew that much from radio shows like "Gang Busters" and detective movies. But *the Lord*? I didn't get it and so would always manage to steer the conversation away from the subject. One thing about being a blabbermouth, you could always make conversations go where you wanted them to go. At least most of the time.

The day finally came for kindergarten to start. There were girls mostly, and children who were content to talk to one another and use crayons and build things—mostly little pots—out of modeling clay. I could tell that this was going to be terribly boring so I walked outside and around the corner to where two men were digging a very deep ditch. I started talking to them, and this turned out to be a very lucky thing.

One of the men said:

"Do you know that you can see stars from down here?"

"Stars?" I asked. "What stars? Where?"

I was looking into the bottom of the trench, wondering if stars could be like diamonds and exist as points of light in the dirt.

I didn't see anything. Just dirt.

"If you stand down here and look up you can see the stars."

Three weeks earlier, Don Doyle had sent me on a wild goose chase to Charley Long's store for a bucket of "Red-and-White Striped Paint." I was surprised when Charley laughed at me, but then he explained the joke. Ha! Some joke. Rico-level humor.

This looked like another joke of about the same propositions.

Stars from the bottom of the ditch.

Sure.

I looked up at the blue sky from where I was standing. There were no stars. There was nothing.

I started to walk away.

"Wait a minute. Come back, kid," they said. "Climb down the ladder and take a look."

I agreed. Anything seemed better than crayons even if it was another joke on yours truly. So I climbed down the ladder and looked up.

THERE WERE *STARS!*

The sky was much, much darker and you could actually see stars.

"Wow!" I said, "When did you find out about this?"

"I've always known about it," one of the men said. "It's just a fact."

A fact? I knew nothing of the kind! I was sure there was not another person in the whole town who had ever heard of such a thing. It was a startling and important scientific discovery. I started my rounds to get to the bottom of it—to discuss it with people.

Almost everybody knew. And, among those who didn't know about it, there were a number who didn't care.

I couldn't figure out why a person wouldn't care about such an astonishing thing.

I went back to the ditch to go down the ladder again but some clouds had rolled in and the sky was obscured. Also, the minister's wife was looking all over for me thinking that I was lost. It was Nap Time, she said, and all the children were expected to stretch out on blankets. I told her that my mother was suddenly taken sick and that I was supposed to report home immediately. An ambulance was coming down from Bandon and my mother might have to be put in an iron lung or have something amputated. She bought this story and I went over to T.J.'s.

I told him about the stars and he solemnly and seriously agreed that it was literally the goddamndest thing he had ever heard of. He also volunteered that Nap Time was "A Lot of Happy Horse Shit," a phrase that I immediately taught the other kids in town whether they felt like learning it or not. What an excellent term to describe a stupid activity.

I sat on a stool at the end of the bar and ate a couple of Fig Newtons out of a new package. Life, as Moran would say later on, was pretty much what you made of it. Stay on course. Steer to your Pole Star. (But I got this kind of star mixed up with Poland and couldn't figure it out for years.)

The Writer

My grandfather was always the big shot, the historian, the "writer." He was always telling everybody about all the writing he was doing. History books allude to Frank Tichenor's unpublished "history." But he didn't do it. I have inherited the gene for not doing it. I understand the frustration.

My grandfather abandoned his family at the end of the 1920s. He took off. Searching for freedom? I don't know. But it wasn't to write. It must have been to shoot off his mouth. He left Mary behind, his wife, my grandmother, a shy person who had always been forced into the background.

I have a wedding picture of the two of them. It's one half of an oval picture. I've always wondered who in the world was standing in the other half.

In early 1937 it was my grandmother who wrote and published a little book. It must have angered Frank at great deal. Mary—a book! How dare she!

She wrote a book about the battleship *Oregon*, which had been docked in Portland for many years as a museum and a wonderful place for visits, dances, and receptions. It was a turn-of-the-century battlewagon and had served in the Spanish-American War. I remember it as one of the most beautiful places in the world. It had lots of mahogany and brass and maroon velvet. It was a Victorian masterpiece. It was loaded with military displays in glass cases. My Auntie Marnie remembers going to dinner-dances there and whispering under the moon up on deck.

Real Home

One day T.J. Collins was standing in the window of his bar & grill and noticed me walking by.

He ran outside and yelled at me to return.

"Hey, Johnny. Come back!"

He had a news flash for me.

He told me that I walked like an Indian!

I don't know what T.J. knew about Indians, but it didn't matter. I didn't care. What he said was really terrific news for me. I didn't seem to be doing much else right at the time. T.J.'s news more than offset getting my face slapped that morning by my mother. But now I was an Indian Walker. T.J. came out on the boardwalk and recreated my erect, straight-line walking.

This information led me to try to *run* like an Indian. Soon I was running all over the place. Up and down the beach. Over hills. Up the highway toward the can dump. Running like blue blazes—going lickety-split. My parents thought it was time for me to have a chat with somebody. They selected Doc Pugh, who, as you know, was the town dentist, not a psychiatrist, and he declared that I was probably sane. At least as sane as anybody needed to be in Curry County in those days.

Next I tried to *think* like an Indian. I would climb trees and try to imagine what it had been like for the coastal tribes who used to live there. What did they eat? Where did they go during the storms? Did they have recess? What did they do for fun? I started wondering about Indians in the same way I had wondered about the far-off Japanese.

I had the incredible good luck one day to run up to a special place I'd found on a cliff above the ocean—a place with a view of the offshore rocks and the coastline all the way down to Humbug Mountain. I was absent-mindedly digging in the ground with a stick and suddenly turned up a bunch of old clam shells and ashes. I was sitting on a place where Indians had eaten meals! Talk about signs and symbols! Holy Smoke!

At about this time I had a couple of friends who were truly interested in what I had to say about Indians: one was Fletcher, the arrow-maker, and the other was a woman who worked at Red's. It was Fletcher who told me that Indians believed that everything was possessed of spirits! A mind boggler, but it all fit together. It made sense. Fletcher called it *mana*, an unseen spiritual force present everywhere. In everything.

Rocks? Trees? Birds? The water in Garrison Lake? Fletcher assured me that it was true. Thistles. And the wild blue irises in the spring. _95_

I tried to bring this up to a few others in town. Log truck drivers were too busy; the fishermen didn't give a damn that day; and it just made the local Methodists scornful and nervous. No doubt they thought all this Indian stuff was a fantasy that was bad for me spiritually. Kids my own age wanted me to return to being a cowboy or a soldier. So I kept my thoughts to myself and strapped my cap guns back on. It was an important lesson in life. If frogs had spirits, I guessed that was going to be my own personal business.

I didn't bring it up again until Moran came to town. He agreed. He said he believed he had felt the spirits of people in places where he'd lived—people for whom that place had been a home; people for whom that place was just a house. He said he thought about the laughter that might have been there. Dancing. Children playing on the floor. Christmas trees and fudge. Fires in the fireplace on the first cold days. Colored eggs. Screen doors slamming all summer.

Some spirits were generous, I later found out on my own, while others were mean. I lived in some mean rooms one time in the gables of a gray house Back East. No amount of lamps and candles could ever illuminate the place. It was determined to be dark and, eventually, to darken me. People started saying I was brooding too much, so I moved.

You didn't need to be an Indian or a wizard to know that some places have never had much good happen in them. No bouquets. Rooms in which people have never been very much in love. Rooms in the back. Rooms where it's impossible to see the moon. "Dead-end rooms," you might say.

The quality of our lives is as much a matter of where we spend our time as how. And it's not just finding bigger or better houses or apartments, but of being lucky and patient enough to discover a special room or place in which you can feel alive and free. A place where you are always pleased. Maybe it's the view. Maybe the light. The colors. Nobody knows, but it's connected to the concept of real home. Where things are easy. Where things are right.

The woman I mentioned? The one who worked at Red's? Her name was Dorothy. I loved her for several reasons. Because she was beautiful and always smelled so good. Because she gave me nickels and listened to me. And I guess chiefly because I was never supposed to talk to her at all. Ever! This on account of some mystery I was never to know about in connection with the rooms above Red's Bar. Sailors laughed a lot up there at night was all I knew. The blinds were always pulled down just after sunset.

I ran away one time because the palefaces at home couldn't understand me. They didn't for a second share my deep concern about how Indians got along without tennis shoes and candy bars.

I ran off to Red's, where Dorothy smuggled me into a booth and ordered ginger ale for me. I asked for it in a beer mug and got it, just like at T.J.'s. Also some pretzels. She scrunched up next to me and held my hand. A heart of solid gold, sang a guy named Harvey from behind the bar, making up a ditty that he crooned in a falsetto voice as he waltzed with a bar towel. I remember his name because it was the same as my Uncle Harvey, who was a taxicab driver in Portland and the younger brother of my dad.

We chatted for quite a while and then Dorothy explained that I had to go back. That people would be worried. And that I belonged at home.

I was on my second ginger ale and Glenn Miller was playing quietly on the jukebox and I told her that it felt more like home right there with her in that booth. Real home.

Well, she didn't say anything, but held my hand and looked out the window at the highway and then, in a way that I hadn't seen up to that time, managed to smile and cry at the same time.

Real home.

The spirits there.

It can be a helluva long hunt.

Frank and Indians

My grandfather wasn't impressed at all when I told him about my new-found powers as an Indian Walker. I think I demonstrated by walking around the Weather Station in his yard seven or eight times in a gradually expanding circle.

"You walk like a Tichenor, it seems to me," he observed. "Not like an Indian. I have seen very few Indians walking. And I don't think T. J. Collins has ever seen any at all. So I don't know what he's talking about."

There had been the same controlled response about spirits.

I gently alluded to the subject one day. I don't know what I said. I certainly didn't blurt out something like: "You hate Indians, don't you?"

I felt him out on the point and he said:

"Come here. I want to show you something."

We rummaged through a desk drawer that was filled with loose correspondence, bills, and, mixed among them, old photos.

"Here. Take a look at this."

It was a photo of my grandfather taken many years earlier, but there he was all decked out in his official blue suit with the buttoned-up vest and the watch fob on it. He was standing in a back yard with an old lady. I remember the small size of the old lady in the picture because the top of her head was exactly level with the top button of Frank's vest.

"Who's that?" I asked.

"That is Sarah Root. I knew her. She was the last full-blooded Indian in the county. And this clipping is from the *Curry County Reporter* of October 4, 1928, that reported her death. She was never able to give her exact age; it was between 85 and 90. She came up to what is now Gold Beach from California in about 1852 or 1853. I knew one of her husbands, a man named Fry."

"An Indian?"

"No. A white man. She had three husbands, all of them white men. She had nine children. She was a fine woman."

He paused for a moment and then continued: "Now *my* grandfather! There was a person who could have told you about Indians!"

I hoped he would start to tell me more. But he suddenly found a reason to become very busy on some of his Official Business.

I knew there had been some Indian troubles in Port Orford because Battle Rock was so named because of an ancient battle there. There was a sign at the little parking lot above the rock. It was next to Pugh's drugstore and dentist place and said that Battle Rock State Park had been dedicated to the explorers and pioneers who prepared the way for the settlement of the southern Oregon coast. Captain George Vancouver sighted and determined the latitude of Cape Blanco on April 24, 1792, naming it Cape Orford. The name didn't stick to the Cape, but it moved down to become a Port. The *Sea Gull* landed on June 9, 1851, for the purpose of establishing a settlement.

The Kid Who Couldn't Read or Write

Kindergarten you could walk away from. I'd proved that.

The First Grade could not be walked away from. You went into the first-floor room in the southeast corner of the grammar school and you were under the control of Mrs. Grant. Period.

(Yes, the First Grade. I know a lot of you Eastern people are fond of saying things like: "Third grade was hard for me" or "I met Tony in sixth grade." In Oregon we put the word "the" in front of grades. That's just the way it was.)

There was a morning recess. Then there was lunch, when most kids who could went home to eat. And afternoon recess. Those were the times when you were permitted to leave the room. Those, plus Emergencies.

If you could overcome your embarrassment, you could raise one finger (meaning Pee) or two fingers (meaning Dump) and you were permitted to go to the bathroom. The girls, at first, could not overcome this awkwardness and would wet their pants. Talk about mortification! Mrs. Grant would have to rinse out their panties in the janitor's sink and hang them to dry behind the wood stove in the classroom.

Even the biggest liars among us soon realized that we couldn't signal three or four dumps in the same day.

At hand signals I was fine. Perfect.

At talking, as I have indicated, I was just great; a Master. I could talk to anybody about anything. I could even read lips a little bit.

But a great darkness quickly descended on me in Mrs. Grant's classroom. The individual things in "the Alphabet," the glyphs, were a complete mystery. Unsolvable. They were simply not distinguishable, one from the other.

Within days, the other children were spelling "CAT" in upper-case printed letters.

They would write down the letters and then, later on, decode what they meant.

I faked it. I scrawled meaningless symbols which I hoped meant CAT but meant nothing: to Mrs. Grant, other kids, or to me. I would look at the stuff a few minutes later and not know whether it was CAT, DOG, SALLY, or RUN.

I didn't get it. I didn't get any of it.

I was utterly unable to comprehend writing or reading. Everybody else did. Every other boy. And every other girl, including all the panty-wetters. We were all about six. 18 kids in all. 17 got it. I didn't.

Notes were sent home with me. The shit hit the fan. I was going to be thrown out of school. Oh, my God. Nobody really cared that much about me, I don't think. The adults cared about their reputations. Nobody wanted a dumbbell on their hands. Something had to be done.

An actual Tribunal was called to find out what to do.

Several grownups went to Mrs. Grant's classroom and had a discussion about it. About me.

I was in the hall trying to hear what they said.

My grandfather had the loudest voice. He said that I had learned English grammar almost perfectly and made very few mistakes for a person my age. My parents had nothing to contribute. My sister testified that she'd been trying to teach me how to read for the last two years but concluded that I wouldn't, not that I couldn't.

T.J. Collins blew my cover about swearing when he said that I was plenty smart enough to differentiate between Home Talk and Bar & Grill Talk. In other words, I would say stuff like Cripes and Darn and Fiddlesticks around my parents, but could say Happy Horse Shit and Son-of-a-Bitch at exactly the right times over at T.J.'s. Thanks a lot, Collins. A big help.

Dr. Baird had no opinion on the matter, but Doc Pugh, the only other medical-type person, thought that it was "just a matter of time."

"But whose time?" Mrs. Grant wanted to know. "My time? The other little kids' time? Johnny's time? When? How? What are we to do?"

Mrs. Grant had a real flair for the philosophical at some moments. The rest of the time she was a meaningless blob.

Finally Dr. Baird said something after all.

"Don't threaten him," he said. "That's all I can tell you."

Then he went home. He passed me in the hallway without saying anything to me. That guy was really puzzling. Smitty said "the Great War" had screwed him up.

But the adults followed his advice about not threatening. This took quite a bit of doing by my mother. She rolled through life on little ball-bearing threats.

There were no entreaties or bribes, I'll say that for them.

Meanwhile, the others kids teased me. "How are you doing, Dummy?"

Some old guy, probably in his thirties, came down from the high school a week or so later and stayed with me for an hour or so after Mrs. Grant and the other children went home. With the handle of a broom he pointed to a chart near the top of the ceiling at the front end of the room. It showed the mysterious Alphabet. At the far left-hand side of the chart was A. Stacked one above the other was a Capital Printed A, a Lower-Case Printed a, a Handwritten Capital A, and a Lower-Case Handwritten a. It was complete nonsense.

He took the time to explain to me *that they were all the same thing!*

This was quite a breakthrough in itself since I had previously concluded that they meant four entirely different things—as different as macaroni, fish, lumber, and rocks.

Not only did they stand for the same Letter, but the Letter was a Signal to Make You Say *AH* or *AY!*

"No shit?" I said, quite involuntarily. Like I was talking to T.J.

"No shit," he said dryly. "That's the deal."

Amazing! He worked his way down the alphabet: Signals to Make Sounds.

He took his time.

Whatever Mrs. Grant was trying to do, it wasn't phonics.

I quickly caught on about CAT—its C sound, its A sound, and its T sound.

From there on in it was a cinch.

"I thought it was a lot harder than this."

"Then it was," the guy from the high school said. "Wasn't it?"

I didn't quite get his meaning for another few years. Maybe 43.

The man must have had a word with Mrs. Grant because she continued a similar style with me.

I very soon caught up with the others and then passed most of them.

I'd wait for special opportunities when one of them goofed up.

"How's it going, Dummy?" I delighted in asking them.

Mrs. Grant hit me with a ruler for doing this and asked me to remember how it felt when people called *me* a dummy.

I said I couldn't remember.

This was toward the beginning of my career as a really big liar.

1937 & 1938

This is what I remember from 1937, when I was six and seven: Running. Trying secretly to become an actual Indian.

The *Hindenberg* crashed and I saw it on the newsreel, especially the Zeppelin's black skeleton (there's that word!) shown in an aerial shot taken the day afterward. A woman pilot got lost while flying an airplane in the South Pacific "near Howland Island."

Somebody was highly sillahsee about "the little chickenshit, Mussolini" (Crawford Smith's words) doing something bad in Africa.

Sister named our two new banty roosters Mussolini and Hitler because they would puff out their chests and strut around.

"War clouds," remarked Grandfather Frank, and I promptly went outdoors but couldn't spot them.

In Portland, however, I was fortunate enough to see and hear the dirigible *Los Angeles* closer up. I told you that it was the sister ship of the *Graf Zeppelin* which most people didn't know flew all over the world for nine years, went a million miles (actually!), made 144 ocean crossings, carried 13,000 passengers, and was finally broken up for scrap in 1938. What a dumb thing to have done. Do you know how much people would pay for a ride on the *Graf Zeppelin* today? Plenty! Tons of people would be lining up.

The *Graf Zeppelin* made a round-the-world flight before I was even born.

Here are some more things to to remember. The Japanese invaded China. The Golden Gate Bridge opened. *Newsweek* magazine started.

Movies: *The Good Earth, Captains Courageous, Lost Horizon, The Hurricane.*

The first Bugs Bunny cartoon was shown in a movie theater (which my sister remembers as "Porky's Hare Hunt").

Music I clearly remember: "They Can't Take That Away From Me," "Let's Call the Whole Thing Off," "Nice Work if You Can Get It," "A Foggy Day in London Town," "Blue Hawaii," "In the Still of the Night," "Sweet Leilani," "Too Marvelous For Words," "Johnny One-Note," "That Old Feeling," "Once in Awhile," and "Harbor Lights."

Nylon was patented. Spam was introduced, which I liked (to the distress of my father, a butcher). Kix—the Corn Puff Cereal—came along and I ate it.

The New York Yankees won the World Series.

I wrote a Radio Log of some of the shows my family listened to and put it in My Journal (with help)—1937.

Take a gander at the chart on the next page. (Gander? That's about as confusing as the first time somebody tells you to "keep your eyes peeled!")

There was also Believe-It-Or-Not by Ripley, all kinds of music and sports shows, Phil Spitalny and His All-Girl Orchestra, Guy Lombardo, the Ink Spots, quiz programs, Ted Weems Orchestra, Renfrew of the Mounties, Gabriel Heatter doing the news, H.V. Kaltenborn doing the news, and a lot of other stuff. My grandfather would listen to classical music when he could find it. Kids would say: "Believe-It-or-Rip by Notley" to be funny.

1938.

Peace In Our Time, said Neville Chamberlain after leaving Munich. Hitler then annexed Austria and made Chamberlain look like a jackass, Grandfather Frank said. Teflon was invented at DuPont. Fiberglas was invented at Owens Corning Glass Company. *Superman* comic books hit the stands at Doyle's. Orson Welles did "The War of the Worlds" on CBS radio and scared the tar out of a bunch of people all over the country. "Crazy Assholes," T.J. called them, and wondered why they couldn't take a joke.

Movies I remember clearly: *The Dawn Patrol, Adventures of Tom Sawyer,* and *Little Miss Broadway* with Shirley Temple. The big one: *Snow White and the Seven Dwarfs.* We "Whistled While We Worked" until parents were driven nuts.

Other songs of the time were: "My Love is Here to Stay," "You Must Have Been a Beautiful Baby," "Thanks For the Memory" (as sung by Bob Hope), "You Go To My Head," "Two Sleepy People," "Flat Foot Floogie (With a Floy Floy)," "A-Tisket–A-Tasket," "Spring is Here," "I'll be Seeing You" (greatly re-popularized when World War Two started).

Bumble Bee tuna was introduced in Astoria, Oregon, in this year. A big hurricane hit Long Island and New England. The New York Yankees took the World Series again.

Add Frank Morgan and Fanny Brice's radio show (Maxwell House). Likewise: Dr. Christian; Big Town: Edward G. Robinson; Alias Jimmy Valentine; Mr. Keene, Tracer of Lost Persons; and The Shadow.

Radio Log

Show	Sponsor	How Long	What Day	What Time
Fibber McGee & Molly	Johnson's Wax	30 min.	Mon	8:00
Lux Radio Theater: movie adaptations	Lux Soap	60 min.	Mon	9:00
Al Jolson: guests	Lifebuoy Soap	30 min.	Tue	8:30
Kate Smith Bandwagon	Atlantic Oil	60 min.	Wed	7:00
One Man's Family	Tenderleaf Tea	30 min.	Wed	8:00
George Burns & Gracie Allen	Campbell Soups	30 min.	Wed	8:30
Fred Allen Program: Town Hall Tonight	Sal Hepatica	60 min.	Wed	9:00
Gang Busters	Palmolive	60 min.	Wed	10:00
Rudy Vallee Varieties, guests	Royal Gelatin	60 min.	Thu	8:00
Bing Crosby Program, Bob Burns, guests	Kraft Cheese	60 min.	Thu	9:00
Death Valley Days	Pacific Borax	30 min.	Fri	8:30
First Nighter	Campana Balm	30 min.	Fri	9:00
Bob Hope Program: Red Nichols Orchestra	Atlantic Oil	30 min.	Sat	7:00
Your Hit Parade: Harry Salter Orchestra	Lucky Strikes	30 min.	Sat	9:00
Grand Hotel: drama, Les Tremaine	Campana Balm	30 min.	Sun	6:30
Jack Benny Program	Jello	30 min.	Sun	7:00
Jimmy Durante: Jumbo Fire Chief	Texaco Oil	30 min.	Sun	7:30
Major Bowes Amateur Hour	Chase & Sanborn	60 min.	Sun	8:00
Manhattan Merry-Go-Round	Dr. Lyons	30 min.	Sun	9:00
Walter Winchell: Broadway gossip	Jergens Lotion	15 min.	Sun	9:30
March of Time: dramatized news	Remington Rand	15 min.	Week days	9:30
Lum and Abner	Horlick Malt	15 min.	Week days	7:30
Amos 'n' Andy	Pepsodent	15 min	Week days	7:00

The Fine Art of Managing Your Expletives

My father swore if he cut himself with his butcher knives, but that was the only time, and then he'd look around to see if anybody heard him. He knew how to swear but it made him ashamed. It also annoyed my mother. So that was another reason. There was no point in annoying my mother, we all knew that.

My mother was once stepped on by a horse and all she could muster was: "For Crying Out Loud! *Shoot!*"

This was as high as she got on the scale of strong language.

Her mother, who lived in Portland, was even more conservative.

Several languages, all different, have to be learned by little kids. I learned four.

There was Home Swearing which consisted of some of the following, not necessarily in order of their intensity:

"Crime-en-Itley!"

"Gol (or Gosh) Darn!"

"For Pete's Sake!"

"Lord Love a Duck!"

"Holy Smokes!"

"Hell's Bells! (Or a variant: "Hell's Bells & Buckets of Blood!")

"I'll be darned!"

These expressions were far too strong to use at Grandma's house in Portland. When you were there you could use nothing stronger than:

"Shucks!"

"Fiddlesticks!"

"I'll be Dag-Nabbed." Or "I'll be Switched."

When truly agitated (having a hissy fit or going into a tizzy), she would venture:

"Drat! I think I'll walk into the lake until my hat floats!"

These languages seemed to work okay for me until, as I told you, I met T.J. Collins over at his Bar & Grill. Also Lou Monescu and the fishermen in town (the most notorious of whom for bad language, of course, was Smitty—not on account of his deliberately wishing to offend anybody, but because his voice was so loud and carried so far that nobody could help overhearing him).

It was from these people that I learned the good stuff (for which I would get thrashed or slapped if I accidentally used it in the house— expressions like Happy Horse Shit, Turd Bird, and Jesus H. Johnson! Also, Crawford Smith's famous: "Well I'll be a Two-Toned Son of a Bitch!")

There was also a fourth approach I learned from Frenchie, the Nova Scotia fisherman, that could be used at home.

I had been taught—under threat of physical harm—never to criticize anything that was served at a meal, including the hated spinach, liver, dumplings (those big, horrible white-snot dumplings my mother made), corn bread drier than the Oklahoma Dust Bowl, and a few other items that I would have to smuggle out of the house in my pockets or leave the table in a Fake Emergency and spit them into the toilet.

"How's the liver?" my father would ask.

"*Maird dew ko-shawn.*" I would smile, looking down at my plate where a pool of ketchup engulfed the obnoxious, hideous, weird-colored meat.

They were quite pleased that I seemed to be on my way to becoming a refined person. Maybe it wasn't such a bad idea that I spoke to some of those unmarried guys after all, at least the ones who spoke foreign languages (and could say "pig shit" without getting caught.)

Following is stuff we thought was funny.

Knock-Knock jokes were popular, and among the first I heard was this one: Knock knock. Who's there? Eyleen. Eyleen, who? Eyleen over and you kiss my ass.

Confucius-Says jokes were popular and I got slapped for repeating one that I didn't even understand at the time. It was: Confucius say "Woman pilot who fly airplane upsidedown have big crackup."

Then there is the inevitable attempt to sneak one in on everybody by pretending that "Kay" is a girl in your class. So, blithely in front of both my mother and father, I told a departing Matt McCormick: "Hey, Matt, Eff You See Kay, tell her to give me a call."

It didn't fool my mother. She smacked me so hard I fell into the woodbox.

Here is a "poem" everybody learned and laughed about: "Fuck a duck and screw a pigeon; go to Hell and get religion."

Peter dick cock prick weenie pud wee-wee dong dork. A few words for a boy's thing.

Saying (about bad luck): "Fucked by the Fifth Fickle Finger of Fate."

Another bad-luck saying: "Dicked by the Dangling Dong of Destiny."

Limericks were big.

I think it was Eddie Baker who discovered the concept of hidden dirty words. Or maybe I discovered it and told Eddie Baker. I can't remember. It was Eddie who concentrated on the idea and spent hours peering at words in the big dictionary in the classroom. By "hidden" dirty words all I'm talking about is the fact that in the name "Sturdavent," for example, the word "turd" is buried. Turd is also found in such words as sTURDy and SaTURDay. Eddie was curious to find out if other of our favorite expressions could be discovered lurking in commonplace, longer words. FUCK, he decided, existed nowhere and he couldn't get CUNT to work either. The "prick" in prickly barely counts at all. Class is simple-minded and so is titular. But Eddie kept looking. Lying in wait for the big one. As much as I hated Eddie, I had to admire him.

It is sometimes good to have somebody really good to hate—somebody you can always depend on, practically like a friend.

What else? Oh, yeah.

"Chuck you, Farley!" is something I learned in an early grade, I think from none other than Eddie Baker. He made a typical kid error by saying this out loud at home one time and got knocked on his can by his father.

Another thing we *did* get away with, however, was the frequent remark: "Well, you're really a Smart Feller, aren't you?"

Mysteries (Not to Be Discussed)

It began, as you might have guessed, when I reported the strange behavior of Mr. & Mrs. Spence doing something on their hands and knees with all their clothes off on the living room floor behind the office at their tourist court. I tried to treat this in the same manner as other local phenomena, like the observation that a Dungeness crab is green until you plunge it into boiling water, at which time it turns red-orange. Nobody knows why; that's just what happens.

I was told never to talk about the time at Mr. & Mrs. Spence's.

I was told not to talk to the women who worked at Red's. Which was a real puzzler, since, as I've said, they were awfully nice to me and looked better and smelled better than most of the other women in town. Especially Dorothy. None were fat. None had chipped fingernail polish. None had messy hair or appeared in public with their hair up in curlers. They wore pretty dresses even on weekends while other townswomen only dolled up for Sundays. (That was an expression from those days, by the way: to get "dolled up" or "gussied up," instead of merely "dressed up.")

Don't talk to those women! That was the injunction. Don't even say "hello" to them. I couldn't figure it out.

Another class of person they kept harping on (as I've said before) was Strange Men. Actually it was singular, since it was emphasized that the Strange Man I was supposed to avoid always appeared alone.

"Do not talk to a strange man," was the ruling from both parents, "especially a sailor. If they say hello to you, don't say hello back. Just come home, or go the other direction."

To a little kid, these are vague instructions. What, after all, is the test for "strange?" What is the "other" direction?

Do strange men ever appear in twos or threes or larger groups? Does the condition of strangeness disappear when they're together? Can you spot strangeness in the eyes of these men or do you tell it from their hats or their pants?

Also, what is the "other" direction? North was toward Bandon and south was toward Gold Beach. West was toward the Tichenor Cemetery, and east meant the hills beyond the reservoir. I had those figured out. These directions had been authenticated by various townspeople and older kids. So the new, "other" direction was a puzzler. I figured that it wasn't straight up in the air, but that's about all I could imagine.

"Why?" was always the question from me. "Why not talk to those women?" I'd ask. "What would the Strange Man do to me?" I wondered out loud.

Answer:

"Never mind. Just do as you're told and don't talk to people like that."

They couldn't tell me about their horrible fears—they couldn't explain it. They just warned me that such men were capable of doing terrible things to me. Which led me to ask my usual "stupid" questions such as:

"If these guys are so awful, then why are they nice to me?"

"Ah, ha!" my parents would exclaim, "there you *have* it!"

There I had what?

What did I have? A person who is going to be mean to you does just exactly the opposite and is nice to you and makes time for you and seems to care what you're talking about? Are those the things to look out for? This is a bad guy?

And the good guys are the ones who don't have time for you and call you stupid and lazy and a fool? Is that it?

I overheard a conversation about this general subject in which the word "unnatural" was used, but this didn't shed very much light.

I continued to secretly talk to the women at Red's. And I secretly talked to people who sailed on lumber ships and would wander up to town for a look-see and maybe a couple of beers.

I got to know one of these sailors, a man named Harrison, who was on a regular run from Port Orford to Long Beach, California. I discerned nothing Strange about Harrison who had a lot of stories to tell me about China, including one about a woman that he was in love with who had been kidnapped by her family and taken to the interior with his son (who was about my age, he said). He needed to get promoted in order to save enough money to go find her and bring her back to California, she and the boy, where they would live in a bungalow, whatever that was. From the sound of it I reckoned a bungalow was something like a pagoda, a picture of which I had seen in our 15-volume *Stoddard's Illustrated Lectures* with the purple leather bindings.

There was an amazing conversation at dinner one night in the breakfast nook of the house when we lived on the hill below Mrs. Lenieve. (Here was another riddle, by the way—how people could legally have lunch and dinner in a breakfast nook. But nobody had a satisfactory answer for that one, either.)

"I saw you talking to that Strange Man on the corner this afternoon," my mother said, in a menacing voice.

"What Strange Man?" I asked, not knowing what she was talking about. I would have certainly remembered having finally met a Strange Man.

"The man with the black cap."

"Oh, him," I said. "That was Harrison."

"Harrison?" my father demanded.

"Yes, Harrison," I said. "He works on a ship that takes lumber down to California. He's trying to become a Third Mate. I don't know what that is, exactly, but that's what he's trying to do. He needs to save money because he's going to China."

I was trying to be nonchalant in my response since, at that moment, I was trying to feed a piece of one of mom's horrid dumplings to Blackie III under the table. The cat wasn't having any, though. Smart cat.

The conversation shifted to other matters.

Time passed and we got to the Jello part of the meal at which time I asked a question.

The question had to do with a concept that a new kid in town was trying to promote among some boys his age. I had heard part of a conversation in this kid's sales pitch. I looked at my father and asked:

"What does cornhole mean?"

My father's head spun around like a phonograph record.

He gave me an astonished look, not warranted by my question.

Have you ever stuck your finger in a light socket, either intentionally or accidentally? Well, that's the look my father had—electrocuted looking.

"HARRISON!" he shouted and banged his fist on the table top.

"What about Harrison?" I asked.

"He used that word, didn't he?" my father asked.

"No, he didn't."

"Well, who did?" my mother asked me, her eyes starting to take on that squinty cat look that preceded a smack on the face.

"Some new kid," I said, "who just moved up from Crescent City."

They both sputtered.

"Don't talk to him," I was advised in very loud voices.

"About cornhole?" I asked.

"About anything!" my mother said. "Ever!"

"That will be hard," I said. And I wasn't lipping off. I asked how I was supposed to avoid talking to somebody in my own school, or anybody else for that matter, for the rest of my entire life?

"Do it anyway!" was the advice.

"Well, . . . " I said. "Okay, but what does it mean?"

"It doesn't matter," my father said.

"Obviously," my sister said, "it has something to do with planting."

"You shut up!" my mother snapped at her.

My sister could either cry or shrug at such an outburst. She was in a shrugging mood, however, and calmly ate the rest of her Jello.

"And stay away from that man Harrison!" my mother added in the same tone of voice to me. "Understand?"

"Why?" I asked.

"Because I *said* so, that's why!" my mother hissed. She had now turned completely dangerous. My sister and I looked at one another and shared the same thought. We had agreed some time earlier on a description of this behavior, one which we would use behind mother's back. She had just "Turned Tiger" on us and became the kind of creature who could kill its own young. And probably *would* if provoked further. We shut up and went to our rooms.

This sort of scene was replayed several times with the same unexpected intensity when I asked about queers, clap, and "shacked up," and my sister inquired about "Syph." My mother also Turned Tiger when my sister was thwarted in her attempt to discuss a few details about enemas. For boys. And for girls. (This was one of our mother's favorite "treatments" at the time and terrifically unpopular.)

My sister started with a harmless remark having to do with the real need for enemas.

"Not at the dinner table," my father said.

"Not any time!" my mother commanded, starting to get that look.

My sister plowed ahead anyway.

"Who thought up enemas, anyway?" she asked (and then, in what I thought was the best question of all:) " . . . and after he thought it up, who wanted the first one?"

"You shut your mouth!" my mother yelled.

(Think about it some time. You've just invented the Enema and now you want to persuade somebody to have one, let's say a stranger. What would you say? What would be your sales pitch?)

So this was our Sex Education—a maze of confusion and misinformation, embarrassment, mystery, fear of punishment, . . . you name it.

We were left to figure it out for ourselves.

Some boys were helped, a couple of years later, when a cook from a lumber ship showed them pictures from a book printed in France. I didn't see it and, therefore, had difficulty in believing their eyewitness reports.

We were on our own.

Here's a secret. Not as big as the one involving Laureen (which I"ll tell you about later), but I'd still prefer it didn't get around too much. As they used to say: "Keep it under your hat."

I have had assorted careers, including a 10-year stint at a big consulting firm in the East. One of the questions we used to ask business executives was: "What is the most serious miscalculation you could make?" It is the question I wish I'd understood when, at the age of about six, I thought I could steal selected pieces of my mother's and my sister's lingerie and get away with it. They were greatly puzzled by the disappearance of these items and even more distressed by their discovery under a corner of my mattress one afternoon. My sister was troubled. My mother was speechless.

Sensing that I was expected to say something, I summarized my experience by saying:

"They feel good."

Anybody who has ever felt lingerie knows this to be true.

"That is not the point!" my mother said.

"Did you wear any of these things?" my sister interrupted.

"You keep out of this!" said my mother, eager to control this desperate, perhaps hopeless, situation.

"No," I said to my sister. "Of course I didn't wear them!"

This was a lie, of course, because I had worn a pair of her underpants to school one morning, but found the difficulty associated with their having no fly too great an obstacle to their continued use, feel good or not. Now the word was out that they weren't supposed to feel good. Oh, yeah, then why were they made out of that material?

Later I figured out that "slip" meant just what it says.

At dinner that night my father didn't look at me funny so I figured that my mother and sister were keeping mum on the subject of the Little Weirdo in their midst. By keeping so still about it, they scared me and I remained scared for a long time. There was nobody like a Moran in town to tell me that there were guys in major world capitals walking around in silk shorts. Why? Because it was practical? No, because the fabric felt good on their weenies.

This subject never came up again and, for your information, I have never stolen anybody else's underwear. I have *felt* lingerie, however, at every opportunity—on women when they'd let me, and quite blatantly on mannequins in department stores. None of the usual male business of "accidentally" brushing against the nightgowns and chemises. Absolutely not. I take stuff off racks to feel them and dip into the panty bin in pursuit of the best ones, the feelyest.

Call it the silk-nylon trajectory if you want to. I was catapulted toward the feely stuff.

Ed Rowland

Ed Rowland had sandy red hair and was a cousin of ours. That's how he was always introduced.

"This is our cousin, Ed Rowland. He's from California, but he's all right. He's a good friend and we're also related."

Ed didn't do much. He didn't have to do much because he was going to inherit the Ranch. That's what they called it. The Ranch. It was family property between Lafayette and Walnut Creek, towns east of Oakland. Although he really didn't have to do much more than wait, he had a job. He got a little job to keep him busy while he waited to inherit the Ranch. He was so good at the little job, they gave him a bigger one. Then he became a supervisor. It was in a sugar factory somewhere in the area.

Every summer when I was a child, Ed would drive from California to Portland to visit other relatives and stop for a day or two to visit us in Port Orford. It was in these early visits that I became aware of Ed's propensity to kiss people and also to drink lots of whiskey.

Ed was an enthusiastic kisser. He would lay big movie-style kisses on my mother, my aunt Margaret, and my twin aunts, Anna and Marianne. Big ones. These kisses looked serious; like they meant business. The women would flush a little and hurriedly explain to onlookers:

"Cousin. He's my cousin. From California."

And that made it okay.

I learned the words "kissin' cousins" at about this time and thought this was an example, Ed kissing everybody that way.

And speaking of aunts, Ed had grown up in the Bay Area where there is, or at least was at the time, a dialectical convention which made him pronounce the word aunt as "Ont." All of *us* said "Ant." So it was several years before I realized that when he said he frequently visited his Ontz, he was actually visiting his three Ants.

When I was little I believed that Ed's Ontz was maybe an animal of some kind, perhaps a fabulous creature with one horn or multicolored fur or the ability to sing.

"I drove into San Francisco," he would always begin, "to see my Ontz."

Maybe I always left the room at that point, sensing adult conversation, so I never heard details. There was an Ontz Place in San Francisco. And Ed went there now and then to see his Ontz, presumably contained in a sturdy cage. A child's mind is good at filing mysterious information in compartments where it won't cause mental harm. It's not unlike a hazardous waste site where people can safely bury dangerous things and then get on with their lives.

Ed's cousin-ness worked this way.

You will recall that Captain William Tichenor brought his family to Port Orford when it was safe to do so. He brought his wife, Elizabeth, his son, Jacob, and two daughters: Anna and Sarah Ellen.

Sarah Ellen, whom most everybody called simply "Ellen," followed her brother, Jacob, into the teaching profession, and was the first teacher in the Eckley District of Curry County.

Sarah Ellen Tichenor married Mr. Edward Walker McGraw in Port Orford on June 4, 1869. They didn't live there, however. Mr. McGraw received B.A. and M.A. degrees from the University of Michigan and was admitted to the bar in Detroit in 1860. Later that year, he migrated to Portland, Oregon, where he was U.S. district attorney for Oregon and the district attorney for Portland during the years 1862-1864. He then settled in San Francisco in 1868 and practiced law for more than 50 years.

Sarah Ellen and Edward Walker McGraw had five daughters, the last of whom was born in 1875 and was named Susie Lois. Susie married Edward Richard Rowland in 1902. They had one child, Edward M.

Left to right: Aunty Marnie, Cousin Ed, Aunt Marion

Rowland (our California Cousin, Ed, with the sandy red hair), who was born in 1906. Ed's mom willed her remains to a medical school so nothing of her was buried in the Tichenor Cemetery. But Sarah Ellen Tichenor and Edward Walker McGraw, Ed Rowland's grandparents, were buried there.

Ed, as you can easily see, was a great-grandson of Captain William Tichenor.

So my mother and Edward were distant cousins. 2nd? 3rd? I don't know. I get confused when it comes to cousin stuff. And the "M." in Edward M. Rowland's name stands for "McGraw." So there you have it.

The whiskey. One of the very first times that Ed ever visited (and the first and last time he ever tried to give me one of his big, slobbery kisses) I went into his room on the first morning of his stay to tell him that breakfast was ready. Ed had finished dressing and was puttering around. He was smoking a Lucky Strike cigarette and working on a third of a water glass of straight whiskey. An "eye-opener," he called it. Subsequent shots during the day were called "Pick-Me-Ups."

I believe this whiskey emboldened him to kiss my mother more than was really necessary. I think it bothered my father. It didn't seem to faze my mother. I wondered if she had an angle. I wondered if something was brewing.

Introduction to Luck

I happened to be in the store one afternoon after school when Oscar Chase, the Heinz salesman, came to the store to take my dad's order.

He asked how things were going.

My father said: "So far, so good; knock on wood," and with that he rapped the wooden counter with his knuckles.

Huh?

I asked what that was about. I had never noticed him doing that before.

Nobody knew what it was about. They just did it. For luck.

Well, okay. Anybody, even a little kid, can handle small doses of ambiguity and mystification.

At about that same time, two men built a combination garage and wood shed for my father and, as a final touch, nailed a horseshoe over the door to the woodshed. Not only was it for luck, I was told, but it was hung the way it was, with the horns up, "so the luck would not run out."

I asked if luck could be seen and was told that no, not really, it could not be. But it was there. Like the one-way current that flowed in the ocean from Japan.

Oh.

They started building Greyhound buses in the shape of Velveeta cheese boxes instead of with hoods sticking out in front, and they actually drove one of the new models into town to "christen" it. When I was told of this, I winked and said:

"Oh, sure they are."

Ha ha ha. Big joke. Christen a bus. Older people were trying to monkey with my mind again.

Well, of course not only did they "christen" the City of Port Orford and make a speech to the dumb thing, the Mayor was invited to smack a bottle of champagne on the front of it! I knew very well that if a kid were to try a stunt like that somebody would have knocked the bejeebers out of him.

"Why is this happening?" I asked a bystander.

Answer: "For Luck!"

The next few episodes flip-flopped for me. First good. Then bad. Then good again.

"Watch out, Johnny!" shouted my sister. "Black cat! Back up! Go the other way!"

"Oh, aren't you in luck!" said a stranger. "You found a penny!"

Distant sound of breaking mirror followed by: "Ah, shit! Seven years bad luck!"

One of the first times I was in the forbidden premises at T.J. Collins' Bar and Grill, I witnessed a curious event and promptly asked:

"Why'd you do that, T.J.?"

"Do what?"

"I just saw you throw salt over your shoulder. How come?"

"It could be very bad luck if I didn't."

"Why?"

"Because it's what you're supposed to do when you spill salt. That's why."

You can see that there wasn't much going on in Port Orford at that time to develop a person's critical thinking abilities. I certainly couldn't figure out what was going on.

Another stranger shouted in alarm when I walked down the sidewalk in front of the movie theater.

"Hey, don't do that!"

Do what, I wondered. I was walking on the sidewalk. I wasn't going to the bathroom on it. I wasn't hurting it any. I was just going someplace.

"You walked under that ladder!"

Yes, it was true that a tall ladder was standing unoccupied in front of the marquee. Nobody was on it. It wasn't doing anything. It didn't have sharp nails sticking out of it. Of course I walked under the ladder. I couldn't walk through the solid walls of the box office. I didn't want to step off the curb into the mud. What was the commotion?

"Don't you know that's *Bad Luck?*"

There I was, getting a lecture on superstition from an agitated stranger, probably one of those sheep ranchers from up Sixes River way. I told him that I didn't know anything about it. And I could deduce nothing about it. I had, only a year or two earlier, deduced that rain was nothing more than water broken into very small pieces.

– 117 –

My destination was Doyle's. I mentioned the ladder business to Eve, expecting her to laugh at such behavior but instead she frowned and agreed that it was indeed a dangerous thing to do.

I thought at first the issue was about the ladder falling on me. No, no, I was told, there was a lot more to it than that. A lot more. "It's just very bad luck, Johnny, that's all there is to it."

A few weeks later, Uncle John came to town in his police captain's uniform and squawked at me because I had tried to put his hat on a bed. "That's bad luck, Johnny! Didn't you know that?"

Whatever you guys say.

Sometimes it's a lot more economical to go along with people than to get involved in a lot of conversations that go nowhere.

Superstition is a lot like politics and everybody has his own opinion. If you're a kid, don't argue. That's my advice.

The Goose Feast

Here is a bird-death true story.

Jack Pruett was the town's artist. He would occasionally paint a respectable seascape that he would exhibit on a blank wall behind the cash register at the Orford Restaurant. A tourist would usually buy it within a matter of a week or so. Ten or fifteen dollars would stretch quite a distance for Jack at the time. He lived in a small house that had once belonged to somebody in his family. Taxes and electricity didn't amount to much, and Jack didn't pay any fire insurance, saying that if the house burned down it would probably be the Lord's way of telling him to get out of town.

It was Jack's house that a Canada goose crashed into one Saturday night.

But, before I get to the goose, I have to talk about the storm. As I told you, once in awhile you get a Pacific storm that slams straight in from the ocean, south to north, with winds strong enough to make it almost impossible for grown fishermen to walk against them. White foam blown from the ocean collects like snow at the base of buildings. Chimneys blow down and windows cave in. All traffic stops. And, if it's bad enough (and this one was), the electric lines go down.

There we were in the dark with the screaming wind and everybody in town had to wash dishes by candlelight in their kitchens.

That's what happened in this particular storm.

Motorists were stranded and it didn't take long for the only two motor courts (soon to be called motels) in town to fill up solid.

A roof blew off the house next to the old Lenieve place and the people who lived there were taken in by neighbors. Water blowing off Garrison Lake forced the evacuation of a dozen homes and suddenly a whole bunch of other people were in need of shelter. We took in a young couple and their little boy, and they slept in sleeping bags in the front room. The boy had a cold and coughed a lot. He slept on the couch.

The wind was still blowing pretty hard the next morning—Sunday—and the town was a mess. We were all eating corn flakes and drinking hot tea with the couple and their little boy when there was a knocking at the kitchen door. It was Jack Pruett with a huge goose in his arms.

Lots of birds of all sizes and types can be blown into trees and buildings and telephone poles where they are stunned and frequently killed.

Jack's goose looked dead.

"It slammed into my roof," Jack said. "At about four in the morning. Felt like a truck hit the place. Or a small airplane. Really. I didn't know what it was until daylight. I went out and there it was. Enormous, isn't it?"

I had never been that close to a Canada goose and I hadn't realized how big they can get. This one weighed a ton.

"Anyway," Jack continued, "I felt it and it was still warm, and then I realized it was alive. I didn't know what to do. I thought you'd know what to do, Al, you know about poultry. So I came over here."

My dad didn't even touch it.

"Kill it," he said simply. "Kill it and eat it."

"But it's not dead!"

"I can fix that," my dad said, getting that White-Chicken Massacre look and glancing around for his hatchet.

"Well, I don't know . . . ," Jack said.

"Take him to Dr. Baird's," my sister suggested. Little Nurse Nightingale.

"He's not there," Jack said. "I already thought of that."

"How about Doc Pugh?" my sister continued.

"He's a dentist," Jack said.

"That's true," she said. "But he might know something."

Jack walked over to Doc Pugh's and my sister and I went with him.

Doc came to the door and it was one of those situations where talking wasn't necessary. The story was right there, plain as day.

Doc took the giant goose and placed it on his kitchen table.

After examining the bird, Doc delivered his judgment.

"This here is what is known as a Gone Goose," he said. "Busted neck. Paralyzed. In a coma. Don't know how it lasted this long. Other than that, it's a perfectly healthy bird and ought to make a first-rate goose dinner."

"A Goose Dinner," Jack repeated. "Yes, I could do that, I suppose. How would you people like to attend a Goose Feast?"

It was an invitation.

We said we would. Doc said he would.

"Since I am a little short of cash at the present moment, it would be nice if everybody could bring along some leftovers or a salad or something."

"How about macaroni salad?" my sister asked. She had just learned how to make it in her Home Eck class. "I think macaroni salad would be okay at a Goose Feast? Don't you?"

"More than just okay," Jack assured her. "It would be perfect. Make a whole bunch."

"We could bake two or three kinds of potatoes," Doc suggested. "Yams, Idaho, you name it."

"Great," Jack agreed.

I volunteered that my dad would dress the bird, which he did. And that my mom would stuff it.

Three o'clock was supposed to be the appointed time, mid-afternoon. It was then nine-thirty in the morning.

A lot happened in the next few hours.

Jack was very unselfish and, as he walked along, he would ask the people he met if they wanted to come to the Goose Feast. They all said sure.

Then Jack would add:

"Bring anybody you want."

The electricity came back on. The phones started ringing all over town.

"Pruett's having a Goose Feast and he said I could invite you. Bring some deviled eggs or something."

People out past the mill were getting invitations.

The word passed among workmen building the new Coast Guard station.

A watchman down at the Cannery got a call and said he'd bring a few cans of crab meat.

Jack's phone started ringing off the hook and he called my father to say:

"Jesus, Al, half the people in town are coming to the Goose Feast and I don't know where to put them all. You got any ideas?"

He didn't.

"Also," Jack continued, "this is a big goose, but it's not going to feed everybody—not dozens of people. This is getting out of hand. This is getting as big as a 4th of July party down on the beach."

"Well," my father said. "We can't have it on the beach in this kind of weather."

"I know it."

"I'll tell you what," my father said. "Find a place big enough to have the dinner and I'll bring along some extra hamburger or something and we'll make sure everybody gets enough to eat."

More phone calls.

More people got involved.

Finally somebody suggested that the townspeople convene in the Sixes River Grange Hall. It could hold a lot of people, there were all kinds of tables and folding chairs, and it had a couple of big stoves and a grill in the kitchen area. So that's what happened.

At about two-thirty, dozens of cars and pickups converged in the Grange Hall parking lot.

People piled out with covered dishes, boxes of stuff, and pans of fresh bread and biscuits. There were jugs of cider and cases of beer. Somebody brought a huge ham. There were dozens of different kinds of vegetables and salads. Pickles. There was Crawford Smith's World-Famous Smoked Salmon. Celery stalks with Philadelphia cream cheese spread on them. Radishes. My dad brought weenies and hamburgers and T.J. and Cliff helped prepare them on the grill. There was plenty of Kool-Aid and Orange Crush.

It was a marvelous time. It got real hot inside and the doors had to be opened. There was an accordionist and two fiddle players. Somebody went back for his drums. Two real good singers sang songs.

The Goose Feast was an enormous success and the party didn't break up until after ten at night, late for me. Everybody was stuffed and exhausted.

Driving home, my father said:

"Whew! What a dinner. But you know something, I didn't get a taste of the goose. How was it?"

My mother said she hadn't tasted it either.

"How about you, Sister?" she asked Alida.

"I didn't have any, either," she said. "How about you, Johnny?"

I told everybody that I'd looked for it but hadn't seen it.

Similar conversations were being held in other vehicles.

"Did you have any of the goose?"

"No."

Jack had forgotten to bring it. In his excitement, he had taken it out of the oven, covered it with a dish towel, and got distracted by having a beer with Crawford Smith. Then Crawford, Lottie, and Jack piled in Crawford's truck and went to the Grange Hall.

Everybody agreed, however, that it was the best Goose Feast in the history of the entire county.

So what if there wasn't a goose?

A Great Time Was Had By All.

Fool's Hill

I don't know whether it was indifference or a mild form of cruelty that characterized so many of the relatives on my mother's side of the family. They were a big lot, all of them: tall and loud, and always jostling and pushing for action. They would urge one another to hurry the hell up, even when getting ready to go to a picnic at Humbug Mountain or to

Janzen Beach, the amusement park in Portland; hurrying up to have fun. They passed through their whole lives with great speed and alacrity.

My namesake, Uncle John (actually a great-uncle) was a police captain in charge of the Morningside Division in Portland, Oregon, and, as I've told you, he would wear his uniform on vacation when he came to visit us. Honest to God. Big, portly Captain John Tichenor with his hawk nose and his navy blue uniform splashed with gold, striding around town with wide gestures and a loud voice, in absolute charge. It would irritate the constable, Gene White, but he'd never complain about it. The Tichenors founded the town, after all. The Tichenors were big shots.

Uncle John was visiting with us the day I was made a substitute on the second grade baseball team. Sports were not a big part of life in our town, so I didn't know what a substitute was. I presumed, however, that it was a fairly big deal.

So I ran all the way home with the news:

"I am a Substitute!" I shouted with pride.

Well, Uncle John laughed until he cried. He chortled and gasped and turned red, and slammed his hand repeatedly on the wooden counter of my father's grocery store. His laughter spread to everybody else: my mother, my father, and some customers who were waiting at the cash register. Everybody had a huge laugh at my expense.

The opportunity for revenge came two days later. (Only the *opportunity*, mind you, not the revenge itself.) John was still in town and a friend on my team caught a bad cold and had to stay home from school. This meant that I got to play right field: Domain of the Least Talented. As I stepped up to bat in the second inning, some of the kindly spirits residing in the clouds above Curry County—perhaps the luck-bringers and wish-fulfillers we silently appeal to when blowing out candles and pulling on wishbones—must have looked down and said something like: "Let's give this kid a break, what do you say?"

In a wild swing, I smacked a fair ball through the stratosphere above the astonished third baseman. It sailed clear over the left field fence, across a big patch of weeds, and onto the highway where it took a big bounce and disappeared into a ditch on the other side! The kid playing left field ran through a gate to retrieve it and I took off around the bases. A Home Run! A Home RUN! Just like in the World Series Games I'd listened to the previous fall on the big console radio at my grandfather's house. The one with short wave.

But, no. No. It was not to be. That would be too sweet; too much of a good thing. It would have fixed Uncle John's wagon too completely.

Dave Studley, a small-minded teacher who was officiating that day, announced that I had failed to step solidly on second base!

So off I went again, out of breath and half-frantic, jumping/stomping on each bag until the dust flew out of them: Wham; Wham; Wham; all three bases and I was on my way to home plate for the second time, literally running my heart out, when the ball whizzed past my ear on its way to the glove of the catcher who was a couple of steps away from home plate.

"SLIDE! SLIDE! SLIDE!" came the cry of staunch friends and deadly enemies alike—even from Eddie Baker, who jumped up and down on the sidelines, rooting for me like I was his best friend in the whole world. So I slid. Low and hard. And fast. I ripped a hind pocket on my corduroy pants.

"OUT!" cried Dave Studely, the town's leading stickler for details.

I was too stunned to speak, but a moan came up from all the others—the students and teachers alike—probably including the gods above (who must also have penciled some notes about Dave Studley to pass further up so that Saint Peter or somebody could have a few hard words when the Time Came).

Out at the plate after one complete Home Run and 99% of a second!

Two home runs in the same day! Two home runs in practically the same minute! Nobody had ever knocked the ball across the highway! But I was out. From substitute to batter in seconds. From total obscurity to Most Valuable Player, just like that! And then it was all taken away. Back to the shadows.

I was disgusted. I did the "incorrect" thing. I went home. It was wrong politically, and I knew it. But I did it anyway. I would do it again. It was the right gesture: the silent message of "screw you, who needs it; you can keep your ball and your bases and the kind of a rule that disallows a Home Run for a little kid because he missed second base by one inch!"

This was Port Orford's grammar school playground, not Yankee Stadium. It was an ordinary Tuesday afternoon in the spring, with mud puddles still brimming in the outfield; not the final game for the American League pennant.

I took my time walking home. And a phone call got there before I did.

The big people were ready for me. Primed. Pissed off. Dishonored. Because they knew all about Sportsmanship, and how Good Sports were supposed to act. How Tichenors were supposed to act. Smilers and shruggers, those Tichenors. Just smile and shrug, and don't let it get to you. Hurry up and get back in the game. Play. And, above all, be a Good Sport. I stood there next to the cold stove in the store and took it. All this crap. From parents; from disapproving customers (which made the humiliation even more complete, since it was now beyond a family matter and open to the entire public); and—of course—from Uncle John, the perfect figure of justice and Right Thinking in his police uniform. All of them had an angle. Everybody had a news flash about Sportsmanship.

Nobody acknowledged the Home Runs. Nobody took into account the ball that went clear across Highway 101 and into the ditch. Nobody thought Dave Studley was a big jerk. I had failed. I had failed the Tichenors in the private cemetery on the hill beyond. I had failed my team. I had failed my home town. I had failed organized baseball. I had maybe even failed America and her dreams for greatness.

There was no way out for me; nothing to do but wait it out. I remember thinking what it would be like to stow away on the next lumber ship and go anyplace at all—maybe Australia—or take my life's savings out of the bank and get on the southbound bus to California.

John then put the cap on it. Uncle John. My namesake and godfather. He summarized everything in a bitter concluding statement. He looked down and said to me:

"Let me tell you something, Johnny. It's a long walk up Fool's Hill!"

It was the final clod from the dump truck. The grownups looked at me with disdain, and then once more placed the weight of the entire world upon their capable shoulders. Some went on about their business of examining the pork chops, inspecting them for freshness, or strolling—as John did—down to the barbershop to resolve matters of international importance.

Having thus been "talked to," I was then ignored. I became invisible. Which was far worse, even, than being the ridiculed "Substitute." I had been the Substitute all right; followed by the Hero, shining and important; then—on the second trip around the bases—the Loser; consequently: the Bad Sport; and, finally, the Fool.

– 125–

Such was the pinnacle of that particular Tuesday, and—for that matter—of the rest of the spring. As best I could, I erased the memory of the lectures and the adults, but tried to keep vivid my memory of going by the bases on that first Home Run.

I remembered the cheers. I had driven in two kids who had been on first and second, and they were clapping their hands at home plate. That was good. It really affected the score. It counted. People were jumping up and down. The third baseman was at the edge of the highway, remembering to look both ways before he ran across the blacktop to search for the ball in the ditch. That was the instant to remember: when things were exactly perfect and the homer was a cinch. The brightest moment.

It's still bright.

But so is the memory of Uncle John's big cop voice telling me about the long, hard upward journey that awaited boys like me.

The one up Fool's Hill.

People On the Point of Land Extending Far Into the Ocean

Because of my persistence in talking about what the local Indians might or might not have been like, my sister happened to discuss it with the principal of the high school. He dropped by the store one Saturday to talk to me about the subject.

"So," he said. "You're interested in Indians, are you?"

"Yes," I said.

I had talked about it so much that a couple of weeks earlier Smitty had started calling me "Chief." A few other people started doing it, too. Saying things like: "Hello, Chief." "How're you doing, Chief?" Stuff like that. Two or three days earlier I was having a 7-Up float at Doyle's and somebody made me laugh and I blew 7-Up out my nose. Ever do that? It foamed right out.

Don Doyle piped right up and said:

"Heap Strong Medicine, huh, Chief?"

Everybody laughed.

The principal lighted a big curved pipe and said:

"You know something? I'm interested in local Indians, too. And I'll tell you what. I have to go up to the University of Oregon in Eugene a couple of weeks from now and I have a friend whose husband works in the university library. I believe they have a big anthropology section there. Do you know what 'anthropology' means?"

I said I didn't and he explained it to me.

"So," he continued. "I'll go up and see what I can find out. Then I'll come back and tell you."

In the coming weeks I became a celebrity without trying. I told everybody that the principal was going to the University of Oregon to find out about Indians—our own former Indians—and that he would tell me about them. Give me a report.

A small groundswell of interest got going and people said they wanted to be around when the principal made his report.

At first the principal agreed to talk to a few people standing around the big wood stove in my father's store. But too many people voiced their interest, so Mr. Wight, which was the principal's name, said he would speak in a small classroom at the high school. He created a sign-up sheet, just like for a real class. People came into my father's store and put their names on it. A number of them didn't really give a damn about Indians, past or present, but didn't want to be left out of anything. So they signed up.

The principal looked at the final list and moved the planned talk to the biggest classroom in the whole school. 43 people signed up. Including the minister and his wife.

The day came.

We went to the classroom and saw the strange words written on the blackboard in the front of the room.

At the top was the word Athapascan. Wight said that they were the major tribes that were once found between the Umpqua River in Oregon to the north and as far south as the Eel River in California.

Then there were tribes within tribes. On the Umpqua and the Coquille rivers lived the Mishikhwutmeunne tribes. (This was the longest word on the blackboard).

The Kusan tribes (who spoke a different language) once lived in Coos Bay and the lower Coquille River.

Nasumi was a Kusan village in what is now Bandon.

Next was a village between the Coquille River and Flores Creek: Natutshitunne.

East of us were the Taltushtuntude people on Galice Creek.

South were the Takelma tribes who lived on the Rogue River, and the Chasta Costa, Chetco, and Tututune tribes near the river.

North from the Rogue was the Yukichetunne (People at the Mouth of the River) Tribe. Next were the Kwausathlkhuntunnes (People Who Eat Mussels) who lived near Humbug Mountain.

Wight was working his way up the coast, building excitement and suspense as he got closer to our town.

Then came the Kwatami tribes who claimed all the country between the coast and the Coast Range from the south boundary of Nasumi to Humbug Mountain.

Kwatami, Wight said, means "On the Gulf." That was us, all right. The natural harbor. So the clam shells and ashes I'd dug up were Kwatami!

But there was more!

"There were three villages nearby. One at Sixes called Kthukhwuttune, which means 'People Where Good Grass Is.'"

He let that sink in a minute. All of us knew of the bright green fields near the Sixes River Bridge.

"The next-closest one was called Kosotshe, a village on Flores Creek between Sixes and Port Orford."

He paused.

"Finally," he said. "Right here. Right here in Port Orford was the village called Kaltsergheatunne. And this means: 'People On a Point of Land Extending Far Into the Ocean.'"

"Yes! Yes!" A number of people exclaimed.

"In 1854, the tribe—the Kwatami—was governed by Hahhultalah, who lived in the Sixes area and by a sub-chief, Tagonecia, here at Port Orford."

He then said that he had borrowed a couple of books from the University library that showed pictures of local Indians. The crowd hung around for awhile to study the pictures and then went home.

For only a day or so, people tried to get the nickname Tagonecia to stick on me, but it was too hard to remember.

I also feared that I would be demoted to Sub-Chief, but I wasn't.

The nickname Chief stuck. But not for long. I was soon back to "Johnny Bee."

But Wight's interest in the subject had conferred Heap Strong Medicine on me and my concerns, including what Fletcher had explained about spirits, especially later when we buried Skychief.

Running With Winnie

My grandfather was, I believe, the tallest person in town.

He lived in a white house down an alley off the town's main street. He was, among other official duties, the Official Collector of Information for the U.S. Weather Bureau, so he had a rain gauge on the lawn in a little white hutch, a thermometer, and an instrument to measure wind speed. For some unaccountable reason I urinated in the rain gauge one time. My grandfather suspected me, but couldn't prove anything. Time passed. I eventually confessed and I remember a hazy conversation about whether I thought I was being funny or if I was trying to be mean. It was neither. The rain gauge was there. I peed in it. Probably driven by exactly the same compulsion that makes people climb mountains that were never climbed before or try to go to the North Pole for the first time. Peeing in a rain gauge is a smaller example, to be sure, but something along the same line. I had to stand on a box to do it, I remember.

My grandfather left the room, but not before I saw him starting to laugh. Grandpa Frank lived with his housekeeper, a situation which would have been scandalous had it not been for his stature (both height-wise, Justice-of-the Peace-power-wise, and being-grandson-of-the-founder-of-the-town-wise). His housekeeper had a daughter about my age. A lot of people thought the daughter was his. I never had an opinion on that, one way or the other. I didn't care. Winifred was the girl's name and she was my friend. Winnie. What difference did it make?

– 129–

We would sit by the fire gong in the middle of town and talk. The gong was a huge ring of iron, five feet across, suspended by a chain tied onto a log framework—an arch. A crowbar looking piece of metal was tied to a log upright by a piece of rope. If the iron ring was struck energetically with the crowbar the sound could be heard for miles. No kid ever worked up the nerve to whack it, even once. We knew that Gene White would be on us in seconds. It was no longer used to signal fires. There was a new siren on the volunteer fire house for that. The gong and the arch had once been painted red, but the paint had largely chipped away and the remaining red was faded to about the same rust color as the iron gong.

Frequently, one or the other of us would sit on the gong itself—the bottom of the suspended circle—and the other would sit on a rock next to it. It was at a place where the highway turned on its way through town, so we could watch any traffic going by.

Winifred, Winnie, was smart and cute. Brown curly hair. (Three people, Moran, Crawford Smith, and my Aunty Marnie, all swore she looked exactly like Shirley Temple, but I never quite saw the resemblance.) We spent a lot of time talking about things, a lot of which I'd never thought about before.

Funny thing. We would pause occasionally to run someplace. (This marked, by the way, the beginning of my Running Phase, accountable, I think, to my yellow Keds.)

We would run up the hill or to the cliffs or no place in particular. Just run. For the sake of movement, for the release of stored-up energy and enthusiasm. Then, finally out of breath, we would resume our conversations. We went up all the way to the can dump one time and I showed her the chrome bumper and she understood what I was talking about. Anybody else would have probably beat me up for dragging them all the way to the can dump to see an old bumper.

In our last talk together it was a coincidence that we talked about death. Winnie and I spoke of where you went and what you did when you got there. Winnie thought that heaven was probably out past the universe somewhere beyond all of the visible stars. Mostly we expressed our concern and awe about just not being around town any more. Not being. Winnie seemed concerned that if something happened to us we wouldn't be remembered. By anybody. We'd be forgotten.

Within three weeks of this talk, Winnie got pneumonia.

I heard about it and wanted to see her but nobody would let me. She was in her room in my grandfather's white house. Under the care of Dr. Baird.

I didn't know what pneumonia did to people. Whether it turned them a weird color. Or made limbs fall off. Or what. It was impressed on me that the illness was frightful and terrible. And that some people had a helluva time pulling through.

I kept asking to see her and finally my grandfather said I could. But only for a minute.

It was in the afternoon and it was raining. Water ran down all the window panes. I was taken to the door of her room and told not to stay very long. My grandfather went back to his study where the shades were drawn and the piano lid was shut.

Alone, I stood in front of the door to Winnie's room, afraid to go in. Afraid of what I might see. I had recently seen pictures of people wounded in the European War, people with their faces wrapped in bandages with only little holes showing to let them breath. I was afraid of seeing Winnie this way. Or seeing her in an Iron Lung or something.

I finally went inside and stood at the end of her bed.

She was propped up on pillows and was pale but very pretty. Nothing appeared to have fallen off. Her hands were intact, attached to her arms, resting on the quilt that covered her.

She smiled at me.

She asked how I was doing and I said, "Fine," and then I asked how she was doing and she said, "Fine."

We looked for a way into a conversation but couldn't find one. I felt like running. The way we had suddenly used to do. Not away from her, you understand, but with her. Just start running. Across town. Down the hill to the beach in front of Battle Rock. Then maybe run all the way down the coast to Hubbard Creek, jumping the rivulets, flying by the blue clay deposit, racing past the rusted boiler of the shipwrecked *Joan of Arc*, raising clusters of gulls, and leaving our footprints in the wet sand closest to the waves. Footprints that would be gone when we returned.

I sat down in a chair next to the bed.

I feared she would mention the subject of our last conversation together.

And she did. Right off the bat. Death.

She said the thought of going away wasn't too frightening after all.

Then she asked me this: If she died, would I be sure to remember her?

I couldn't say of course I would. I couldn't say anything because of the seriousness of the moment. Thoughts came to mind: of our eating canned peaches in the kitchen, running, talking, interpreting clouds in the sky, lying in the sand.

"The Red Gong," I said, trying to concentrate all my thoughts into a common image. And she said, "Chrome."

We didn't say much else I can remember and I was asked to leave. We said good-bye. We waved. That was it.

Within a few days I expected to run around the base of the hill and she'd be there, probably trying to pick a dried-out dandelion without shaking loose any of the seeds. Flicking the fire gong with our fingernails or small stones to get a slight deep ringing noise.

But that night she died.

When I heard about it I was troubled but not shocked or surprised. Not like when Ted Sauers died later on, which was much harder for me to comprehend. I think the difference was that Winifred was ready in some way—intellectually prepared in an adult-like way. Maybe spiritually. She was smart. Ted was dumb. He was a dumb kid for whom death should have been an absolute impossibility. He was clearly not ready. In no way. It would have taken another 50 years for Ted to get anywhere near ready for something like that. Winnie was composed, I guess you could say. If not prepared at least composed. Ready in that sense.

It was no problem remembering her. I didn't need the red gong or the chrome bumper. She was buried in the family cemetery and a small white stone marked her grave. But I didn't need to trudge all the way up there to be reminded. It was no chore to remember her. It was not like chopping wood, stocking shelves, or doing other duties in exchange for my miserable 25¢-a-week allowance.

If Ted had come back to life, I would have been so shocked that I'd have died myself—like of a heart attack. I wouldn't have been a bit surprised, however, if I saw Winnie suddenly appear next to the cannery on the dock or wading in the big mudpuddle in her red rubber boots. It would have seemed quite natural. We would have started talking and running again just like that.

Beacons

The old fire gong reminded me of the only other thing that rang: the bell buoy. Nobody heard the harbor buoy because it didn't need to be listened to. During the day there was other noise to cover it up. Rain. Wind. Trucks and other traffic. On a quiet night you could hear it easily if you listened for it. Otherwise it wasn't there. If you were a fisherman, of course, fogged in on a flat white sea then it was as loud as Westminster Abbey and twice as inviting, so said Crawford Smith. When the fog rolled in when it wasn't supposed to, there you'd be, busily hauling in crab pots and suddenly you couldn't see the closest end of the boat. Then it was time to listen for the Cape Blanco fog horn. If it was loud, Crawford said, then you would steer south by compass for what seemed like the right number of minutes and then turn off your engine to listen for the bell buoy. It would be exactly like that time I was telling you about when I was stuck in the fog in between the barber shop and the store and needed a voice to keep calling so that I could be guided home.

Along with North Stars in our lives, the distant places to steer toward, we all have our buoys—close in, familiar guides. A favorite piece of music or an old chrome bumper or a picture is a bell buoy. It helps us from getting too far lost. Crawford said that no sailor he ever knew felt lost out there in the fog. Fog always lifts, he said, and a person was perfectly safe. The reason to want to get ashore was to bring in the catch while it was fresh and to get to the Pastime to soak up a couple of schooners of Olympia Draft. Fog is not about danger. Storms are about danger.

Old Home Week

My grandfather Frank came over to the store one day when I was supposed to be putting dusty Idaho baking potatoes into five- and ten-pound paper bags, weighing them on the scales and making sure that equal numbers of small, medium, and large potatoes were going into each bag.

"Come on," he said. "We've got to go somewhere."

"But I'm supposed to be working," I said.

"I'll fix it," he said, and had a few words with my father.

He came back and repeated.

"Come on. Get your jacket on and let's get going. And grab your rain hat. There's a cap on Humbug."

"Where are we going?"

"Never mind," he said. "I'll show you."

We walked a short way to the road that goes to the Coast Guard station and the Tichenor Family Cemetery. We went to a junction where one road turned left to the Coast Guard station and the other veered toward a collection of summer cottages a couple of miles farther toward Agate Beach and the south end of Garrison Lake. It was a well-known fact that the little houses were haunted before the Crazy People moved there.

"There are ghosts in this direction," I cautioned, when we made the right-hand turn.

"Poppycock!" he said. "There are no ghosts in there. There are people."

"The Crazy People."

"Who calls them the Crazy People?"

"I do, . . . all the other kids do," I explained.

"Did you kids dream up the idea, or did parents?"

"I don't know," I said, "but everybody knows they don't have jobs and they don't work."

"They don't have to, Johnny. Enough of them are retired. They don't have to work if they don't want to."

I didn't know what "retired" meant and I didn't care.

"Well, anyway," I said, "it's a well-known fact that they're all crazy."

"Have you ever met any of them?"

"No. They stick to themselves."

"That's their right," my grandfather said. "It's their perfect right to do what they please. As long as they don't harm anybody. Which they don't."

"How do you know that?"

"Because, " he explained (in what was a standard explanation for a great many things), "I am the Justice of the Peace."

So I said nothing, but just kept tromping toward what the Crazy People now called "Where the Woodbine Twineth." Can you imagine such a name for a cluster of cottages?

We got there. And something big was going on.

About fifty yards from the buildings was a small sign hand painted on a piece of cardboard that said: GRAVEYARD. It was around a bend from the houses and out of everybody's line of vision. Also, there was a big blackberry patch along the front and you couldn't have seen the gravestones if there had been any, which there were not.

A slow procession was heading toward this imaginary cemetery. It was led by somebody driving a pickup. Hooked onto the pickup was a homemade two-wheel trailer upon which was a long, narrow box covered with an American flag.

"My God," I said to my grandfather. "Somebody died."

"Shush," he said.

A man in a cap said quietly to my grandfather:

"Major Bentley specified this touch, not wishing to be sent to the graveyard inside a hearse. He wished to be borne upon a catafalque," the man in the cap said, "I think he'd seen the word used in a Portland *Oregonian* crossword puzzle."

"It is not properly a catafalque," my grandfather explained. "Maybe a limber or a caisson or something else that's horse-drawn. I think a catafalque is a structure inside a church. But what the hell does it matter? If Major Bentley wanted to call it a catafalque, what difference does it make?"

"Right," the other man said. "The word won't get used in the service, anyway."

So the "catafalque" rolled slowly around the corner toward the "cemetery."

Everybody in Woodbine walked along behind the trailer.

The driver parked in the vacant lot graveyard and stopped in the middle of it. He turned off the engine.

"The driver's name is Rodge," my grandfather whispered. "And the woman is named Sylvia."

The woman stood next to the catafalque and spoke:

"As the newly elected mayor of Where the Woodbine Twineth, it is my solemn duty to record the passing of Bentley of our community."

There was a muffled sound—advice from an audience member.

"Major Bentley," Sylvia corrected herself and then continued.

"The Major was an Artillery officer in the Great War. And our friend."

"More than seven years!" someone else coached.

"Yes," Sylvia agreed, "of more than seven years, . . . and a great contributor to our plans, activities, and entertainments. Including picnics and playing bridge in our tournaments. His request was to keep this service very short and he recommended that we all go back to his place and have some Martinis, the fixin's for which he—the Major—so graciously provided. Not only that, but many ingredients for the first picnic of the season which will include Bentley's favorite cucumber-and-tomato salad, and the baked beans of Irma Dolge. My potato salad this year will not contain horseradish, despite the advice and counsel of John Henry to the contrary. So that's it."

More muffled advice.

"Oh, yes," she added. "Major Bentley was not a patriot; only an ordinary American who saw his duty and performed it."

Sylvia looked at the group of people to see if she'd left anything else out of the Eulogy.

The crowd smiled.

She proceeded.

"Roger, if you will, please."

Roger drew a .45 cal. service automatic from the glove compartment of the jeep.

"Okay, folks," he said. "Cover your ears. This is the salute fired by the firing squad that would normally be a part of a military funeral. Everybody would fire three times after the officer in charge of the burial party would say: 'Ready, Aim, Fire.' Okay? Only I won't say that. I'll just fire. So hold your ears if you want to. Here goes."

Roger shouted "Fire" and then discharged three shots without too much pause or ceremony. Just BLAM, BLAM, BLAM, and it was all over.

"Good," Sylvia said after the echoes died away. "Perfect."

Another muffled conversation in the group.

– 136–

Roger and three other men each grabbed an end of the big American flag draping Bentley's catafalque and marched outward so they could fold it up. They revealed a big refrigerator carton lying on its side on Roger's trailer. The top side was open. Inside the "coffin" was a man lying flat on a lawn chaise. It was Bentley in his World War One major's uniform. He opened his eyes.

I wasn't terribly surprised since he didn't look very dead to me. Then he spoke:

"Not bad," he said, as Sylvia and the others helped him out of the carton and back onto the ground. "Not bad at all. Just the right length. I want to thank everybody—and you, Frank."

The small crowd murmured, "You're welcome," as did my grandfather.

It was the fourth year of the Bentley Funeral.

It happened every May 21st. And served as the kickoff for regular picnics with potato salad.

The people of Woodbine knew they'd made it another year when they "buried" Major Bentley.

"Let's go have a drink," Bentley said. And that's what they did.

As we were walking along, the Major said:

"You must be Johnny Bee."

I admitted that I was. I'd much rather have been "Chief" and had people say it with the same respect as they called him "Major."

We then had a half-indoor, half-outdoor picnic.

The Woodbine people made sure that I got a drumstick.

I'll say that for them.

Tannenbaum Express

There were no Christmas tree lots in our town prior to the holiday season. There were no long faces of people looking at trees they couldn't afford. No jokers doing their phony strangling scenes and saying things like:

"Auuugh! . . . How much a foot?"

"What's this tree made of for Cripes Sakes—*Gold?*"

If you wanted a tree you drove out to the woods and found exactly the tree you wanted, cut it down, and brought it back into town. Simple as that. To get to our family's favorite place we had to take a longish drive on a dirt road out toward the lighthouse at Cape Blanco. We would have to pass the Hughes Ranch with its Victorian house built by Patrick and Jane Hughes at the turn of the century. (One of their children, Alice, married Patrick Masterson in Port Orford, and they were the parents of my friend, Pat.) There was an abandoned church nearby and a graveyard, plus hundreds of spruce trees that were just the right size for a Christmas tree in your house; ones that were seven or eight feet tall.

So we'd go out there, walk around in the drizzle for awhile, and select just the right one. My sister, my father, and I weren't too picky. We could spot one almost immediately. But my mother needed time. It was like comparison shopping. We could get pretty damp by the time she finally made up her mind. My father would then chop down the selected tree with a hatchet and tie it on the top of the car.

Anybody in town who wanted a Christmas tree was never much more than 40 minutes away from having just the right one. Their idea of the perfect tree.

"At the perfect price," my father would always add.

Then it was upstairs to the attic to find the boxes of ornaments and the strings of Christmas tree lights while my dad nailed a couple of boards to the bottom of the tree.

There was also holly growing in the woods so you could get plenty of free holly to hang up.

So there you'd have it: mirrored ornaments, colored lights, red-and-white peppermint candy canes, and the smell of the fresh needles. And, one by one, brightly wrapped packages would appear under the tree as the Big Day drew ever so slowly closer.

There have always been two schools of thought about Christmas and presents. There are the people who feel they must wait until Christmas Day to open their presents. And there is the other camp who opens presents on Christmas Eve. We opened presents on Christmas Eve. All the presents. That way there was none of the business of staying awake half the night waiting for Santa Claus. We knew there wasn't a Santa Claus anyway. Especially one who came down the chimney in the middle of the night when there were still hot coals in the fireplace.

So, by Christmas morning, we'd already opened everything. Christmas Day was to play with toys and loll around. Parents could get up late. I felt it was the sensible way to do it. Wouldn't you know, however, that I would grow up and hang around with people from the other camp, the Christmas Morning-ers. Those for whom Christmas wouldn't be Christmas without presents being opened in the gray light of dawn. What kind of gaiety and spirit is that? Puffy, tired faces trying to reflect enthusiasm as they said the usual stuff. Oh, my, look at this. This is perfect. My, my, my. Yawning all the while and looking perfectly miserable.

There is 20 times more enthusiasm on Christmas Eve, always stoked by bowls of nuts and lubricated by Tom & Jerrys and eggnogs. I remember the exuberant, reckless kisses from aunts with their sexy rum-and-cinnamon lips. They wore dresses that smelled of perfume but their breaths smelled like cakes. There was a lot of dashing around and loud talking even while the presents were being handed out and opened. It could be black and raining outside, but inside there was every color imaginable in the living room and the kitchen, what with the clothes and the ribbons, the tree ornaments and the Christmas cards arranged in rows on the mantle, the fat candles and the lamps, and the fire in the fireplace (where people sprinkled increasing amounts of Colored Fire Powder from a tall can to make the flames new colors of robins' egg blue, magenta, and green). There was lipstick and fingernail polish, feely flowered dresses, tree lights reflected back in the mirror, and wrapping paper up to your ankles everywhere. There was music on the radio and glug-glugs from bottles in the kitchen. There was tinsel—some of it draped over door frames with mistletoe tied on it with ribbons. People modeled new clothes by holding them in front of themselves and posing like they were in magazine ads. Men put on women's hats and batted their eyelashes. Women grabbed kid's cap guns and stuck them in the ribs of the men, saying: "Stick 'em up, Buster!" and "Do what I say or you're a goner!" There was laughter of every kind, chortles and hee-haws, deep department-store-Santa Ho-Ho-Hos, and edge-of-control laughing that sounded almost like crying. This mayhem went on for hours at a stretch.

I have never seen anything on the part of the Christmas-Morning celebrants that could match this in any way. As I said, they have always been lumpy, sleepy people in their dressing gowns and slippers, listlessly opening gifts. Non-manic kids. No booze. No spirit. Cleanliness fanatics folding wrapping paper the moment it was unwrapped "so that sparks don't jump out and start a terrible fire" from their two-bit little one-log and two-log fires. No hurtling across the room. No maniac hugs. No tripping and falling down in the paper and empty boxes. No getting hoarse from yelling. No. Just tiny gray mornings and stupid Christmas carols on the radio (when Christmas is over, for crying out loud). Then a solemn procession to a table to eat cardboard waffles and zombie-cold scrambled eggs.

I have observed that Christmas-Morning people are much more controlled and buttoned-up than Christmas-Eve people. As I've suggested, Christmas-Morning people don't get things rolling with a few Tom & Jerrys. Christmas mornings at our place were always fairly quiet to start. My sister, myself, and cousins were careful not to waken anybody. We opened the extra presents from the stockings pinned to the mantle of the fireplace and then played quietly with toys and games until grownups started to appear. The living room was still a shambles, with plenty of colorful reminders of the night before, ribbons and stuff scattered everywhere. We'd start a new fire while the grownups debated the sensibility of having A Little Of The Hair Of The Dog That Bit Them. Having reached a dignified, sedate decision, they would agree that One Short One could do no harm. One short one then followed another short one until murmuring turned to hollering and somebody like my Uncle George would yell from the kitchen:

"Johnny Bee! You wanna pancake?"

"Sure," I'd say.

And—Whiz—he'd sail one across the room toward me in blatant disregard of the sacred Do-Not-Throw-Food Law.

Within an hour, the group would achieve the same volume and intensity of the night before and then maintain it all the while a turkey was roasting and other food was prepared for a mid-afternoon dinner. Long naps were then part of the proceedings—naps during which aunts, unaccountably, giggled and squealed in bedrooms with uncles.

One Christmas Eve sticks out for me because of its perfection. It possessed just the right amount of heat, closeness, and noise, and I was right in the center of the warm sweet-smelling herd. We had a "Hollywood" fire (Uncle Bob called it, on account of its perfection, like it was in a movie about rich people skiing in Vermont or Sun Valley and then hanging around the Lodge) and a fat tree that had required two extra strings of lights. There was a new angel on the top of the tree with her own orange light bulb. Aunt Anna forgot herself completely and Frenched me. (She looked at my surprise, laughed, and said I'd get over it.) George was throwing walnuts across the kitchen into an open paper grocery bag, trying to score points against Aunt Margaret, his sister-in-law, for a silver-dollar bet. A succession of eggnogs had apparently dimmed his memory to the fact that Marnie was a former high-school basketball champ. She waxed his ass and kept the silver dollar.

I was playing a game with someone until I finally noticed that the room was half empty and nearly quiet. My mother and my aunts were waiting for me to notice this. Something was going on. My father, my uncles, and the other men were gone. Since it was raining, they probably hadn't gone outside to smoke cigars or something. The noise level had diminished to practically nothing.

Then I heard an odd sound, a kind of a sustained whoosh with a cadence to it. It would whoosh for a few seconds, then briefly whir, then whoosh again, and then whir. I couldn't recognize it. I started walking toward the source of the noise. It wasn't in the kitchen, but I was getting warmer. It was louder in the hall toward my bedroom.

My bedroom door was closed. There was no light on in there, but it was where the rhythmic whooshing and whirring was coming from. Wait a minute! I could see a periodic flash of light under the door! What was it? A flashlight? No, . . . it was happening in a too regular a way.

"Go in, . . . go in," the women urged.

I went in.

The men were sitting on the floor in the dark. None looked up at me. They were in a circle and Uncle Bob said to a grown-up Tichenor cousin:

"My turn. Let me have it."

It sounded like a kid's voice.

The cousin handed over a control—the transformer.

In front of them, on an oval track, was an electric train!

But it wasn't any ordinary electric train with a caboose and freight cars and a tank car or two. This was a passenger train! A streamlined silver passenger train. The important part about it was the lights in every single car. There was even a light in the enclosed cab of the locomotive where the engineer sat. There was a bright red warning light on the back of the observation car at the rear. There was a bright headlight on the front of the locomotive. There it was on the floor—the floor of my room! Humming along, running perfectly, each car tick-tick-ticking over the track connections.

"Not so fast, Bob," someone urged. "You'll run her off the track on the curve."

Bob backed off on the control handle.

I squatted down to get a better look.

It was amazing. It was perhaps the most wonderful thing I'd ever seen. I had observed electric trains in department stores, but never anything with so many lights. It must have been one-of-a-kind. They built this one and then quit.

There were two things about this experience that I will never forget. First was the fact that I had no idea, absolutely no idea, that the train was mine. I thought it was a gift that belonged to one of the men. I suppose I got this idea because of the concentration of everybody crowded around the train—the fact they didn't look up and acknowledge me.

The other thing was that I was not one bit envious of whoever it was that owned the train. I was content to just look at it like everybody else—in absolute amazement. It was like being high on a cliff looking down on an actual passenger train. That's how real it looked, being there in the dark.

As a matter of fact, I was quite stunned when everybody looked at me and said "Merry Christmas," like sort of a choir—and with gestures which suggested that We-Here-Assembled now present you with this astonishing train. It was the After-You gesture that people make when they want you to go through the door first.

"What do you think, Johnny?" somebody asked and it was obvious to everybody that I was beyond being able to speak.

This made everybody laugh for at least a minute and the men, still on the floor watching the moving train, became engineers again.

Finally, it was Aunt Margaret who insisted:

"Don't you think Johnny ought to have a turn?"

So I got a turn on the control. But it was a short turn and I soon gave it up to a grownup.

In a Perfect Heaven I believe there is a wingless angel in a gray suit—a distinguished English-looking gentleman who looks more like an accountant than an Angel and who wears silk rep-stripe ties. This is the Person who keeps a record of all the electric trains that anybody ever got anywhere, including China and South America. There is a nice bronze plaque in the end of his office with big raised letters spelling the names of the Top Ten All-Time Winners!

At the head of the list, in undeniable first place (perhaps with an extra gold star or a small jewel for emphasis), it says:

Johnny Bee's Train. Christmas Eve, 1938. Passenger-Type in Silver. With Lights.

There may be Christmas-Day winners on the list.

But I would tend to doubt it.

Along Came 1939

La Guardia Airport opened in New York. Ford introduced Lincoln Mercury, and DuPont made their big announcement about Nylon. The New York World's Fair opened and was telecast by NBC. (Seen by 1,000 viewers.) Simultaneously, the Golden Gate International Exposition began in San Francisco where they dumped a lot of dirt in the bay and created Treasure Island. FM radio receivers were marketed for the first time.

"This is London," said CBS correspondent Edward R. Murrow on the radio news. "Batman" comics appeared at Doyle's. Low-priced Pocket Books started, the country's first paperbacks. My grandfather read *The Grapes of Wrath* and tried to get me and my sister interested in listening to parts of it. No go.

Grandma Moses started her (paid) painting career at age 79. Two huge films were: *Gone With the Wind* and *The Wizard of Oz*. Others: *Gunga Din, Beau Geste, Four Feathers, Boom Town,* and *The Hunchback of Notre Dame.* My sister was crazy about *Intermezzo, Wuthering Heights, The Philadelphia Story,* and *Mr. Smith Goes to Washington.*

The trumpet player, Harry James, left the Benny Goodman orchestra to form his own band and hired an unknown singer named Frank Sinatra.

Big songs that year: "I'll Never Smile Again," "Somewhere Over the Rainbow," "We're Off to See the Wizard," "South of the Border," "Three Little Fishies (in an Itty-Bitty Pool)" "Beer Barrel Polka," "Brazil," "I Didn't Know What Time It Was," "All the Things You Are."

They let Al Capone out of prison but his mind, according to Crawford Smith, "was wrecked by the Syph."

Precooked frozen foods were put on the market by Birds Eye ("but the idea is not for us," says my father). 5-minute Cream of Wheat, however, hit our shelves. Lay's potato chips were introduced.

WARNING: If you have never heard the music to the following jingle, don't ask some older person what it is because it will haunt you for the rest of your life, maybe longer: "Pepsi Cola hits the spot / Twelve full ounces, that's a lot / Twice as much for a nickel, too / Pepsi Cola is the drink for you!"

The Dinah Shore Show started on radio. So did the Charley McCarthy Show with Edgar Bergen (with permanent guest Don Ameche who most kids thought invented the telephone because he was in the movie about Alexander Graham Bell), Sponsor: Chase & Sanborn coffee. Other new radio shows included the Frank Morgan–Fannie Brice Program (Maxwell House), Orson Welles Mercury Theater (Campbells Soups); Green Hornet (Palmolive Soap)—and a real thriller LIGHTS OUT (Kelloggs).

Hitler marched into Austria. The Big War started in Europe. Germany invaded Poland. France and Britain entered the war. Russia invaded Finland. All hell broke loose. By the end of the year, Germans were bombing British cities and towns.

Moran showed up from nowhere (Boston, actually); some tourists had a helluva time; and Eddie Baker, in one of the intervals when he was a friend instead of a deadly enemy, found a human skull.

Farm Devils

Things were hard for me, my father would say, because I had no real experience with hard. What he meant was that I had never experienced real work, not the way he had on the farm in Kansas.

I thought I was working hard bagging dirty, dusty potatoes, but he assured me that it wasn't hard work at all—certainly not as tough as working on a farm.

I didn't believe him because I had seen lyrical little farms in picture books with their smiling cows and freshly painted houses and barns. What could be so hard about a farm? There would be a few more eggs to collect and tomatoes to pick. A farm looked to me like a place that pretty much ran itself.

I asked a few people what they knew about farms. Most of them didn't know a single thing. They had never lived on one.

I discovered that the Methodist minister had grown up on a farm in Iowa and he really let me have it.

Earlier when I had asked about spirits in the trees and the lake, he denied the possibility. Then suddenly he tells me that he had searched for any profession or craft that would keep him away from farms and the feeling that there were devils in the wind and the ground there. Devils? I listened intently because it was fun to see him became so fervent and lunatic like, just like when he talked about Jesus and the Resurrection. It was interesting because it was like a volcanic eruption or a geyser suddenly breaking loose. His face would get very red and his hands would tremble.

He said that nothing was for sure on a farm and with that he thumped his fist on the table. If you raised crops, he said, you were at risk because the crop could die because there wasn't enough water and crops could die because there was too much water. Floods? I asked him and he said, yes, exactly. Crops could grow just dandy and you might even have a bumper crop but the market price could fall and you wouldn't make any profit at all, as a matter of fact you could lose money. If you raised animals they could get sick and die. Or the market would be glutted or the animals would be rustled or run away.

Every day on a farm, he said, the Rust Devil was at work trying to ruin all the iron metal and the wire and the chains and, just as relentlessly, the Rot Goblins worked on wood, trying to crumble the fenceposts and the farmhouse and the outbuildings and make them sink into the ground as tan powder.

Gravity was a hidden monster trying to pull everything into the center of the earth including the grass, the seedlings, and the feet of the chickens themselves. Humans could feel it in their boots on muddy days and, in the summer especially, anything you had to carry could double its weight between a nearby field and the barn.

New rope would fray and harness would break, rain would begin to fall from clear skies and tractor engines would fail like broken hearts deep inside. Great winds would blow for days and the grit driven by them could enter small cracks and settle on the mantle and in food and into your teeth.

The minister was taking on the look of one of the humping animals that my father said were only playing.

There were days and weeks at a stretch, he said, when nothing went right, where lameness and accidents and failure heaped up like a snow on a porch and a person couldn't walk a hundred steps without mishap or snakefright or the dread of something else breaking.

He concluded that farm work was a nightmare of endless repetition until, quite suddenly, almost any effort was likely to blow up, backfire, or collapse. A steel pump handle would fracture like a popsicle stick and the only bolt of lightning in four adjacent counties would strike your pigpen's roof setting the shingles ablaze and causing great swine hullabaloo.

He said there were endless nights that were too cold or too hot to sleep and the devils attacked your bones and you got up weak and stumbling.

It was work that never ended, jobs that were never finished, terrible boredom, and Sunday was not a day of rest because it, too, began in darkness and the cows didn't know any better since they would assemble in the barn and low for hay and relief just as always. Milking could not be adjourned for the convenience of the milkers; the milkers milked and the mowers mowed and the plowers, like robots, made their furrows up and back and up and back.

The frosts came and snows fell hard but the repairs went on, the hammering and the oiling, the sewing and the pickling of root-cellar extras. A farm genie lurked at the entrance to the county road to hypnotize anybody who went to town, to reinforce the myth this was the Life so don't you dare get on the train and try to leave because we need you slaves on the place to wage the constant war against the weeds and a return to naturalness. Saplings and brush could spring up in a season. They lurked just one breath under the grass waiting. Criminals should not be sent to prisons, the Minister raged, they should be banished to farms. Then they would know the meaning of hard labor and punishment. The farmers themselves could then be released to other useful work. He concluded by saying that farming was an agony and a crap shoot and there was no doubt about it.

I could tell by the look on his face, angry and contrite at the same time, regretful at having gone quite so insane, that I had better conclude my visit and my investigation. I exited quickly. I had learned more than enough about farms. Even if the preacher was only half right, there shouldn't be farms at all.

I went over to T.J.'s place where he was supervising the making of clam chowder in the kitchen for the lunchtime trade. I told him that I had been talking to people about farms and that some unfamiliar terms had been used.

A "bumper crop" wasn't what it sounded like. Neither was a "crap shoot."

T.J. laughed at that one until tears streaked his face.

I observed my father with a certain new respect. I had seen him shaving in the bathroom and I knew that his torso skin was snow white, and that his arms and neck and face were deeply tanned. The contrast was amazing. When I had asked about it earlier I had been told that he had a "Farmer's Tan."

After the minster's harangue about farms I could now deduce that there were indeed powerful forces at work there.

I knew that my father had not been on a farm for many years but there it was, evidence as clear as day, the deep tan that had been tattooed on by some marvel elf of sun.

In a later conversation with my grandfather Frank that merely grazed this subject, he respectfully acknowledged that my other grandfather, the Kansas Frank, must be a strong, brave man what with his having to be the soldier that he was. In the constant fight against the elements.

What Do You Want to Be?

People become true adults when they have forgotten virtually everything about being a kid. For example, adults are fond of leaning down to children and asking the question:

"What do you want to be when you grow up?"

This is a stupid, pain-in-the-ass question but they don't remember it because too much time has elapsed since an adult bent down to them and asked the same question—about a subject they couldn't yet imagine.

I was frequently asked this question by family members and other grownups and quickly learned that the simple answer of "I don't don't know" is not satisfactory to a true adult. It is unacceptable since they have long forgotten what it was like to have no concept of ever growing up because time passed so slowly.

An adult will always prompt a kid who doesn't know. Always.

"How about a fireman?" they would ask.

In my case I would said no, I didn't want to be a fireman. I could remember only one fire in Port Orford and the fighting of it had been unsuccessful. Who wanted to be a fireman? Bandon, after all, had burned completely to the ground.

"How about a doctor?"

Since I couldn't imagine ever being as old as Dr. Baird, such a possibility was entirely out of the question. No.

"A fisherman?"

"Maybe."

A maybe makes an adult's eyes light up. They think they're on to something.

"How would you like to run a store like this one?"

I thought not but didn't wish to offend so I said "maybe."

"How would you like to be a Police Captain like me?"

Not if it meant gaining that much weight and shooting off my mouth all the time. But, once again, being diplomatic, I gave it another "maybe," knowing that Uncle John would then go away to tell another grownup the good news that I was probably going to be a cop. Almost certainly. Apparently an adult's hopes need to be kept alive.

After intense questioning of this kind I determined that I didn't want to be a lighthouse keeper or a full-time garbage collector. No. Being the projectionist in the movie theater had some appeal because it would have enabled me to see lots of movies and eat popcorn up by the machines. I didn't want to be a taxi driver in Portland like my Uncle Harvey, but I enjoyed the sights and smells in the kitchen of Margie's Cafe and so becoming a cook like Cliff seemed a possibility. I didn't think I wanted to be in the Coast Guard unless I was a Captain or something and didn't have to ride in the back of the truck with the men. I didn't want to fly an airplane in the early days because I had never really seen one. The China Clipper in the newsreels could have been trick photography and actually no bigger than a kite. It had four engines and was unbelievable.

I asked if I could be a reader and was informed that it wasn't a profession.

Since reader had been knocked down as an idea, I figured that looker was also not likely to be regarded as a possibility so I didn't bother mentioning it.

Being in the movies was a remote possibility. Not as a child star like Shirley Temple but as a cowboy or a detective.

One thing for sure was that I didn't want to be what any of my ancestors had been, with the possible exception of sea captain. I couldn't think of any relatives that I wanted to be like. I didn't want to do what they did. I wanted to be somebody else. I wanted to have more fun than them.

In one of the *Books of Knowledge* or another illustrated book I saw a rope-making machine in which a whole bunch of tiny filaments of hemp were being woven into small lines and then braided into a huge rope similar to the ones used to tie lumber ships to the dock, rope as big in diameter as a small melon. It was as if a whole bunch of spiders were extruding dense material into a huge solid line for web.

I got it into my mind that I was, in my own way, a machine which created strands of information and experience—everything I heard from people or saw and read or felt on my own—and then slowly but inextricably wove them and braided them into a strong rope that was being coiled somewhere in the center of my person. This was My Rope and it contained all of the individual strands of my life and I knew it could be used to pull myself along or hoist myself out of danger.

I never said anything about this to the adults who asked me what I was going to be when I grew up. It would have been a little too puzzling to them to hear that I already was something—a kind of rope-maker; a cognizant device that is humming along most of the day. And, of course, nobody ever had the imagination to ask:

"What *are* you?" Meaning right now; this minute. "Not what are you going to be at some unknowable time in the future, but what are you right now? Please tell me."

They probably thought they knew the answers.

Such as: You are a kid who runs. A kid who picks up things on the beach but not in his room. You are a kid who goes to school but frequently stares at the world outside the window instead of doing the work. A kid who likes movies and candy bars and soup. A kid who is fairly true to his friends.

But what adult could have ever dreamed that some kids are conscious machines that are silently and invisibly fabricating the very ropes of their lives, ropes up which they may climb triumphant cliffs; or, sadly, ropes with which they will later hang themselves from trees.

A more interesting question to ask a little kid is: "What do you remember about being a little kid?" because five-year-olds can remember when they were two and a half, even though it was half their lifetimes ago and now ancient history.

Or: "What would you do tomorrow if you had the chance?"

Here's the scoop. Until the Rennaissance, philosophers worried about being and then shifted their concentration to knowing. Both of these subject areas are hard, and certainly beyond the comprehension of most children.

Kids focus on going and doing, in that order. As in: "I'm going to cross the room now and play with that toy," or "I'm going over to Pat's now and we're probably going to climb a tree." But anything could happen on the way.

Focuses and directions could change.

Most people growing up these days have it emphasized that they must first *know* before they can go and do. They must get an education and master a body of knowledge in order to go into the world to practice a craft or a profession.

My father's generation was the last in which a tall child could go and do, just as Al went and did—with nothing much more than the strength and determination to succeed.

There is one thing more. At another time I remember asking a question about growing up and wondering if there was the grownup equivalent of a child's cry of "king's ex!"—a truce, a demand for safety, a simple declaration, that would save you.

No, they said, there was no such thing. Life was hard.

Yet I continue to think about this king's ex idea. Immunity. Time out. Cease fire. Safe at home.

I wish to be immune. I wish to be the one who cannot be touched; the one who is somehow magically protected.

There is one other thought having to do with ropes and webs and it must be filed under the heading of "Creepy, Crawly Spiders."

I concluded at a young age that spiders didn't like to get wet and that's why they chose to live in Port Orford basements, garages, and sheds. I knew that at least one or two lived in the woods because you could be running as fast as you could down a path and run smack into a web, scream, and have a minor shit hemorrhage (one of T.J.'s expressions) as you brushed off the spider that wasn't there.

One of the deepest secrets I ever had was that I would capture insects and toss them on the web of a huge brown spider in the corner of the woodshed. He would dutifully race up and mummy-wrap the insect in silk. It was a secret, that is, until Masterson walked up (snuck up would be more like it) behind me and said:

"Fun, isn't it?"

According to him, he said (after the shock which caused a Level Two Shit Hemorrhage of its own) that everybody in town fed insects to spiders. Always had. Always would. As if spiders had been placed on earth for the amusement of latent sadists of all ages.

From the brown spider I observed the Up-Down Escape Trick. Want to go down, go down—just like an elevator. Want to go up—up she goes! From then on I daydreamed about the capability of spinning, of going up and down on lines, and of making elaborate webs. Some of the webs were History Webs.

Ted (Which, Coincidentally, Rhymes With Dead!)

As a child, especially in a small town, death is a known quality, even though it runs counter to logic and comprehensibility. Every week, it seemed, somebody's dog got run over by the Greyhound bus. Or one of my cats by a lumber carrier. And I mean really flattened.

Also, and you know this, certain kittens in a litter don't make it at all. They are scrawny or deformed and their death is not a mystery. Runts die. And big sea birds get whapped into the sides of walls and chimneys during fierce storms—and everybody knows that you don't get whapped real hard into the side of a chimney and then fly off as if nothing had happened. If you're a seabird in this situation, you die.

And old people die, too. Like Mrs. Lenieve. First your hair gets all white. Then you walk with great difficulty until finally somebody (guess who!) has to lug groceries up the hill to your house from my Dad's store. Then you can't walk at all. And then it gets so bad that you can't talk. That's the way it was with Mrs. Lenieve.

So, when Janeen Carson walked into the store and said: "Mrs. Lenieve is dead," my mind didn't do cartwheels. There was not a great deal of shock. And it certainly wasn't a surprise.

When you get into Mrs. Lenieve's shape, there aren't too many alternatives besides out. You do not, for example, decide to move to California and try to get a job in the movies. So it was sad, okay, but clearly not a surprise. Doc Pugh summed it up when I told him her latest symptoms just before she croaked and he said: "She's a Goner."

The only other way that people died (at least during the time I'm talking about as I was growing up) was to get killed in some kind of a terrible car or truck accident—like when Jack Powers lost the brakes on his logging truck coming down the side of a mountain and crashed into a tree and had the load of logs come forward and sheer off the cab and also Jack Powers' head. The rumor went around Grade School that the Constable, Gene White, could only find one of Jack's front teeth and that was all they could find of Jack Powers' entire head! Pulverized. We went to the funeral and all the kids in town wondered if they'd stuck the tooth in the coffin with Jack's headless body. It really gave you something to think about for a few days, I'll tell you. My sister said it gave her the Willies. Another similar affliction in those days was the Heebie Jeebies.

So, up to the time I'm about to describe (which was maybe when I was in the second grade) any death was explainable. Puniness. Oldness. Whapped into chimneys. Or great blood-and-guts deals where people died instantly in wrecks, or like the time a drunken sailor from a lumber boat fell off Fort Point.

What we're talking about here is the quality of abruptness.

Then along comes this thing with Ted Sauers.

As a kid, at least when I was little, there were a couple of things that could haunt you if you let them. Infantile paralysis was one of them. Because if you got infantile paralysis you either (A) died or (B) wound up in an Iron Lung, lying there flat in a big machine looking up into a mirror at nurses in uniform. Forever! We knew this was a true fact because we'd seen it in plenty of newsreels. (That was when I caught on that my mother had been lying about the spinach. Can you imagine?)

The other Dread we faced was called "Mastoid." Kids speculated that it was something that you got somehow from lake water, but it never prevented anybody from swimming. A kid had died from Mastoid up in Coquille a couple of years earlier, but that may as well have been on the moon or New York City or Japan for all the difference it made to those of us in Port Orford. Coquille was two hours away on the Old Highway and this appeared to be a substantial margin of safety, at least the way we saw it.

It was around the end of June that Ted Sauers—our own Ted—got Mastoid! It was unbelievable. Ted! Just like the rest of us in every respect. Same grade. Same height. Same weight. Owned a pet. Swam in both of the favorite places on Garrison Lake (including the part with the big, wind-blown waves at the south end).

Daryll Sauers' cousin, Ted. Teddy. Theodore.

It got very quiet. And not just in classrooms at school. But in the hallways and on the school ground at recess. Everything was hushed. Parents had taken Ted up to the little hospital in Bandon (which I remembered all too clearly from the tonsil operation that wasn't supposed to hurt) and he was in one of those white rooms. Daryll was permitted to see him from the doorway but couldn't go in and Daryll told us that Ted looked in his direction but didn't say anything and maybe couldn't even see him.

That was Mastoid for you. Down, . . . then out.

Ted was dead in three days flat.

And the whole town was silent.

The funeral was silent. And then the town was silent again afterward.

It wasn't like Mrs. Lenieve's funeral. Do you know what she did? She left a will and some money for everybody in town to go to T.J. Collins' Bar & Grill or Red's "Saloon" and have a good time. Have a chicken-fried steak (which was right at the top of T.J.'s menu for high price), or a few drinks. Whichever you wished. Because Mrs. Lenieve had lived there from almost the time the place started and this was her way of saying "So Long."

The town was noisy and laughing all the rest of that funeral day. "Just the way she would have wanted it," my grandfather said. "Exactly!"

But Ted Sauers? What could you do about that? What could you even think about that?

It was horrible.

In the eulogy, a minister used the expression, "conspicuous by his absence." Which turned out to be exactly true! You'd look around a classroom and the non-presence of Ted was painfully apparent. He was not there. He would never be there again. Because he was at the south end of town buried in the graveyard, dead. A kid! In a box. In the ground. Perfectly okay one minute and then, lo and behold, deader than a chimney-whacked albatross!

– 153–

Him. Ted. One of the best kids in our group. Croaked. Kicked the bucket.

Which was the other thing—the fact that there were eight of us who played together after school and on weekends, and—in the summer—dug caves in the cliffs and built sand forts on the beach. Eight of us. Four on a team. And Ted was one of us. And then we were seven. Which we didn't literally realize until we tried to choose up sides the next time, and then it got quiet and hard to have any fun.

My inquiry into this matter persisted for some time. Other people gave it up and went on about their business almost as if Ted had been that unknown kid who had died in Coquille. But Ted was not some unknown kid in a distant town. He was Ted, a good friend of mine. Of ours. Who had been born in our town!

The biggest letdown in my whole investigation was from the Methodist minister. I remember the whole thing exactly, even where I was standing when he said it. On the porch of his house next to the church. On the corner closest to the goldfish pond. He said—and his wife agreed with him—that it was God's wish! That God had wanted Ted! And The Lord Called Him.

Ted? A kid that was practically in the first grade before he could tie his own shoes? A kid that had to be reminded four times every day to cut the kindling and haul wood into the wood box next to the stove? That Ted? I wondered what God could possibly need Ted for. Things were going just fine. Berries were coming on. There were plenty of fish to be caught. The mill was hiring. Ships from all over the world were taking on lumber. So I'm supposed to believe that God, in the middle of all of this, suddenly has a great need to have some dumb kid named Ted leave his old friends and his new dog and Garrison Lake which was only then just getting really good to swim in?

No.

I could not believe it. I wouldn't believe it.

It didn't wash.

The minister and his wife invited me inside to talk it over. I declined. The major weapons in the Methodist arsenal in those days consisted of cookies and cups of hot chocolate served up with earnest conversations and vague threats about Salvation. But I resisted them and resumed my own personal inquiry into the untimely death of Ted Sauers.

My grandfather simply didn't know.

Crawford Smith, a trustworthy individual with respect to most mysteries, would not even guess.

Fletcher couldn't say and Dorothy was baffled.

So I gave it up. I didn't discuss it again until Moran got to town and everybody realized that Moran knew everything.

I asked just why it was, in Moran's opinion, that Ted Sauers had died. Because it sure as hell hadn't made any sense to me. Even over time.

Moran said two things: first,

"Don't tell anybody I told you this, okay?"

I agreed.

Then, second:

"It is a shame that Ted died. He had an inner-ear infection. And there is research underway right now for new drugs that cure infections like that. If Ted had been close to one of the research facilities in the East they might have given him an experimental drug and saved his life. Ted was just unlucky. Very soon, I predict, nobody will ever die from such a problem."

It was a truly astounding and satisfactory answer.

The mystery had been cleared up for me. Ted's case could then be entered with that of Jack Powers and the storm-blown birds. Crappy luck. Not old age or retribution or anything of the kind. Just plain bad luck.

The point is that Ted was unlucky and the Methodists were wrong.

Ted was not "called." He died of a bacterial infection that swept through him in a hospital room in Bandon. God may have been watching a Yankees game in New York City at that very minute and was probably just as upset as everybody else when He received the news.

But I got the answer. That's the important part.

You have a certain amount of your own luck and you can share—in certain circumstances—in the luck of others. (Moran talking.) It's what you do with your luck that counts: making the best you can of it.

Because, you never know, you could get picked up by a sudden gust, a tornado, and whapped into the side of a chimney! BOING! Just like that. Unlikely? Sure, it's unlikely. Yes, it sounds like Dorothy and Toto.

But it's possible, isn't it? It's entirely possible.

Don't kid yourself.

Hating Paprika

Magyar Paprika was the name on the little Schilling can. It sat on a shelf in our kitchen with a few other spices and was always in the very front. "Magyar," my grandfather explained to me, meant "Hungarian." Three cans of it mysteriously disappeared before I was apprehended, charged, tried, and convicted of the theft of this spice.

Was I stealing Hungarian paprika because I liked it?

No, I was not.

Was I stealing Hungarian paprika because I hated it?

Yes, I was.

Our family was big on mashed potatoes. We had mashed potatoes almost every night at dinner. (Which is another subject, by the way. My father came from a farm where nobody said "dinner," they said "supper." He tried to persist in this practice but my mother always corrected him. "No, Al! It is dinner! Supper is something people have after going to the theater—a late supper." Although she meant movies.)

The potatoes would be mashed and plomped onto plates and then my mother would sprinkle a huge amount of paprika on the mashed potatoes for effect.

"To make them look nice," she would explain.

Well I hated the taste and I told her so.

"I don't like the taste of this," I would explain.

"Paprika has no taste," she would argue.

"Yes, it does have a taste and I don't like it."

"It is only decorative."

"I don't like paprika."

"You can't even taste it. Al, can you taste it?"

Al wouldn't even look in my direction. He knew what he was supposed to say and he said it.

"Naw. It doesn't have much taste."

But I knew that this was an admission on his part that it had some taste. I knew he lied. Paprika has plenty of taste. He knew that. He just didn't want to get caught crosswise with my mother and endure upwards of three or four days of the cold shoulder. (The Cold Shoulder was something people gave one another in the 1930s. It wasn't pleasant, believe me. It meant several days of silence and mean looks. My mother was very good at this technique.)

I would try to scrape my paprika off before the plate even got to the table. This, my mother would lecture, "ruined the effect." She would sprinkle more paprika on my mashed potatoes. How things looked was important to her. Vital, in fact.

I would scrape the top of my mashed potatoes in an effort to get rid of the paprika.

"Eat it," she would command. "You're being silly. It has no taste."

I knew it had plenty of taste.

Maybe her taster was screwed up.

"Eat it and stop being a fool."

(This was a contradiction that was quite apparent even to a child. If you deliberately ate something that you knew was terrible, then that was the exact moment you started being a fool. Who was she trying to kid?)

We went to dinner at a restaurant in Portland one time and they served mashed potatoes with just a smidge of paprika on them. I mentioned this to my mother in the hopes that in the future she would reduce the huge amounts she used. Some people don't use a whole can of paprika in their lifetimes. I'll bet she'd go through at least two cans a year!

"They should have used more," she said. "They didn't use enough. It would be a lot prettier with more."

I was at an age when I was getting cagey. Not just smart, but a little bit clever.

I went to the town's acknowledged Best Cook. I went to Margie's and walked back to the kitchen where Cliff was making something for the lunch menu. I tried to approach the subject obliquely.

"What about paprika?" I asked him.

"What about it?" he asked me back.

"What do you think about it?"

"It's a spice. You know that, don't you?"

"Yes, I know that."

"It is a necessary ingredient in Chicken Paprika, a famous Hungarian dish."

"Is that so?"

"Yes. That's so. Have you ever tasted Chicken Paprika?"

I winced.

"No."

He saw me wince.

"You don't like paprika?"

I didn't answer. I asked another question.

"Do you put lots and lots of paprika in Chicken Paprika?"

"No, not lots and lots. Paprika has a strong flavor."

There! I knew it! I knew it. I had her.

I told Cliff that my mother sprinkled paprika on mashed potatoes for decoration.

Cliff said that he sprinkled paprika on mashed potatoes for the same reason.

"How much?" I asked him.

"Here," he said. "I'll show you."

He had just thrown away a few slices of stale bread. He retrieved a slice and sprinkled a little bit of paprika on it.

"There."

It was about one-fifth the amount my mother would have used. Maybe one-sixth.

I asked Cliff if he would have a few words with my mother, being sure to include the fact that Hungarians made a chicken dish flavored with this spice. Cliff said that he would not. Cliff said that he would not get involved in family disputes.

He also said that when I got big, I could do what I wanted with respect to spices. I could use as much as I pleased or as little as I pleased. I could do without paprika altogether.

When I got big.

I was never going to get big. Nobody ever got big. Everybody was frozen in time in Port Orford. I was going to stay little. I was going to stay little and defenseless and I was going to eat paprika whether I liked it or not because my mother was all-powerful and because there was an endless supply of paprika in the world and because she thought it was pretty on mashed potatoes and I would just By God have to put up with it.

Maybe my sister would knuckle under and eat it and my father would knuckle under and eat it, but I was going to continue the fight.

I thought I gained some ground once when my father had made some scrambled eggs one Sunday and put too much pepper in them. My mother squawked at him:

"There's too much pepper in these eggs."

"The pepper's just perfect."

Al liked a lot of pepper. He put it on everything.

"No, it isn't," she said. "You used too much. Remember, pepper is always something you can add later, but you can't take it out. People should be able to adjust the amount of pepper in their food."

I seized this opportunity to point out that, according to this logic, people ought to be able to adjust the amount of paprika on their mashed potatoes.

She told me to shut up.

Town Bully— Metal Boat

In the street in front of Bennett's store was the town's biggest mud puddle. From there, heading south, you would come to a vacant lot, Charley Long's store, then the place where they used to have three bowling lanes for ten pins. Next was Lou Monescu's Garage, an alley, the barber shop, Pugh's drugstore, and—finally—the little state park commemorating the Rock.

After the first big rains in the fall, the mud puddle would fill up and offer a great place in which to sail boats. Although shallow, maybe only ten inches deep, the puddle was nearly twenty yards long and ten or fifteen yards wide. It was in the middle of a street that led to a part of the cliffs where nobody lived, so there was no great need to fill in the puddle and keep the road in repair.

One day after school I went to the puddle to sail a boat that I'd gotten on my birthday. I didn't much like the boat, but decided to sail it anyway. It was made of metal in the shape of a rowboat and was stupid looking. I rigged a piece of cardboard for a sail and put it in the puddle. I hoped it would sail across and then I'd walk around the puddle and retrieve it. I would have had boots on but my boots had become suddenly too little and also they were the wrong color. They were dark red when all boy's boots were—by ancient tradition—supposed to be black. They were embarrassing to me. My mother had found them on a trip to Marshfield. They had been on sale.

The boat didn't have a rudder on it. I didn't know the purpose of rudders at that time. So the boat went in tight circles and wasn't getting anywhere.

At about this time, Richard Pugh and Pat Masterson arrived on their bikes. Pugh was a known bully. Pat was normally my friend. But, I'd noticed, when somebody hung around with a bully they themselves suddenly took on bully-like characteristics. So when Richard started throwing stones at my metal boat, Pat joined right in.

"Hey," I yelled at them. "What are you trying to do?"

"Sink it!" Richard said jubilantly.

"Yeah," Pat chorused. "Sink it!"

"Well, cut it out," I said.

"Screw you," Richard said and threw a large stone that hit right next to the boat and swamped it. It sank and left the cardboard "sail" floating on the surface.

Richard and I looked at one another and had the same idea at the same moment.

It was as if two big neon signs were facing one another and suddenly lit up with the message:

GO HOME AND GET YOUR BOOTS!

That was the solution. Run home. Get boots. Wade into the puddle and rescue the boat. Like I said, I really didn't care that much about the stupid boat, but I didn't want Richard Pugh exercising any salvage rights to it.

I took off running down the boardwalk toward my place. Richard got on his bike and pedaled frantically in the other direction.

We found our boots and returned to the puddle at the same moment.

Richard had a pair of his father's waders draped over the handlebars. I had my stupid red rubber boots.

We each took off our shoes. Richard struggled to get into the way-too-big waders. I pushed my left foot into my way-too-little boot. Both of us panted and struggled.

I was barely into one boot when Richard rose and clomped into the water. I said the hell with it and followed with one boot and one stockinged foot. We both went to where we thought the boat had gone down and started fishing around for it.

The stones in the bottom of the puddle hurt my right foot and the water was intensely cold.

I felt for the boat and found it.

I grabbed it. Richard saw me and whacked my hand from underneath. The boat spiraled in the air, bailed itself out, and landed right-side up behind me, floating perfectly. I tried to grab it again but Richard knocked me down. The whole left side of me went into the water. Richard grabbed the boat and hurried out of the puddle. He and Pat got on their bicycles, laughing.

"That's mine, Richard!" I shouted. "Give it back!"

Futile.

Richard was having trouble getting on his bike because of the waders and also because of needing to hang onto his shoes and the boat.

I reached in the puddle for a bunch of mud to throw, but grabbed a tomato-sized stone. I threw it as hard as I could at Richard. I came close to hitting him. It bounced off one of the rubber grips on his handlebars and rebounded straight into the side of Pat's head. To my horror, Pat fell off his bike and collapsed flat onto the ground. Out cold. He looked dead.

When things don't go well for bullies they're apt to reveal themselves as cowards. Richard did. He dropped his shoes and my boat and peddled home as fast as he could. It was no particular surprise that by the time I got to Pat, Gene White appeared in his green pickup. We both kneeled down to see if Pat really was dead. He wasn't. He opened his eyes and asked what happened. Blood started leaking out of his head.

"You got hit by a rock," I said, hoping to create a belief in Gene White's mind that maybe Richard threw it, or that it had fallen from the sky like the Gold Meteor that Crazy Parker had spent most of his life looking for in the hills far behind the Sixes River Grange Hall.

Gene was more concerned for safety than justice in that moment so he paid no attention.

"Stay down for a minute," he instructed.

As luck would have it, Doc Pugh was driving from the other direction. He stopped and got out.

"Is he okay?" Gene asked.

Doc Pugh looked at Pat's eyes and said that Pat was okay. Probably wouldn't need stitches or anything but Dr. Baird should probably look at him.

They put him in Doc Pugh's car to drive him there.

Pat leaned out the window and, without any memory or malice concerning the event, said:

"Bring my bike over, would you, Johnny?"

I said sure.

I forced the other boot on my wet foot and rode Pat's bike to Dr. Baird's two-story house where he lived upstairs alone and had his doctor's office on the ground floor. T.J. told me that it was his belief that Dr. Baird "visited women" in Portland. This didn't surprise me all. I visited women in Portland myself: my grandmother, three aunts on my mother's side, and an aunt on my father's side (Aunt Hester who was married to Uncle Harvey).

Baird cleaned off Pat's head and put a small bandage on it. Everybody in town knew that Dr. Baird didn't work for nothing. Ever. He always got paid in money and, if not that, in chickens, smoked salmon, fresh crabs, vegetables, or something.

"What do I owe you?" I asked Dr. Baird.

"What do you mean?" he replied.

"What do I owe you for fixing up Pat? I'm the one who hit him with the rock."

I felt okay in saying this, knowing that Dr. Baird kept confidences and didn't hold too many grudges. He was all the time fixing up drunks who threatened to kill him because they claimed he was "hurting" them when all he was trying to help them, for crying out loud.

"Fifty cents," Baird said to me.

I didn't have fifty cents. Not with me. I doubt that I had fifty cents, altogether, back in the pig in my room.

I held up the boat. Despite its adventure it still looked just fine. The enamel hadn't been chipped.

"How about this?" I gave it to him to examine.

After studying it carefully, top and bottom, he handed it back.

"No," he said. "I don't think so. I can't use a metal rowboat."

I got creative.

"How about these boots?" I asked him. And then I added something that my father always said to somebody who was interested in a particular cut of meat in one of his butcher shop meat cases: "Especially nice."

He looked down at the stupid red boots.

I pulled them off for his further evaluation.

He inspected them thoroughly, saying "Hmmm" a couple of times in the process.

"Yes," he said after a while. "Yes, these will do. I'll take the boots."

Psychology. By taking the boots, he was forcing a confession about Pat and the rock. Nobody, but nobody, ever lost his boots.

I gave him the boots, put on my shoes, and left—me walking, Pat riding his bike.

I felt sorry for Pat, so I gave him the boat. Which, I'm sure you will understand, was no big gesture on my part since I've already reported how little I really cared about the boat.

He thanked me and went home.

As I passed the puddle, I saw that Richard's shoes were still there, so I took them home with me. To hold them hostage. His shoes were certainly more important than some dumb metal rowboat, and there were two of the shoes.

I walked up the kitchen steps to the kitchen door of the house. I hoped nobody would be there, but I was mistaken. My mother was sitting in the breakfast nook having an afternoon cup of coffee. She looked as if she was in one of those moods where she might whack me so I tried to get right to my room and change my clothes.

"What happened to you?"

"I fell in a mud puddle."

"You fell in a mud puddle?"

"Yes. A mud puddle. Fell."

"What were you doing?"

"Sailing a boat."

"What boat? The one you got for your birthday?"

"Yes," I said. "That boat."

"Where is it?"

"Where is it?" I stalled. "Where is what?"

"The boat," she said. "Where is the new boat?"

Oh, Lord, I thought to myself.

"You know Pat Masterson," I began.

"Yes, of course I know Pat Masterson," she replied.

"Well, a bunch of us were playing at the big mud puddle, you know the one on the other side of Bennett's big fence?"

"Yes, yes."

(I had to be careful. The Tiger Woman was lurking in there.)

"We were playing there and some kids were fooling around throwing rocks. Well, here's what happened. A rock hit Pat Masterson right on the head. I mean, really hard. Doc Pugh showed up in his Plymouth and Gene White showed up in his pickup, you know, the green one, and decided that Pat needed to get looked at by Dr. Baird. So I took his bike up there—Pat's bike that is—and waited while Dr. Baird put a bandage on him. On Pat's head. It didn't need stitches. But it needed a bandage. Only. So that's what happened to Pat in Dr. Baird's office. Pat's going to be all right. That's good, isn't it?"

I had discovered on my own that a highly detailed story will sometimes divert a line of questioning from a parent. They'll get interested in one of the details and pursue it, thereby forgetting what they were talking about in the first place. This technique failed on this particular occasion.

"So what happened to the boat?"

"Didn't I mention about the boat?"

"No."

"The same people throwing rocks hit my boat with a rock and it sank in the middle of the mud puddle."

I thought I was through the worst of it. No.

"So now," my mother continued, "you're back to get your boots so that you can wade into the mud puddle and find it? Is that right?"

"No," I said. "That is not exactly right. What happened was this: I was here already to get my boots. I got them, in fact. I put them on at the mud puddle and tried to find the boat. I couldn't find it."

I could see from the look in her eyes that I was going to lose on this story, and that my lying was far too evident and the story was far too flimsy.

I had been playing rummy with my grandfather a few days earlier and he had given an impromptu lecture on Hitler and other liars. The main theme of his talk during the rummy game was that the bigger the lie, the more apt it was to be believed. I wasn't sure about this idea, but knew that I had to do something, and fast, so I went for it.

"Here's what happened next. Richard Pugh came along and saw me fishing around for the boat. He asked me what I was looking for and I said my boat. He said that any time a real boat was lost then anybody who could find it could keep it. Something about salvage rights. So I told him that this was not a real boat. And he said: 'Well, what is it then, an unreal boat?' And I said it was a toy boat. And he said, 'I'm going home

- 164-

to get my boots and I'm going to look for it. And, if I find it, I'm going to keep it.'"

Since my mother wasn't poised to strike, I continued:

"That's what Richard Pugh said. So Richard went home to get some boots and, in the meantime, I found the boat. I saw Richard coming back to the mud puddle on his bicycle so I said to Pat Masterson, 'Here, you take the boat and hide it in your coat where Richard can't see it and we'll see how long he walks around in the mud puddle trying to find it.' Then I pretended to look, too. I fell in. The rock hit Pat. Doc Pugh and Gene White showed up. We went to the Doctor's. Pat got a bandage. No stitches. I went back to the mud puddle and changed into my dry shoes. Richard was still there looking for the boat, by the way. And then I picked up Richard's shoes by mistake instead of my boots and came back home. I'd better change, don't you think?"

I didn't wait for an answer. I went to my room. I waited for a number of horrible seconds to see if I'd get called to the stand for further cross-examination. Luck was with me. My mother had to get back to the store. The whole thing blew over. And soon it was time for new boots anyway. My father, not my mother, went with me to get the next ones and he agreed with me that boys' boots should be black. In every case.

So things worked out. Richard quickly suckered Pat out of the boat. And I blackmailed Richard and made him give me the boat in exchange for his missing shoes.

I offered to give the boat back to Pat. He declined, saying that Richard would only get it again, either by trickery or by beating him up.

I then secretly re-gave the boat—clumsily wrapped up but in the original box—to my friend Perk's sister, Marge. I gave it to her because, I think, I wanted to do something secret with her at some point in the future. Exactly what, I wasn't too clear about but I knew it would be deep in the woods. and I knew the gift of the boat would surely soften her up.

For what, I was unclear. Something good, though.

1940– A Turning Point

My grandfather saw an ad in a magazine and sent away for a zillion little flags that mounted on pins and could be stuck in maps. Grandpa Frank had two maps in his office/study: one of Europe and North Africa, and the other of the entire world.

Once the War really got going and Germany went on the march, he would change flags as each country fell and was occupied by the Germans after their blitzkreigs.

One by one the national flags changed to Nazi flags: France, Belgium, the Netherlands, Luxembourg, Denmark, Norway, and Romania. What I didn't learn in *My Weekly Reader* I would get from my grandfather and from listening to "The Richfield Reporter" news summary which was the last thing I was permitted to listen to on the radio at night.

Grandpa also stuck red Soviet flags into Estonia, Latvia, and Lithuania.

Bunches of men were evacuated from Dunkirk.

Winston Churchill says: "We shall not flag or fail. We shall fight in France, we shall fight on the seas and oceans, we shall fight with growing confidence and growing strength in the air, we shall defend our island, whatever the cost may be, we shall fight on the beaches, we shall fight on the landing grounds, we shall fight in the fields and in the streets, we shall fight in the hills; we shall never surrender."

(I mention this speech only so you will understand Frenchie's derivative speech—proclaimed while under the influence of Olympia beer and straight shots of whiskey—the night of the Port Orford "Invasion.")

Italy declared war on France and Britain. Germans marched into Paris.

The Blitz began in London; the night bombings. Newsreels showed kids having to leave home and go into the countryside.

The U.S. draft started. The first one in peacetime. All males from the ages of 18 through 35 had to register. They drafted my Uncle Harvey up in Portland, but not until later. He went into the Army. You'll never believe the job they gave him.

In exchange for 50 old destroyers given to Great Britain, the U.S. got some naval and air bases in British waters.

The man at a gas station in Silver Springs started handing out pictures of military airplanes at the rate of two new ones every month, but you had to bicycle all the way out there to get them. British planes. German planes. U.S. planes. P-4's, Spitfires, etc. I received permission to pin them on the walls of my bedroom. Also that year, the Mustang fighter was designed and produced in 127 days flat at North American Aviation. The MIG-1 fighter was produced and flown by the Soviets. The first Jeep was built.

Prices of cars? Chevrolet coupe = $659. Studebaker Champion = $660. Nash sedan = $795. Pontiac station wagon = $1,015. Packard (get this) = between $867 and $6,300! (T.J. Collins said: "Six Grand, My Ass!")

Penicillin and sulfadiazine came along. No surprise to you-know-who.

Movies: *The Grapes of Wrath, They Drive by Night, Pride and Prejudice, The Thief of Baghdad, My Little Chickadee, Boom Town, Fantasia,* and Pinnochio. My sister liked *Ninotchka,* and *Foreign Correspondent.*

Radio's "Truth or Consequences" started with Ralph Edwards as host. New shows of interest to my grandfather: the Metropolitan Opera of the Air, and the Bell Telephone Hour. Other new radio programs (and remember that all of the shows on that first list were still on the air as well): Fannie Brice "Baby Snooks" Program (Maxwell House), Milton Berle Program (Quaker Oats), Gene Autrey (Wrigley's Gum), The Aldrich Family (Jello), Blondie (Camel Cigarettes), I Love a Mystery (Fleishmann's Yeast), Sherlock Homes, with Basil Rathbone (Bromo Quinine), Spy Stories (Wonder Bread), plus two new Hollywood gossip reporters: Jimmy Fidler and Hedda Hopper.

Songs included: "It Never Entered My Mind," "When You Wish Upon a Star," "It's a Big, Wide, Wonderful World," "Fools Rush In," "How High the Moon," "Imagination," "The Nearness of You," "Taking a Chance on Love," "The Last Time I Saw Paris," "Beat Me, Daddy, Eight to the Bar," and "You Are my Sunshine."

Muzak started getting piped into factories, stores, offices, restaurants, you name it.

The first nylon stockings were sold and were an instant hit.

The Cincinnati Reds won their first World Series. T.J. Collins bet the other way and had to buy a round of drinks for everybody in his Bar & Grill.

Insect Lore and Old Wives' Bullshit

Even in a very small town you can pick up a lot of amazing information about what's lucky and unlucky just by paying attention. For example:

To kill a beetle brings rain, thunder, and lightning. (Old Lady Beck.)

When ants are unusually busy, foul weather will follow. (Mrs. Pugh.)

Butterflies flying at night presage death. (Mrs. Leneive and my grandma.)

Gnats flying low foretell rain. (Mr. Fletcher.)

Ladybugs are lucky. (Everybody. And they also agreed: "Don't kill daddy-longlegs! That would be very *un*lucky!")

If you find a small gold-colored spider on your clothes, "The Money Spider," you will receive unexpected money soon. (Mr. Spence.)

A flea-bite on the hand is a precursor of good news, or it foretells that you will be kissed. (I don't remember who told me this. It doesn't make any difference because it simply isn't true. There were lots of fleas in Port Orford and if I'd gotten kissed every time I got bitten by a flea my lips would have been smacked right off.)

The buzzing of a bee in a room indicates that a stranger will soon pay a visit. (My great-uncle Carol says he was told this one time by his mother-in-law, Rachel Devlan.)

I already notified you that dragonflies (flying needles) can sew your eyes shut and that everybody in those days knew that if an earwig got in your ear it would burrow into you brain and kill you dead. Didn't I?

If a moth flies around you, you will receive a letter. (Frenchie.)

My grandmother wore a gold scarab beetle as a talisman, explaining that the ancient Egyptians did the same.

This is a nice way to transition into further vital information about luck and superstition.

T.J. Collins didn't much believe in Old Wives' Tales, superstition, and local bits of folklore. Either intentionally or accidentally he referred to such things as "Old Wives' Bullshit." Here are a number of examples that people talked about as if they really believed them.

If you see a dog or a cat eating grass it is a sign of impending rain.

Insomnia can be cured by leaving the shoes with the toes pointing towards the bed.

Luck may be changed by having sex with a person of a different race, color, or social standing. (T.J. didn't really believe this, but thought it was a very good idea anyway.)

If you see three butterflies together it is a bad omen.

Expect trouble if ashes are thrown into a room from a burning log.

Superstitions are very bewildering if you're a little kid until you decide to say the hell with it and just play along with everybody. But you had to think twice when a really good pal pressed something in your hand before you went to the hospital up in Bandon to have all your throat and nose organs removed.

"What is this, Pat?"

"Rabbit's Foot! It's real lucky. You may need it."

Moran, Moran— The Mystery Man

Moran arrived one day on the northbound Greyhound. It looked as if he was one of the passengers going through and was merely using the rest room and having a cup of coffee at Doyle's while the bus was parked in front for the customary 15-minute Rest Stop. But there he was, still sitting calmly at a table, when the bus pulled away. He was wearing work clothes and looked like anybody else. He didn't stick out.

Two historical notes about Moran.

First, this was in the fall of 1940. One would remember this exactly for two reasons. Doyle's was still at the south end of town. It moved closer to my dad's store and the movie theater later that year.

Second, you knew it was 1940 because the town still had a switchboard operator for the telephone system and the switchboard was stuck in the far corner of Doyle's first location at the south end of town, almost straight across the street from Pugh's drug store and dental office.

The next big historical note about Moran is this: if everybody in town who later claimed to have been in Doyle's when Moran came to town had actually been in Doyle's that day, the store would have broken apart at the seams and the floor would have caved in!

Angie Coombs, a waitress, was actually there that day, helping Eve Doyle serve the bus crowd. She's the one who called Gene White and said something like this:

"Constable, you'd better come over here to Doyle's because somebody didn't get back on the bus when it left and he may be a tramp or something. Or a troublemaker."

Non-town people did not make our town a destination. It was only a place to go through. Oh, you could stop for a night. Tourists did, particularly in the summertime. They'd stop at places like Spence's Motor Court. They'd eat at Margie's, the Orford, or the seafood place and then they'd be on their way—to much bigger towns and more exciting places.

Eve remembered the conversation between Gene White and Moran as following these lines:

GENE: "You a fisherman?"

MORAN: "I know a fair amount about fishing, but I'm not what you'd call a fisherman."

GENE: "Would you be looking for a job at the lumber mill?"

MORAN: "No, I would not be looking for a job at the lumber mill."

GENE: "Then what kind of a job would you be looking for?"

MORAN: "I'm not looking for a job doing anything."

GENE: "Then this is probably not the town for you."

MORAN: "Why not?"

GENE: "The only people we need here are people with jobs. We can't have freeloaders here. We can't have people who sponge off others."

MORAN: "That would be a vagrant."

GENE: "Agreed. That would be a vagrant."

MORAN: "How do you define a vagrant in this town?"

FRANK TICHENOR: "One who is without any visible means of support."

My grandfather had stepped in for a cup of coffee and, as Justice of the Peace, had entered into the conversation because he felt it appropriate.

Gene White must have felt the same way because he simply left. He drove off in his green pickup, leaving the whole matter to my grandfather. Gene would let him order the vagrant out of town; Frank had more authority in such matters than Gene. When it came to actual power or pull in the town, Gene was probably only a Nine; while my grandfather was a King or an Ace. So that's why Gene probably said the hell with it and let Frank take over.

Moran and my grandfather introduced themselves to each other and had the following conversation.

MORAN: "You seem like an educated person. What would you make of these suitcases? What would you deduce from them?"

My grandfather loved puzzles, so this was an interesting challenge for him.

He looked at the two large suitcases sitting next to the table. He pulled them closer to him and inspected them carefully.

FRANK: "You are obviously not a vagrant. You are not even a wanderer. You are someone with at least some sense of purpose."

MORAN (politely): "Please explain."

A small crowd gathered around. Not the full two hundred or so who later claimed to have been there, but maybe six other people.

Smitty was one of them. And so was Doc Pugh.

Another man from Where the Woodbine Twineth (one of the Crazy People) was there to pick up some processed film that had come up from San Francisco on the bus. He was the Crazy People's photographer who would take pictures from the *National Geographic* on slide film and then project them on a screen and give talks, just like he'd been there, these talks having been memorized from the particular story. It was a big part of the Crazy People's entertainment back there in Woodbine over near Agate Beach. That and picnics and bridge tournaments among the eight of them. You remember Major Bentley, don't you?

Anyway, back to Frank, who was being the detective and presenting his conclusions about the two suitcases.

FRANK: "These bags are very expensive and must have come from a big city back East or in Europe. There are hotel stickers on the bags which indicate First Class passage on passenger ships and stays at major hotels in England, Germany, France, Egypt, and other places. One of the bags has a tag showing that it was flown on an airplane from Istanbul, Turkey, to Rome, Italy. Other, newer, tags show they were aboard trains from Boston to New York and then from New York to San Francisco. On a Pullman car. Then there are Greyhound tags from San Francisco with the destination of this town clearly marked. You did not have a ticket to someplace farther north, such as Marshfield or Portland and just decide to get off and see what was going on. You chose Port Orford as a destination."

MORAN: "Very good. Very good, indeed. Now I would like to show you something and ask you a question."

FRANK: "Of course."

MORAN (withdrawing a document of some kind): "Do you recognize this?"

FRANK (after inspecting it): "Yes. It is a letter of credit to the largest bank in the state. In a large amount, I notice."

MORAN: "This clearly indicates that I am not a vagrant, isn't that correct?"

FRANK: "Yes."

MORAN: "Now, take a look at these." (Producing other documents.)

FRANK: "It is a U.S. passport. Your picture. Driver's license. Other forms of identification. You are who it says you are."

MORAN: "A citizen of the United States."

FRANK: "Correct."

MORAN: "And free to do as I please. Within the limits of the law, of course."

FRANK: "Yes."

MORAN: "I can buy property in this town if I can afford to pay for it, can't I?"

FRANK: "Naturally."

MORAN: "Such as the property on the cliff just to the south of the harbor. The equivalent of a city block or so from the old Ice House. The Bennett property."

FRANK: "Yes."

MORAN: "And I am within my constitutional rights to not answer any questions if I don't feel like it. I don't have to even talk to anybody if I don't want to, isn't that correct?"

FRANK: "That is correct. That would be your right."

MORAN: "Then it is my intention to do just that. This is the longest conversation I intend to have for the rest of the year. I have come here not to be a hermit, but to do some thinking. I expect to buy my groceries here and have my hair cut here. I expect to build a small house on that point. I expect to drink coffee and look at the ocean. I expect to drink scotch whiskey and soda in moderation and to obey all applicable laws and ordinances. And I don't expect to talk to anybody if I don't feel like it. And I'll tell you this right here and now, Mr. Tichenor, I do not expect that I will feel like it!"

I think that within two weeks children my age had created a chant that went:

"Moran, Moran—the Mystery Man!"

He would not talk about himself. He refused to. Lots of people tried to get him to talk but they failed.

He designed a house. Not only that, he built a scale model of the house!

Everybody—but everybody—assured him that the cliff property was the worst place on the entire coast of Oregon to build a house.

Absolutely the worst.

Maybe on the entire West Coast of North America.

There was no protection there from the fierce winds, the storms. No protection at all. Yes, the view would be excellent, but the prospects of the house withstanding a major storm were nil, absolutely nonexistent. It would be ridiculous to build a house on that point.

Everybody in town agreed.

The Commandant of the new Coast Guard station said so and he had spend 20 years on or near the ocean.

My father, my grandfather, and Gene White concurred in this prediction.

They even trucked in old Louis Knapp from his farmhouse out toward Elk River and drove him out for a close-up look.

"No, not here," he declared. "It can't be done."

He begged Moran not to try it. That it could cost him his life. Moran smiled at that.

The fishermen all agreed that it was unwise and unworkable. The lumberjacks and truck drivers agreed. The foreman of the cannery chimed in. It was unanimous.

Moran must not build the house.

So Moran built the house.

His design was unorthodox. And the production process was unorthodox.

He employed only people who needed work, who could use the money, and then Moran taught them what they needed to know. One of the guys he hired was Parker, the man who people said had worn out 20 pairs of boots tromping around the hills looking for the Solid Gold Meteor. Parker had walked to town from his place in the swamp near Silver Springs, noticed Moran standing on the cliff with surveying instruments, and had entered into a rare long conversation with Moran. Two hours they were up there talking, with Moran scratching ideas in the dirt with a stick.

The foundation went in.

The frame went up.

The roof presented itself as a smooth angle toward the ocean, to redirect the wind, not stop it, and the chimney was hidden from the prevailing winter gusts. There was a little basement that had an even smaller basement under it that Moran called a Wine Cellar. It was a spacious house, especially for one person, but when it was finished, it looked small. It was as if the finished house just hunkered down one night and got little and inconspicuous. Some say the paint had something to do with it. Bob Forty, who had seen combat in the Great War, said it was camouflaged, the first time most of us had ever even heard the word.

When the house was finished, many boxes, trunks of clothes, cartons, and cases arrived from places like Boston and New York. Their contents were a mystery.

Moran was the greatest thing to hit town in years. He and his house caused more conversation than the time the Coast Guard guy got drunk and tried to kill his wife with a dull butcher knife, chasing her to hell and gone until a bunch of people, a kind of a posse you might say, finally caught up with him and put him in jail. He whacked at Gene White with the knife. If it had been properly sharpened, my father observed (himself a butcher, you'll remember, who had to keep his knives real sharp), the crazy man might have cut Gene's head off! As it was, it just caused a bruise. Can you believe it? He went to the State Prison. The Coastguardsman, not Gene.

People would drink beer in the taverns and speculate about Moran. Was he maybe a big criminal who quit the mob and came to the little town to hide out—one of those syndicate men? Was it possible that Moran was a famous engineer who built a big building that collapsed and killed a bunch of people and that's why he banished himself? Was he a mad scientist?

Was he actually a Wino who was drunk all the time up there where nobody could see him? (No, Doc Pugh said to this, because Moran's eyes were always clear and he didn't have the shakes.)

The talk went on and on.

As it did so, the house seemed to grow even smaller until, one day, we could hardly notice it at all. It blended in. It practically disappeared.

Then the test. A big storm blew up. It wrecked the *Phyllis*, a big freighter, by simply throwing it onto the rocks down near Humbug. (Don Doyle, acting the joker, tried to convice me that the ship was loaded with ketchup. We drove down the coast to the wreck site and looked at it through Don's binoculars. I had never looked through binoculars until that moment and I had the sensation of falling off the cliff we were on. I was deeply terrified and this made the adults laugh. Even Eve laughed. I went back to the car. The horror of optics.) The same storm picked up somebody's new chicken coop and knocked it to smithereens. It blew off a roof on a house on the far side of town, a house farthest from the ocean.

But Moran's place? You guessed it. Solid as a rock. Not one shingle blown off or one brick displaced from a chimney. Which reminds me that Bob Forty's cousin's place had its entire chimney blown off, not just a few bricks on the top. The whole shootin' match blew clear off the side of the house.

"Zoom" Zumquist, drunk as a skunk as usual, went up to the cliffs to have a look at the storm and the wind knocked him down on some rocks. Moran went to get him and patched up a cut on Zoom's arm, then even helped him back down to the Pastime. Zoom reported that he'd never been in such a quiet house as Moran's. The storm was just a whisper, he said, like the wind wasn't out there at all. And the view from the big windows was perfect, Zoom said, just perfect.

Zoom went to Dr. Baird a couple of days later to have the bandage changed and Dr. Baird said:

"Who in the hell did this?"

Zoom didn't know whether Dr. Baird said what he said because the dressing was good or because the dressing was bad. And he didn't get into it.

Moran truly was a mystery. Yes, indeed. For quite a number of months to come.

Some Fish For Planting

I was up on the bluff standing around, looking at the ocean rocks now and then with a cheap, collapsible "spy"glass similar to what I was told pirate captains used, when I noticed Old Lady Betts walking down the cliff road to the dock.

Once I had asked somebody—probably Moran—why it was that Old Lady Betts was called "Old Lady" when Mrs. Lenieve was twice as old, but wasn't called "Old Lady" but was called "Missus" like most of the other grown women in town. Moran said that "Old Lady Lenieve" would be too alliterative, whatever that meant, so I left it alone.

Old Lady Betts was moving swiftly, head up, eyes straight ahead, walking briskly along in a pair of canvas shoes. Her pale gray hair was tucked neatly under a garden hat and she was carrying a folded burlap bag, a gunny sack, under her arm.

As she cleared the far end of the cannery she shouted something at Crawford Smith. I couldn't hear it, so I started down the path to the dock to see what was going on.

Crawford was in a dinghy under the dock waiting for his fishing boat to be lowered by the winch. He shouted:

"You're going to hit the pilings!"

He had been screaming this for years. It was the expression of a fear, not a fact.

The boat was nowhere near the pilings. But Crawford's yelling had become a necessary part of the ritual of getting his boat in the water. It was now a part of the rite. Any omission might result in his boat breaking in half.

Old Lady Betts walked to the edge of the dock and looked down.

The winch engine chugged and the big pulleys squeaked as the cable ran through them.

"Crawford?" she said.

She couldn't see his dinghy under the dock, but she knew he was there.

"Crawford?"

He paid no attention. His fishing boat was now about ten feet from the water.

"Slow down," he shouted. "You're going to break the hull!"

The winch operator did not respond. He had never broken the hull of anything. He expertly lowered the boat into the water, with barely a ripple.

Crawford Smith rowed from under the dock, tied the dinghy to the bottom of the ladder and climbed aboard his fishing boat, *The Four Aces*.

He lit a pipe and looked at the ocean down toward Humbug. No cap on Humbug, no rain.

The day was uncharacteristically cloudless and calm.

"Crawford?" Betts said for the third time.

Crawford unhooked the winch cables from his boat.

"Yes, what is it?"

"I need some black snappers for my garden," she said. "Please give me some."

"I don't think I have any black snappers," he said.

"Come on," she coaxed. "You've got to have some to bait your crab pots."

"Well, that's right. . . . however . . ."

"Certainly you must have a few extras," she insisted.

Crawford relented.

"I'll take a look," he said, and disappeared into the cabin and went below deck.

He was gone for a while, by which time I was on the dock and standing next to the winch derrick.

The proceedings were enlivened when Henri, the French-Canadian fisherman from Nova Scotia drove down the cliff road in what he called his Dooz-Yem Automobile, an old Model "A" Ford, which was battered, and dirty, and clanked.

This car was the exact opposite of his Prum-Yay Automobile which was kept in a garage that was a good deal nicer than Winslows' place (which was, let's face it, a virtual shack).

The Prum-Yay was quite the most beautiful car in North America and was driven by Henri only on Sundays when it didn't rain, and then only briefly, not to mention slowly and carefully.

To the same degree that the Model "A" clanked and backfired, the Prum-Yay hummed or murmured. His driving performance in the Model "A" was likewise the opposite: fast, reckless, and loud with an abundance of honking: AH-EW-GAH! AH-EW-GAH! The horn blared and Henri braked to a stop about six inches from my foot.

"Chief!" he shouted. "How are you?"

One of the very few people to still call me Chief.

I said hello.

"And you, Madame Betts, *bonjour*."

"*Bonjour*, Henri," she replied and said a few other words in French. They jabbered for a minute or so.

Other than the French teacher at the high school, Old Lady Betts was the only person in town who could speak with Henri in his native language.

Henri and the winch operator then walked to the end of the dock where several heavy fishing lines stretched tautly into the water. Henri tugged at one of them. He then pulled up the line, hand over hand, until the catch appeared. The "catch" consisted of two cold bottles of Olympia beer.

Nobody I knew called one of these beers an "Olympia." I'd been in T.J.'s when people would order one by saying either, "Give me an O-lee" or "Let me have a Limpee." These nicknames may have been split about fifty-fifty. But not the elegance of "May I have an Olympia, please." It wasn't done.

"Ah," Henri said in anticipation of the beer, and produced a church key from the pocket of his shirt. ("Church key?" Who thought *that* one up?)

The two men returned to the area of the winch and looked down at Crawford's boat. Henri offered me a swig of beer. Like I was not merely some kid, but a Nova Scotian associate.

Crawford appeared in view with several dead, slippery black snappers.

At this time a late-model sedan appeared on the cliff road. It descended cautiously (at maybe one-third the speed of Henri in the Dooz-Yem) . . . perhaps fearfully.

Crawford yelled at Old Lady Betts:

"Have somebody come down the ladder and I'll hand them these fish."

Old Lady Betts looked at me.

The two men drinking their beers looked at me.

Crawford appeared to be looking at me.

I was to be the somebody: the Kid Who Happened to Be Standing Around.

"I'll give you a nickel," said Old Lady Betts.

Which was what I was hoping to hear.

The nice-looking car stopped at the edge of the dock and some people got out, tourists obviously.

Locals would have parked on the uphill side of the cannery where it was safer from seagulls.

The people who got out of the car included a tall man with a mustache, an overweight lady in slacks, an adolescent girl in shorts, and a kid, a boy a couple of years younger than me, who was wearing a cheap straw cowboy hat emblazoned with the message: *I'VE BEEN TO JOHNSON'S CEDAR BEACH AQUARIUM!*

I, too, had been to this so-called aquarium. My parents, my sister, the Doyles, and I had snookered ourselves into stopping. It consisted of only three or four cheesy little tanks, a bunch of ordinary fish including a ling cod, and a small red octopus that we must have watched for ten minutes until Don Doyle drew the conclusion that it was dead. No wonder it wouldn't move—even when we tapped the glass.

Don reported this to the man he thought was Johnson but who turned out to be the guy who bought the place from Johnson and who deeply regretted having done so. He walked over to the tank, took one look, and said:

"Yes. Shit! You're right."

Then he told us that it was a good thing the "aquarium" was also a gas station because that was the only part of the business that made any money. We asked what he was going to do with the octopus.

"Leave it," he said. "Who'll know the difference? Californians won't."

The tourists advanced, gawking around and wrinkling their noses at the fishy smells of the dock.

The young girl took a snapshot of the two beer drinkers and the winch. She was shooting into the sun, which will give you some idea of her relative swiftness.

"Well, " Crawford shouted from down below.

It was my cue.

Old Lady Betts handed me the gunny sack.

I tucked it in my belt and started down the ladder.

"What is he doing?" the kid asked his dad.

His dad said he didn't know.

The kid approached the top of the ladder and looked over.

"You're going to fall in the ocean!" his mother yelled at him.

"I'm not going to fall in the ocean," the kid said to her and then called down to me. "What are you doing?"

"Getting some fish," I said.

"He's going fishing!" the kid inaccurately reported in a loud voice back to his parents and his sister.

He again leaned forward and spoke to me.

"Where's your pole?" he asked.

"I don't need a pole."

"Then how're you going to catch them?"

"I don't have to catch them."

"What are they going to do, jump out of the water into your pockets?"

I sensed this kid was a comedian. A smart guy. Probably from California.

I got to the bottom of the ladder and pulled out the gunny sack so that Crawford could drop the first of the black snappers into it.

He held up the first fish.

"Wow," said the kid's dad on the dock, "look at that swell fish!"

Black snappers look okay, but they aren't worth anything.

"Yes," the overweight woman agreed.

"Gee," the sister said.

Black snappers are fairly good-sized fish. These were maybe 18 inches.

"They look like good eating," the tourist man said, self-assuredly.

I'd heard of stories where fishermen sold worthless black snappers to smart-assed tourists for the same price as red snappers which, indeed, are very good eating. This was not to be one of those days, however.

Crawford boomed at him in his can-be-heard-all-the-way-up-to-the-ice-house voice.

"These are not good to eat. They are not good for anything!"

"Except bait," Henri interjected.

"Yes, bait," Crawford agreed, " for crab pots."

"And planting," said Old Lady Betts.

The tourists looked at her like she was nuts.

"Planting?" asked the man, the woman, and the kid. All at once.

The winch operator said to Henri: "Listen, it's the Andrews Sisters."

The young girl said:

"You can't grow fish!" Pause. "So why plant them?"

Tourists.

Everybody looked exasperated. Except Old Lady Betts.

"It is a known fact that Indians planted fish with their corn."

"That sounds stupid," the kid said.

"Here, here," scolded the mom.

"As it turns out," Old Lady Betts continued with far more patience than anyone expected under the circumstances. "The fish decay and act as wonderful fertilizer for the corn."

"What is fertilizer?" the kid asked his father.

The man with the mustache replied:

"It's stuff that helps things grow."

"So fish helps the corn grow?" the kid asked in gawky mock amazement.

"So she reports," the father said.

I came back up the ladder with seven or eight black snappers in the gunny sack.

I figured it was time to get the kid.

There are several ways to handle black snappers. The best way is with gloves. Otherwise you can hook a finger in a gill. Or, as I had learned to do it, by grabbing the end of the tail fin and locking on tightly with your fingernails. Otherwise they're slippery and will get away from you.

"Here," I said to both the boy and the girl. "Take a look."

I quickly handed a fish to each of them.

If they'd been smart they'd have dropped them on the dock. Immediately.

But no.

The kid juggled his for several seconds, the dead fish flopping every which direction, until he finally dropped it. In the meantime, he had managed to rub the smelly fish on his face, his shirt, his arms, and his pants.

The girl instinctively clutched her fish to her bosom, as if it were a baby she knew she mustn't drop. Then she caught a whiff of the fish and dropped it as fast as she could.

I had succeeded in stinking up both of them. Wait until they got back into that hot car and started driving someplace. I glanced at the license plates on the car. Ha! *Yes!* California. "Alhambra Buick" it also said on a little tag.

I gingerly put the two black snappers back in the bag.

The kid and his sister looked at each other with horrified looks and wrinkled noses.

As I walked over to Betts with the sack, the California kid (for whom I must give full credit for initiative) tripped me. He stuck his foot out and tripped me good.

I fell down, the sack dropped, and all the fish skittered ahead of me on the dock.

The father rushed to help.

"Dad, Dad!" the children tried to warn him. "Don't touch them!"

Too late.

He had picked one up. He realized his mistake but there was nothing he could do.

I thought it was worth getting tripped for.

I had scored a three.

The winch guy and Henri raised their O-lee bottles in a toast. Or a salute.

Old Lady Betts, although not really that old, was indeed a lady.

"Over here," she said, directing the tourists. "Here's a water faucet. Fresh water piped down from the cannery. And a bucket. Wash yourselves off."

Henri mumbled something in French that sounded like "futility."

As I gathered up the fish, something very common happened. The fish attracted the gulls which always hovered around the dock. They formed a tight flock and the bravest one came right down and landed on a fish. I shooed him off.

"Oh, dear," Betts said, and adjusted her hat.

The beer drinkers slid under the tin roof with the winch controls.

Down below, Crawford stepped into the cabin of the boat and started the engine.

Old Lady Betts said to the tourists:

"Watch out! Those birds do horrible things!"

She was honestly trying to be helpful. If she'd had a few more moments to think about it she might have added: "So don't look up!"

But the natural instinct of the tourists was to look up at the gulls. So they did.

And one of the natural instincts of gulls is to do a horrible thing. One did.

It took a crap in mid-air. Not at all unusual. Commonplace, in fact.

Seagull droppings, in case you didn't know it, are white and runny.

The substance sailed down to the brim of the kid's straw hat where it splashed onto his face, his mother's shoulder, and the girl's shoes. The father was spared.

One shot. The gull, also, had scored a three.

Each of the targets started to whimper and cry. They dabbed at one another with handkerchiefs, smearing it around further. The man fumed and said something about the fact that there were no gulls in Alhambra. "Thank God," he added.

Henri and the winch man walked to the end of the dock where they could laugh unnoticed.

Crawford chortled out loud and steered the boat out of the harbor.

I put the fish in the sack and Betts offered me another nickel to lug the fish up the hill and to her garden. I accepted enthusiastically since, at the time, I think my allowance was still only a quarter a week. Despite runaway inflation, my father thought 25¢ was sufficient. This was a good opportunity.

We started up the hill.

In a couple of minutes the tourists' car drew abreast of us and stopped.

The man asked:

"Is there a tourist court in town?"

"Yes," she said. "Spence's. Go to the top of the hill and then left onto the highway. It's north about a mile on the left." – 183–

"Much obliged," the man said and drove off.

I noticed more seagull dump on the back window of the car, but it was too late to say anything about it. It's best to get that stuff washed off before it dries hard. That's the advice.

We walked to her garden. The holes had been dug and the mounds formed. The corn seeds were in a new packet from Charley Long's store. There was a piece of pine board and a butcher knife on the ground.

"Since you're here," Old Lady Betts said, "And your hands are already stinky, please cut those snappers in half and drop them in the holes. Can you do that?"

Can the town butcher's son cut a fish in half? Well, I should say so.

It was done in a flash.

She covered the holes with her spade, tapped them down, and watered them with her green watering can with the circular spout which had a bunch of perforations in it.

She stood looking at the ground and then back in the direction of the sea.

"Do you suppose, Johnny," she asked, "that the Indians said some kind of a prayer for the success of their crops? Performed some kind of a ceremony?"

I said that yes, I supposed they had.

"I wonder what they might have said."

"I don't know," I told her.

"I think I'll give it a try," she said.

I waited as she collected her thoughts.

"May this corn be good."

That was it.

"Can you think of anything else?" she asked.

I tacked on a final thought:

"No worms," I suggested.

"Oh, yes," she agreed. "That's a good one."

She resumed her Indian Ceremony Voice and said:

"May this corn be safe from worms!"

She spread her arms and looked skyward.

"So be it," she concluded and gave me another nickel from her pocket.

I went back home, washed my hands, got on my bicycle, and pedaled over to the McCormicks' house under the big cedar trees (where you must be careful not to eat the cedar berries when you climb up there because they're poison as hell and you'll fall onto the ground dead!).

I passed Spence's Tourist Court on my way and saw the Alhambra people unloading their car so they could get cleaned up.

I made a mental note to tell my grandpa Frank about my (and the gull's) success against these enemy Californians. It was likely to be worth a 7-Up float if I strung the story out for a good five minutes.

Grandpa was one for yarns—not news flashes.

Only ten o'clock in the morning and the day was already a huge success—what with AH-EW-GAHs, a taste of Henri's beer, an Air Raid, and a fish ceremony. I could smell the sun on my clothes.

Fossil Words

Moran's furniture and stuff arrived in two different trucks and I happened to be hanging around the day that the second truck drove down from the north, I suppose from Portland.

"Oh, goodie!" Moran exclaimed when he saw some cardboard cartons marked ALBUMS. He was already pretty well known around town for acting like a kid, which, he said, was very important: "The last thing you want to do is grow up," he cautioned me. "There's no percentage in it. It's okay to get old; just don't get atrophied."

"What's atrophied?"

"Dried up. Notice Old Lady Betts. She is very old but she doesn't act that way. She's got plenty on her mind. She's busy. She does things. She will never atrophy."

"Oh."

The moving men rolled various boxes into Moran's place on dollies.

"I wonder if the phonograph still works?" he asked himself. "I hope so."

I was looking at the cartons marked ALBUMS.

"Jeez, Moran, you must have a lot of pictures."

"Pictures? What pictures?"

He started looking around the room for pictures. There weren't any.

"Here," I said, pointing at the cartons.

"Those are records."

"What do you mean, records?" I thought he meant business records like the receipts my father kept in accordion-pleated files.

"I'll show you."

He opened a carton and pulled out something that looked like a red leather book. It looked like a photo album to me.

He opened it up and each page was actually a sleeve holding a phonograph record.

I knew about records and phonographs because my sister had a little phonograph and bought records of her favorite songs. One of the reasons that she was given the room up under the eaves of the Hill House was not because she was being banished, but because the room was pretty well soundproofed and she could listen to the same record 700 times without driving everybody else crazy. She would, too. Frank Sinatra.

"He sends me," she'd say.

"Yeah, where?" I'd reply, being the joker.

Alida didn't keep her records in books. She kept them organized in stacks.

So I pointed at the book and asked Moran:

"Isn't it kind of hard to find things this way?"

"What do you mean?"

"How do you find the record you want?"

"Oh," he says. "all the records in this album are from the same piece of music."

I must have given him that puzzled-moron look that kids are so good at.

"You know about records, don't you?" he asked me.

"Sure."

"What do you know, exactly?"

"My sister has a phonograph."

"Yeah, go ahead."

"She puts on a record and listens to it. Then she may play the song on the other side, but usually she doesn't. Then she puts on another record."

"A different song."

"Yes."

"Well imagine this. See this particular album. It has six records in it, 12 sides, and it's all the same song. It's just that the song is longer than any of your sister's."

Visions of red-and-white striped paint flooded back. And other wild goose chases I'd been sent on by adults. This didn't seem like Moran and he quickly sensed my incredulity.

"Do you know what classical music is?"

I said I didn't.

"When I unpack the phonograph I'll play something for you, okay? Then you'll see what I'm talking about."

It was a few days later before this happened.

I got busy digging a cliff cave fort with some of my soldier buddies so that we could properly defend against the Nazis whom Perk McCormick thought might fly over at just about any moment in their Junkers tri-motor transports.

"They can fly all the way from Germany to Holland, can't they?" he would speculate.

In Perk's mind, any two geographical places on earth were about equidistant: Argentina and Canada; England and Mexico; you name it. I don't think Perk had even been to Portland, let alone a place as remote as Battleground Lake or Jantzen Beach.

I was up very early one morning, almost earlier than anybody else in the whole town, ate some cereal and a banana, and wandered over to Moran's. Oh, sure, I know what some of you are thinking! This guy's a real comedian if he thinks I'm going to believe that he can remember exactly what he had for breakfast on the particular day, decades ago, just before he wandered over to Moran's place! Well, let me just explain something to you! If, when you were a kid, you ate dry cereal and a banana every single day of your life except on certain Sundays when your mother made waffles, then perhaps you, too, would be sufficiently bright to remember exactly what you had for breakfast. Okay?

Now, if I told you with any show of confidence that it was a Friday morning, that might be harder for you to take. But I think it probably was a Friday and I'll tell you why. Because my grandfather listened to the Opera on Saturday and I think it was the next day that I went over to his place to tell him the same thing I'm about to tell you now. – 187–

I knew it was okay to knock on Moran's door because I could hear noise inside. Music.

Moran came to the door and said: "Ah, good!"

He stopped the record player, a great big radio-phonograph combination about the size of a chest of drawers.

A stack of records was poised on a spindle above the turntable. This was news to me. Moran explained that they dropped down automatically and then you turned the entire set of records over to keep playing the same piece. 12 records of the same piece. Who knew?

"I was about to play some music called 'tone poems' and you can listen if you want to."

"Do I have to sit down?" I asked him.

"Why do you ask that question?"

"Because Frank always wants me to listen to Opera and says you have to sit down to listen. It's just the way it's done."

"You can stand up or walk around if you feel like it. If you get bored you can leave. If you decide to stay, maybe we can talk about what you saw."

"Saw?"

"Yes, this kind of music is about more than just listening. It's about seeing—visualizing—and feeling."

I was beginning to think that some of the people in town who thought Moran was crazy maybe had a point.

He started the music.

There was something to watch. I mean, actually, out of the front windows. The wind had come up and there were a lot of small low-flying clouds drifting past.

The pattern of light and shadow was similar to what you see driving a car under a row of trees and the trees act like a shutter to interrupt the beam of sunlight. Brightness. Shadow. Brightness. Shadow. Only this was slower motion than driving.

The sound became the background music for the day. The piece was short, not the whole 12 records, and Moran stopped the machine and went into the kitchen for a cup of coffee. He came back and asked me what I'd been thinking about when I listened to the music.

"I was watching the clouds."

"Have you ever watched clouds that long before; just sitting still and watching clouds?"

"I don't know." (True answer: No, of course not; don't be ridiculous.)

"What did you think of the music?"

I confessed that I really hadn't been paying much attention and this made him smile.

"Here," he said, and he wrote four words on a piece of paper and gave it to me.

"What's this mean?"

They were words I couldn't pronounce.

"Ask the Frenchman."

What was this, I wondered. A puzzle? A riddle? The run-around? Moran did the correct Music-Appreciation thing by saying:

"I'll see you later."

I was dismissed. But it was with a peculiar deference which I later concluded was his recognition of me as the sort of mystical kid Dalai Lama who appeared to him in a the Chinatown alley, only the alley was his own living room. A person through whose eyes he could glimpse the future or comprehend the past. A kid from whom one might get a message or a signal.

The only other people who were up and active at that time of day were the fishermen down on the dock. I hot-footed it down there.

"Hey, Frenchie!"

He was pouring chicory-smelling coffee out of a thermos into the screw-on lid which was a cup with its own handle.

"Yes, Joan-ee."

He always made it sound like a girl's name but I had gotten used to it because he'd let me ride in the rumble seat of the Prum-Yay.

"What's this?"

I handed him the paper.

"It says: 'Clouds' by Claude Debussy. Debussy wrote the music."

He handed it back and asked:

"How do you know this? You *heard* it?"

"Sort of. Yes."

"*Bien.*"

I went back to the fort.

Message. Two, actually. Plural. Messages. First is the business about "fossil" words, ones we use all the time without knowing anything about their origins.

You use the word "album" all the time, and probably didn't know that it used to have a literal meaning—a book with a lot of individual records in it.

And the second message is murky but has something to do with the possibility that you can become an important part of somebody else's decoder.

Debacle #1— The Beachball

My father was not a big man but he was strong. He had grown up on a farm and done hard work. As a butcher he routinely manhandled sides of beef on and off sharp hooks in the walk-in refrigerator. He had muscular arms and shoulders, but skinny legs. There were some things that he did that were predictable. Absolutely. The last thing at night he would go into the kitchen and put a spoonful of baking soda in a glass of water, stir it around, and drink it in one gulp.

"Heartburn," he would always comment aloud, whether there was anybody to listen or not. He would then emit a deep-toned belch and retire.

My sister and I had always used to wonder if the baking soda continued to produce gas all night. This was because every morning it was my father's task to brave the cold of the house to start a fire in the kitchen stove. This fire also heated a coil that made hot water for us to use. My father wore pajama tops, shorts, and slippers on his forays to the kitchen from my parents' bedroom. The slippers would flop. And he would fart.

This farting was quite amazing because it was not a singular explosion—a boom or a roar—at some point along his route through the living room into the kitchen. It was a series of very small diischarges at every step: *blap, blap, blap, blap*—all the way along his path. When he reached the linoleum of the kitchen, his slippers would also flop lightly on the floor, creating another cadence as a counterpoint to the flatulence: *Flop-Blap, Flop-Blap, Flop-Blap,* all the way to the wood box.

A final, louder, fart would punctuate the end of his gas-passing performance when he leaned over to get kindling for the fire. At this point he would say:

"Ahhhhh."

It was over.

"Here comes the *Hindenberg*," my sister whispered one time.

The other things he could be counted on to do were the following:

1. Eat Nabisco Shredded Wheat every morning of his life.

2. Pour boiling water over his Shredded Wheat to soften it up before pouring milk and sugar on it and eating it.

3. Smoke a cigarette while he drank a second cup of coffee after breakfast.

4. Have a coughing fit after the first puff of this cigarette.

5. Make the following comment: "I've got to give up this habit of smoking. I smoke like a chimbley. Look at my fingers." We would respectfully view the yellowish-orange tobacco stained fingers on his right hand.

6. Sit down to read the newspaper after dinner, read the first two pages, then cover his head with the paper and go to sleep, snoring loudly, until he was wakened for one of his favorite radio programs. Inevitable comment: "Just resting my eyes."

7. Insist on having an evening "breakfast" on Thursday nights, consisting of fried potatoes, scrambled eggs, ham (or bacon), and waffles. (The word "breakfast," like "chimney," was not a word that my father could pronounce. When he said it, it always came out "Breffcuss."

"Get up," he would cry out when the fire in the kitchen stove was burning nicely and the farts had dissipated. "Time for Breffcuss!")

8. Always say the same thing after the Thursday evening meal: "Boy, this is great! I love waffles! This is the Cat's Pajamas."

My father believed in a limited number of values, not one of which I was any good at. They were, rank-ordered, Honesty, Hard Work, and Strength. It was hard for him to reconcile the fact that I was sneaky, that I would always expend more time and energy to avoid work than it would have taken me to accomplish a particular task in the first place, and that I was spindly. He would buy small pieces of exercise equipment and leave them lying around near my room in the hope that I would fanatically exercise and bulk into a small Marine. There were long springs with handles that hooked to doorknobs to build shoulders. There were hand-gripper devices.

There was a particular horror I faced every couple of months. It required all the strength I possessed, and somewhat more patience than I had. It was my most dreaded chore.

A small truck would back into our driveway and dump a huge load of wood chunks on the concrete in front of the combination garage-woodshed. It would then drive away and I would look at this mountain of loose wood and wonder how in the world I would ever get it transported and carefully stacked in the woodshed. It seemed impossible.

There was only one Rule about this activity.

I could not do anything I wanted to do until the task was completed, all the wood was stacked in the woodshed, and the chips and sawdust had been swept off the driveway. The first couple of times I was forced to do this job by myself, the task took three days. Most of that time was spent sitting on the ground trying to conceive of a machine that would do the work for me.

A more imaginative and sympathetic father would have looked out the kitchen window and prophesied:

"That kid's going to be an engineer. Look at him struggling for a labor-saving solution!"

Not my father, though. He would fly out the door to deliver a lengthy sermon about sloth and shiftlessness.

I tried endless techniques to make the job "easier." This usually involved moving wood in stages, getting small piles closer and closer to their destination in the shed. It took months for me to realize (on my own) that this consumed much more energy than a direct route in which the given chunks of wood were picked up and put down only once. I also learned that my frequent "rest breaks" were more enervating than refreshing and—in the end—actually unnecessary.

I learned my own form of Zen meditation.

Instead of feeling a sense of hopelessness and loathing when I faced a new mountain of wood, I blocked all thinking about it. I focused only on what I was going to do when I finished. Like playing with friends, flying a kite, riding my bicycle, whatever.

I learned one trick after another.

The most important was to start with the chunks of wood farthest from the woodshed. Save the closest for last, like the cherry on a chocolate sundae.

Also, I learned how to walk from the pile to the door of the woodshed with my eyes closed. I thought about this as a form of resting or cheating—that as long as I had my eyes closed I wasn't really doing anything. At the beginning of the task it might take as many as 12 or 13 steps to get from the far side of the pile to the door of the woodshed, at which time I would open my eyes and go to the far end of the woodshed with my load.

Because I convinced myself that I was resting when I had my eyes closed, it was unnecessary for me to take any rest breaks at all. I would hammer away at the job until it was finished.

My father misinterpreted this form of cheating as Enterprise and was very proud of me. Although he was saddened that all this hard work wasn't producing a flock of muscles as he would have wished.

I also did other work in the store, as I've explained. It consisted mainly of restocking canned goods on the shelves and putting potatoes in paper bags.

One time I complained to my grandfather about all the work I was doing and the piddling amount of money I was being paid as an allowance. Two bits a week. My grandfather decided to bring a Mock Lawsuit against my father for unfair labor practices, especially against underage workers. Everybody thought this was funny. Even my father tried to see the humor in it, but didn't really. Damages were extracted to the tune of four dollars which I received and took over to my grandfather's house.

His housekeeper, Mrs. Lacey (Winnie's mom, you'll recall), asked me what I was going to do with it.

"Buy an airplane," I said.

There was a toy airplane at Doyle's that I wanted very much. It had a wind-up propeller and the instructions on the side of the box said the plane would fly for up to fifty yards. That was for me. Mrs. Lacey said she'd walk over to Doyle's with me.

The airplane was not in stock.

I wanted to leave.

"No," Mrs. Lacey said, "let's look around."

A beach ball took her fancy.

"Look at this beach ball," she said. "Look at all the colors in the segments. Look at this, . . . it's in two parts, a rubber cover outside and another rubber part inside like an inner tube. This must be very sturdy."

Nobody played with beach balls in Port Orford. A gust of wind could pick one up and cause it to dance into the ocean where (because of the coldness of the water and the dreaded Undertow) we couldn't go after it.

Yet Mrs. Lacey persevered in her attempts to get me to buy the beach ball.

I protested.

"But you'd have so much fun with it," she wheedled, "and all your friends would enjoy it as well!"

We stood in front of the beach ball for five minutes at least and she finally wore me down. I relented. I caved in. I didn't want the beach ball, but I spent most of the four dollars on it.

Mrs. Lacey beamed. She raved about it back at grandfather's house. He looked at me. I looked back at him. Both of us looked a little unhappy. Something had backfired. Something wasn't right.

I carried the beach ball back to the store. That was my first mistake. I should have either (A) left it at my grandfather's or (B) let the air out of it and sneaked in the back door and hid it in my room. But, no. I carried it through the store.

My father lost his temper completely.

I tried to explain.

He dragged me into the back room, behind the walk-in refrigerator. He ripped the beach ball, exploding it. He beat me with the shreds of it. He beat me from the frustration of having been humiliated by a Tichenor. He beat me for being stupid. He beat me harder when I said that I hadn't wanted the beach ball. He beat me the hardest when I wouldn't cry. I was too humiliated to cry. I had been duped and betrayed by Mrs. Lacey who, probably, had been denied a beach ball as a little girl. The whole thing was wrong: the joke lawsuit, the money, the ball, and the beating. My father's fury was wrong. But he couldn't stop. It was only my mother throwing herself between us that finally stopped him.

"What are you doing?" she demanded. "He's only a little kid."

(Imagine that, from Curry County's Hardest Slapper of Boys.)

My father and I knew better. We were oddly united at that moment.

"He is a goddamn fool," my father told her.

"Go to your room," my mother commanded.

"Go to hell," my father added, still rose-red and furious.

I went to neither. I picked up the shredded remains of the beach ball and took them to the kitchen of my grandfather's house. Mrs. Lacey was peeling carrots and humming. I threw the rubber tatters on the floor at her feet.

I brushed past my grandfather on the way out and I didn't say anything and he didn't ask me to say anything.

The subject was finished. It was never mentioned again by me, Mrs. Lacey, my grandfather, or my father. It was as if it never happened. It was an event so huge and ugly that it could never have occurred.

It was a debacle. It was Debacle Number One.

For a kid, there is something completely understandable about such a circumstance, and the key to it is its avoidability. I was to blame for what happened. There was no getting around it. It was altogether avoidable. And, once the faulty decision had been made, the outcome was predictable. I was not angry at my father and his opinion that I was a hell-bound fool. I was not angry at Mrs. Lacey and her stupidity, since I had demonstrated my own greater stupidity by paying attention to her at all. I wasn't angry at my grandfather and his role as the cause of the whole incident. The funny lawsuit was unnecessary and pointless, as was everything that followed.

The Jesus Place

If you were like me when you were growing up you had strict limits on how far away from home you could go. When I first moved to Port Orford I was not permitted to cross the street or hide behind the house. I had to be visible. If I was visible I was safe. That was the reasoning.

"We have to be able to see you!" was the injunction. "Then you'll be okay."

I thought for awhile that parents were able to project rays from their eyes and that the rays insured safety. I paid attention.

At around five I was free to journey around town, but needed to have adult supervision to go to the beach or near the ocean. At six or so I was permitted to go onto the Battle Rock beach, but only as far as the blue clay deposits. By the time I was eight or nine, I could go as far south as Hubbard Creek and anywhere I wanted on Agate Beach.

So it must have been after I was eight that somebody introduced me to the Jesus Place. Eight or nine.

Some older kids took some of us younger ones on a hike down to Hubbard Creek. A boy named Frederick then announced:

"As you know, Jesus had the power to walk on water."

Everybody seemed to acknowledge this fact, although it was unknown to me at the time. My folks weren't church-going people but I had heard about Jesus. I had not been informed, however, of his reputation for walking on water. Helping blind to see? Yes. Curing cripples? Yes. Something about loaves and fishes? Sort of. Water-walking? No.

"I, myself," Frederick continued, "have the power to walk on water."

Whereupon he walked on the water. He walked about 25 yards out to a rock, held both arms straight out from his body in the well-known Look-at-Me gesture, and then walked back to the beach.

I thought it was a reasonably clever thing to have done, but Richard Pugh raved about it.

"How did you *do* that?" Richard wanted to know.

"I have mystical powers," Frederick said.

"I want to try it," Richard said.

Frederick shook his head.

"Don't do it, Richard. You'll be killed. You'll drown."

That was enough for me. I had no need to drown. Drowning killed you dead. Then the undertow got you and your body washed up in Honolulu.

"How did you do it?" Richard wanted to know.

"It's a secret," Frederick said. "Although Curley can do it, too. Want to see him?"

Of course we did.

Curley walked out to the rock, bowed theatrically, and walked back to the beach.

Richard was going nuts.

I wasn't.

Richard cared. I didn't.

It was just one more circumstance in my life that was unexplainable. But I was getting used to ambiguity and mystery. I was ready to hike back to town.

"Wait a minute!" Richard said. "I've got to try it!"

"Okay," said Frederick, "But don't say we didn't warn you."

He then suggested that Richard try to walk to a rock that was a good deal closer and from a starting place that was a little further down the beach.

"I can do it!" he boasted, demonstrating some of the bravado shown by his father, Dr. Pugh, who would swim around Battle Rock every 4th of July just to show everybody what a gray-haired man could do if he put his mind to it.

Richard bravely walked into the surf and was almost instantly in water up to his belly button. A wave then broke over him and soaked him completely.

Richard ran back to the beach, completely confused. And also wet and cold.

The older kids laughed.

"I warned you," Frederick said. "I told you it was impossible."

Somebody started a fire so that Richard could dry off.

After a few minutes, the joke became apparent. The tide went out and revealed a gravel bar that connected the beach to the rock. I had never noticed it before. Frederick and Curley had timed their walks at just the right time. The gravel bar was invisible to us and they appeared to walk on the water.

Richard took the news in reasonably good humor. He later told some other kids that he had nearly drowned in at least 20 feet of water. Bunk.

Some time later, I went down to Hubbard Creek with my grandfather to do some fishing. I decided I would show him my "powers" with respect to walking on water.

"Don't make me pretend to be astonished," he said. "I know all about the Jesus Place. I did it myself when I was a kid. My father learned about it from an Indian who, of course, had never heard of Jesus. I think the Indians called it a Magic Walk or something. Did I tell you that my father, Jacob, was one of the first two white children on this part of the Oregon coast?"

That was a zinger for me at the time. White. It was a word you read about but never heard anybody talk about, at least not in my family.

"What do you mean?" I asked my grandfather. "White like Whitey?" Whitey being the name of a near albino fisherman who had lived in Port Orford at the time.

"No, white as opposed to Indian," he said.

This was a new one on me. He saw my confusion.

"That's how they made the distinction. The white men and the Indians. It was the Indians against the white men."

I should explain that there were no black people in Port Orford. Since there were no black people, there was no reason to use words that might be regarded as the opposite to white.

A black tourist from California had come into my father's store one time and bought some picnic supplies. His wife and children stayed in the car. I talked to them through the open car windows and they seemed quite friendly and cheerful, albeit a little hesitant at first.

After they drove away, my father observed that the customer had been a Negro.

"A what?" I asked him.

"A black man."

"He was not black," I said.

"Yes, he was."

"No, he wasn't."

I went on to explain that neither the man nor the rest of his family were black. They looked tanned.

"That's not the point," my father argued. "They are black people. They are Negroes."

"Well, then," I asked, "is Mr. Henner a Negro?"

"No."

"Why isn't he? He's a darker color than the people who were just here."

"Italians are not Negroes," he said. "Henner's mother was Italian or something."

My father pronounced this nationality as Eye-Talian.

He then adopted a somewhat menacing tone when he said:

"You understand?"

This was always a firm clue to say that I understood whether I did or didn't. It was a conversation closer.

I asked T.J. Collins about it the next day.

"What's the deal on Negroes?"

"What about them?"

"I don't get the black part. I saw a guy yesterday who was just about the same color as you are and my dad said he was a Negro—a black man."

T.J. stared at me for a minute.

"Negroes," he explained, "come in a lot of different shades, all the way from very, very black—practically coal black—to practically white."

"What do you mean, practically white?"

"Well, okay then, . . . white. Plain white."

"So there are white black people?"

"Yes."

"Are there black white people?"

"Technically, yes. In India or somewhere."

Practically and technically are two outstanding weasel words used by adults who are unsure of their ground.

"You shouldn't worry about it," was T.J.'s advice.

I must have looked worried about it so he sought to make things clearer.

"Have you heard the expression 'redskins' as applied to Indians?" he asked.

"Yes."

"Indians are not red, you know that, don't you?"

"Yes."

"They are brown."

"Right."

"And Oriental people are not yellow. You know what I mean, like Chinese and Japanese people."

He was correct. I had seen Japanese merchant sailors up close and they were not yellow. Not at all. They looked tanned.

"They are brown," T.J. said. "Everybody in the world has skin and skin comes in a lot of different colors. Except for Whitey, of course, because he has very little pigment and that's why his eyes are almost pink."

This was getting very boring and complicated and I was ready to call it a day. T.J. could see this.

"The hell with it," he said. "It's not important. Here, have a shot of root beer."

–199–

I asked for 7-Up instead because I had recently blown root beer out my nose and hadn't enjoyed it much.

Back at the beach with my grandfather I did not pursue the White People issue. We instead went fishing and, as usual, didn't catch anything.

On a walk with Moran some time later I told him about the Jesus Place and he explained that it was a tombolo.

Don't go running to your dictionary if you don't know this word.

I'll explain it later.

Skychief

Skychief, as you know, is a kind of gasoline. Or it used to be. Texaco. Because of my fixation on the subject, however, I thought it might have been associated with some kind of a local Indian. But the gas station guy there said no, it wasn't. I think it was the very same day that Eddie Baker came over to my house to play and spend the night. This was during a lull in our dislike for one another. He brought along two paper bags. One of the bags had his pajamas and his toothbrush in it. And the other one contained a human skull.

"A skull!" I exclaimed when Eddie rolled it out on my Goofy-the-Dog rug in my bedroom. The skull looked up at me and I said: "Holy *SHIT!*" this being the very latest expletive I'd learned from T.J. in his bar. It seemed to fit the situation exactly.

I caught my breath.

"Eddie," I asked, "where did you get this skull?"

"From an old shed."

"What old shed?"

"An old shed I found in the bushes behind one of the haunted houses between town and Woodbine."

I thought about this for a second.

It was straight out of I Love a Mystery on the radio.

"What are you going to do?" I asked him.

"I don't know. I thought maybe you'd know what to do. You think we ought to throw it away?"

"No," I said. "That doesn't sound right."

"Well," he asked, "what are we going to do with it?"

"First," I suggested, "you ought to put it back in the bag."

"I'm not going to put it back in the bag," he said. "You put it back in the bag!"

"But you got it in there in the first place," I said.

"Yeah, but I didn't touch it," Eddie said.

"Well, then, how did you get it in the bag?"

"With a stick," he explained. "I picked it up with a stick."

"In the eye?" I asked, getting the willies—the real heebie jeebies.

"Yes," he confirmed. "In the eye."

I shuddered.

"Let's go into the kitchen," I said. "Maybe we can find something in there."

I looked around the kitchen. I thought of a dinner fork, but I knew that wasn't a good idea. I opened the dish-towel drawer. There were a couple of ratty looking dish towels tucked in the corner, set aside as dust cloths. I selected one of them, wrapped it around the skull and squeamishly put the skull back in the bag.

"There," I said. "That's finished."

"What do we do now? Who do we give it to?"

An immediate choice came to mind.

"Moran," I said. "Let's take this over to Moran and see what he thinks. If we show it to anybody else they'll probably have a fit."

Eddie agreed and we went over to Moran's place.

He was sitting in his living room reading a book and listening to an album.

"We've got a skull in this bag," I said. I wanted to warn him so that he wouldn't be as startled as I had been and go into a tizzy.

"A skull? . . . What kind of a skull?"

"It's somebody," Eddie said. "A person."

Eddie was clearly rattled.

"Let me see," Moran said, so I handed him the bag.

He took the skull out of the bag, unwrapped it, and held it in his bare hands, just as nonchalantly as you please! Just as if he looked at human skulls every afternoon around five o'clock.

"Well, it's a human skull all right," he said. "There's no doubt about it."

He rotated the thing in his hands and examined it very carefully.

"I've got an idea about this," he said. "Let's take this over to Doc Pugh's dental office. I'd like him to take a look at it before we turn it over to the authorities."

"The Authorities?" Eddie asked, unclear about what this meant.

"The Law," Moran said. "The Law is always interested in human remains. In case somebody was murdered or kidnapped or something. But I think this is different. Come on."

We trooped over to Doc Pugh's.

"Take a gander at this, Doc," Moran said, and handed him the bag.

Doc Pugh wasn't afraid of the skull either. He picked it right up and looked at its teeth.

"Whoever it was didn't come from around here," Doc Pugh said. "The water's poor and people get a lot of cavities."

I could attest to that.

"Look at this," Moran said. He then pointed to some feature of the skull and used words that Eddie and I couldn't understand.

"Why, you're right!" Doc Pugh said. "How did you know that?"

Moran shrugged, and Doc continued:

"What this means is that this person was at least 50 years old," he said and pointed at the teeth. "And not one single sign of any dental work."

Moran continued, saying:

"That age, no sugar, good diet. It seems to me that this could only mean one thing."

"I agree," Doc said.

Moran looked at me and Eddie and pointed at the skull.

"We believe that this person lived here once. That he was an Indian. I'll bet this is the skull of a 50-year-old Indian man."

The sign at the gas station flashed in my mind—Skychief!

"Was he a chief, do you suppose?" I asked.

"Maybe he was. Maybe he wasn't," Moran said. "We don't know. But we have to call in the authorities. Right now."

We quickly learned that the Authorities included the constable, Gene White, and a member of the Oregon State Police. Some kind of a specialist came down from Salem and they investigated the old shed. Doc Pugh went, and Moran, too, but children were not invited. The team found some more bones, an arrowhead, and a few pieces of leather from a moccasin—so that cinched it. An Indian all right. Probably somebody—a local pioneer, maybe—had dug it up by accident and left it under some refuse in the corner of his shed.

I convinced about half the people in town that the skull had belonged to a chief.

A big one.

Next came the issue of what to do with the Remains.

The minister took a one-way position about burying old bones in consecrated ground, as he called it. No deal. And my grandfather, to my regret, didn't rush right in with an offer to use the Tichenor Family Cemetery.

Moran said:

"We'll have to do something else." And then, of all people, he asked me what I thought we ought to do. That was Moran, all right, capable of turning around and treating some kid like he might be a person.

I had an idea. Not only that, Moran declared that it was a good idea.

(I reported this to my parents, by the way, but it did little to offset their conviction that I was lazy, a liar, and probably worthless. It served as just another opening for them to make a further threat about sending me to Military School. Which was an idea that scared me just as bad as becoming a criminal and being sent to Reform School.)

What I did was this: I suggested to Moran that we bury the Chief and the other bits and parts at the place where I had dug up shells and ashes. I figured that if it was a place where Indians had once had meals and looked at the ocean, then maybe it was an okay place for the grave. He said, "Sure."

The Burial Party was formed. It included a number of kids who knew Eddie and me. And also contained a few adults: namely Moran, Mr. Fletcher, Mrs. Lenieve, Crawford Smith, and a history teacher from the high school. My grandfather said he had to go to Gold Beach that day. My sister wasn't interested in what she said was just a bunch of dirty old bones.

There was a problem to be solved. What to put the Indian in. A coffin was ruled out as too expensive and not necessary. And also not natural, the history teacher added. Hardly in keeping with the times. Eddie made a suggestion that his mom had a bread box the family wasn't using any more—one with a hinged lid and a Mallard duck painted on it. This, too, was ruled out, along with a second idea from Mrs. Lenieve regarding a sturdy hat box she didn't need any more since she no longer traveled. Mr. Fletcher hit on it when he said that he had a piece of leather that we could wrap the remains in. It was soft like the chamois that Henri used to wipe the rinse water off the Prum-Yay after he washed it. This turned out to be the choice. The adults agreed on its suitability.

And Mr. Fletcher did something else. He took the arrowhead and fixed it to a special little arrow, about one-third the length of a regular arrow, but with feathers on the end and a notch to fit into a bow. A "ceremonial" arrow, he called it. And Moran said he would think about some words to say at the ceremony.

Moran also went up to the top of the cliff earlier in the day of the burial and dug a nice hole with a pick and shovel. The rest of us, the children and the adults, walked up about sunset (slowly because Mrs. Lenieve was so old) and, even though we were laughing and joking on the way up, things got serious when we got there and quieted down. It was just as serious as when Daryll Sauer's cousin Ted had died or Winnie Lacey. Only this time no minister would stand there and say exactly the same things over them—exactly as if Ted, Winnie, and anybody else who had died recently were the same person. Nobody had any idea of what Moran was going to say. Moran of the house that couldn't be blown down in the worst storm in 60 years.

Mr. Fletcher asked that we form a circle and pass around the special arrow from one person to the next—and hold it for a minute—then each of us think of something happy for the person whose remains we were about to bury.

Since I was the one who had already had the earlier conversation with Mr. Fletcher about Indians and the spirits in things, I thought about that. Eddie confided later that the only happy thing he could think of at that moment was roller-skates, which I concluded was just fine. I don't know what the other people thought and I never asked them.

Moran carefully wrapped the skull and the bones, the arrow and small parts of moccasin, in the piece of leather. He tied it with brown string. He then placed the bundle in the bottom of the hole and shoveled the earth and stones back in.

Moran opened a basket that he had brought along. In it were a dozen or so clams that he had dug that afternoon and other material from the beach directly below the cliff. He placed the clams down in the loose dirt at the top of the grave, added a covering of seaweed, and then arranged and lighted a fire made from driftwood. This is how the Indians would have baked their clams, you see—under the fire, not directly in it.

Moran stood up and we all reformed our circle around the fire. The sun had just gone down.

"Here is meal for you, my friend," Moran said. "A meal you would understand. On a beautiful day that you would have recognized. We apologize for the people who disturbed you. And we hope that you will now rest in peace, which you deserve."

That was it. He was finished. He looked at the rest of us in the circle and asked:

"Does anyone else have something to add?"

Mr. Fletcher and Mrs. Lenieve signaled that they did.

"After you, Mrs. Lenieve," Mr. Fletcher said.

"No, . . . please," she said. "After you."

"Well, okay." He then looked first at the fire and then to the horizon and then up in the sky.

He thought for a minute about exactly what he was going to say and then spoke.

"If you are not already in your Heaven, " Mr. Fletcher said. "Then may you fly there now as straight and true as your new arrow."

Then, after a long pause, after a very long pause, in fact, Mrs. Lenieve simply said:

"Good-bye."

We stood for another minute before leaving and Moran suggested:

"Somebody needs to stay here and keep an eye on the fire. Make sure nothing happens."

He elected himself to do it—to stay there until the fire had completely died down and there would be no embers to hop into the dry grass.

So the rest of us went home.

But we kept looking back at Moran's shadow, growing ever smaller, and the thin line of smoke that meandered upward toward the first stars.

Everything was right.

King of the Mountain

Kids used to play this game. Maybe they still do. We used to play it on a short hill covered with slick grass, pushing "attackers" away from the top and making them slide and tumble down.

My old man played it for real one time, in a grocery store version of the game.

By the end of 1940 my father had the only grocery store and meat market in town: he was King of the Mountain.

The store seemed huge to me at the time. Four big plate-glass windows in the front; two large meat cases; displays of vegetables; and plenty of shelves and aisles of canned goods to keep stocked. My dad's customers included everybody in the community, naturally, since he was the only game in town.

The storefront was white and the big sign above the windows was painted black. It said: QUICK'S QUALITY MARKET. He was serious about the "quality" part of the statement.

The black-and-white sign would have created a somber appearance to the store had it not been for the hand-painted messages my dad would put in the windows: announcements painted in red and blue tempera paint on long pieces of butcher paper. Special Sales. These signs changed frequently, usually two or three times a week.

More than once the principal of the high school would look at these signs and, smiling, walk into the store to say:

"Al, why in the hell are you constantly having sales? You don't need to have special sales! You're not competing against anybody."

My father would smile back at him and say something like: "It's just the way I do business." Besides, he really enjoyed painting those red and blue signs. All caps. In a type style that was all his own. (And, of course, I've said this before, the signs worked; they were good luck.)

There were some other ways he did business.

As an old-fashioned shopkeeper he liked to talk to his customers, so there were always people in the store whether they were buying anything or not. Sometimes three or four people would be leaning on a meat case as my father worked at the butcher block. Others would stand or sit around a big wood-burning stove in one corner.

There are a lot of rainy days on the coast of Oregon. Rainy days with no place in particular to go.

He did some other things as well. For one thing, he extended credit—in some cases a lot of it—and he did it in a way that preserved everybody's dignity.

"Don't worry about the money," he would say to worried people who had been sick or injured. "Take anything you need. Don't go hungry. When you're back on your feet, you can pay the bill."

Nobody stiffed him. Everybody liked him.

He never realized how much they liked and respected him until one stormy night after the war started. Winds of over 100 mph sucked out two of the windows in the front of the store.

There was a pyramid of coffee cans displayed in one of the windows, coffee being rationed and precious at the time, and all the cans blew down the highway to hell and gone. It was the middle of the night and the Coast Guard brought down big sheets of plywood to replace the glass.

The next day was a marvel. People straggled to the store in ones and twos and threes—all of them carrying big red cans of Folgers cofee.

"Here's your coffee, Al."

"I found this one clear down by the grammar school, Al."

"All four of these I found in a culvert in front of Lou's Garage, Al. But good as new."

Anyway, all the coffee was returned, and it was returned by individuals. It was not a group or a committee that got together to do the right thing by Al. Just lots of different people doing what they perceived as their duty.

The economy got better and people paid all their bills. The mill expanded. Business was good.

Enter SAFEWAY.

They found a good location at the other end of town, remodeled an existing building, put in all the fixtures, stocked the shelves, installed a manager from Portland, and hired some townspeople as clerks. By coincidence, the store opened during the summer and there was the appearance of some business. Tourists from California would drive up from the south and the Safeway store was the first they'd come to when they drove into town.

Then the rains came. Autumn.

The workers in Safeway stood in the store without customers and watched the water trickle down the windows. (Windows, by the way, without signs. Why signs? Who needed signs? Who did not know that Safeway stores could have lower prices because of their buying clout? Who did not know about economies of scale? Simple logic told you that Safeway would win!)

But the workers in Safeway watched the cars and pickups driving through town on their way to my dad's place.

After nine or ten months, Safeway called it quits. They packed up and cleared out in the same efficient and correct way they had come. They had done everything by the book: handbills, advertising, a clean, well-stocked store, courtesy, modern management, the whole works.

On his way out of town, the Safeway manager came into our store and shook my dad's hand.

"You know something, Al?" he said. "We could have saved ourselves a lot of money by having somebody come down for a few days and just ask a few questions. They would have found out about the past. The fact that you stuck with people in this town when things were tough for them, and they returned the favor when it looked like things were tough for you. I had the better store; but you had all the customers. Nice work."

He then climbed in his car to drive back to Portland.

There was no celebration at Quick's Quality Market. No smirking. No King-of-the-Mountain superiority.

It was a slow time in mid-morning, so my old man poured himself a cup of coffee and went into the back room. He cleared off a worktable and unrolled a big length of butcher paper. Then he unscrewed the lids on the big jars of red and blue tempera paint and dampened his biggest brush in a pan of water.

He never sketched anything ahead of time. He knew from experience how much room his words would take.

His first two words fit exactly.

Bright red.

"TODAY'S SPECIALS!"

Business as usual.

While the Safeway guy's Chevy motored northward through the rain, tires singing on the metal surface of the Elk River Bridge.

.

Highlights— 1941

Lend-Lease went into effect.

Yugoslavia was invaded by the Germans. (Which forced my grandfather to write back to the company who sold him the little flags to put on pins. He'd run out of German flags. Who knew they'd invade so many places? He also bought some extra Japanese flags. This was smart.)

Greece: invaded by the Germans.

Crete: invaded by the Germans.

British and Free French troops invaded Syria and Lebanon to prevent a takeover by the Germans. ("Finally," my grandfather said, "the opportunity to use a British and a French Flag for a change.")

German troops invaded Soviet Russia. ("Bad mistake," Frank prophesied.)

Iran was invaded by British and Soviet troops. (More flags.)

Two U.S. destroyers were torpedoed by German U-Boats. Port Orford fishermen were pissed off big time.

Pearl Harbor on the Hawaiian island of Oahu came under attack by 360 carrier-based Japanese planes on the morning of December 7th. (This frightened me very much since I was under the mistaken belief that Hawaii was just over the horizon from us. And I had thought Perk McCormick was dumb when it came to geography!) A lot of warships were sunk and damaged.

Dr. Baird got so drunk he was sick. He was found lying on his porch crying: "Oh, God, not again," and Frank said he'd take care of him. Veterans stick together. Bob Forty agreed. Baird took a long nap and they gave him scotch whiskey in milk for a couple of days until he snapped out of it.

Grandpa Frank stuck Japanese pins in Malaya and Siam on the 8th of December.

Luzon got a pin on December 10th.

Guam got a pin on the 11th.

Wake Island fell on the 23rd. Pin.

Christmas Day. Pin. Hong Kong.

"This is making me sick," Grandpa Frank lamented.

Good films: *Citizen Kane, The Maltese Falcon, Sergeant York, The Sea Wolf, Dumbo,* and *Never Give a Sucker an Even Break.* My sister's favorites: *How Green Was My Valley, King's Row, The Little Foxes,* and *Two-Faced Woman.*

Duffy's Tavern premiered on the CBS Network with a guy named Ed Gardner. Every show opened with the same line. Here it is. Ed said: "Duffy's Tavern, where the elite meet to eat. Archie the manager speaking, Duffy ain't here. Oh, hello, Duffy." Duffy would never appear on the show. Other new shows included Pot o' Gold: $1000 Giveaway (Tums); Aldrich Family (General Foods); City Desk (Palmolive Soap); and Inner Sanctum (where you started getting scared the moment a big door squeaked open). Presented by Carter's Little Liver Pills.

Music to remember always: "Lili Marlene," "(There'll Be Blue Skies Over) The White Cliffs of Dover," "I Don't Want to Walk Without You," "Elmer's Tune," "Racing With the Moon,'" "Deep in the Heart of Texas," "Chattanooga Choo-Choo," "I Don't Want To Set the World On Fire," "Anniversary Waltz," "Boogie Woogie Bugle Boy," "Buckle Down, Winsocki," "My Adobe Hacienda," "Waltzing Matilda," and "There, I've Said It Again."

On the grocery store news front, my dad was informed that Gerbers now sold one million cans of baby food per week. Cheerios breakfast food was introduced by General Mills (and was 2.2 percent sugar). The O.P.A. (Office of Price Administration) was set up to prevent profiteering.

Moran saw me start to throw away half of a sandwich to some seagulls. He was walking up from the dock with some fresh crab and I was standing near the ice house.

"I just learned something terrible," Moran said.

"Yes, what is it?" I asked, fearing that somebody had gotten his arm cut off in the machinery down at the cannery.

"This is the worst winter in 30 years in Russia. Leningrad has been besieged—cut off—by the Germans and they don't have any food there. They're eating dogs, cats, birds, jelly made out of cosmetics, and soup made from boiled leather wallets."

"Are you making that up?" I asked him.

"No. That's what I read. Those able to work get a bread ration of half a pound per day. Others only two slices. And the bread is frequently made of low-grade rye flour mixed with sawdust."

"They must be starving."

"Yes. They are starving."

I took the rest of my sandwich home and put it in the refrigerator. I lay awake that night thinking about Wallet Soup. Worse yet, Skippy Stew.

Barnie Winslow was really big news. New-found friends usually are. Pearl Harbor continued to scare us. Moran dropped out of sight. That was a big one. PBY Catalina flying boats went on patrol.

The only Asian person we ever had in town was a cook that T.J. Collins hired. This man wore a pin on his apron that said: "I'm Not a Jap! I'm a Filipino!"

War dogs came to patrol. There was an event that looked like the prelude to an invasion. There actually was a ship sunk by a submarine. We had buckets of sand and shovels in every classroom. This was to extinguish incendiary bombs that the Japanese were going to drop. We blacked out the town.

I listened to Radio Tokyo on Frank's short-wave radio. They talked in calm, pleasant English voices about what was going on in the Pacific (which according to them was none of America's affair, but merely the business of what I remember their calling "The Greater East Asian Co-Prosperity Sphere").

"Bush-Wah!" was what my grandfather called it, which was translated by T.J. Collins as "Total Bullshit."

I didn't know what to call it, but the war seemed to be getting a lot closer.

Lovey Laureen

I got farmed out. Put in a kind of jail. The reason, my perfidious parents said, was that a tourist kid drowned in Garrison Lake and they decided that kids my age didn't get enough supervision. That's what they said to customers in the store and it was complete Horse Hockey. The real reason was punishment, and actual banishment, for being such a liar. Every other kid in the county was free to wander all over the place as before. I'm not going into the lying issue because it wasn't lying as you know it. It was a reorganization of the truth in beneficial and more understandable ways, a philosophical breakthrough that was well beyond the intellectual capacities of my parents and teachers. Winnie would have caught on, but she was dead. So it was called lying and I was to be punished for it.

So, that summer (for part of the summer at least), I was a day-care recipient at a house where people were home all day. I knew it would be very boring and it started out that way, to be sure. The house seemed old to me and so did the couple who lived there—the Schaeffers. They had gray hair. This was the test of true old. They may have been fifty. Not quite as ancient as my grandfather.

They had big berry patches on their property. Raspberries, mostly, and boysenberries. During the growing season they would pack boxes of these berries every Friday morning and put them in their truck. I'd help pick. They would then take them up to Bandon and sell them.

Actually, there were three people in the Schaeffer family. The couple had several children who had grown up and moved away but the last one, a young woman, was still at home. Her name was Laureen and she had long brown hair and was extremely beautiful. She was engaged to a log-truck driver named Bobby Walker and they were going to get married later that summer. On the 4th of July, actually. Right before the fireworks, but after the chowder.

There was a routine at the Schaeffer house. I would arrive and eat a small bowl of boysenberries and cream. This was a new experience for me because I'd never eaten boysenberries before that summer.

After boysenberries, I went down to the cellar to bring up things Mrs. Schaeffer wanted for the day, food for lunch and dinner. There were hundreds of jars of fruits and vegetables down there. Also potatoes in boxes. Not to mention mice that would startle me as they scurried away. It was then my pleasant duty to run upstairs and waken Laureen.

Laureen's room had heavy curtains that I will never forget. I remember not so much the fabric or the design, but their color and what they did. They were a dark mossy green color and all but stopped the sunshine. They created a dim, murky light—a deep bottom-of-the-ocean green. It was very strange and wonderful to be in a room with that quality of light. The curtains slid open on rings and, after I'd stood for awhile in the underwater feeling, I would spread them quickly and fill the room with blinding sunshine. Laureen would hide under the covers and scream. Then would follow a pushing-pulling wrestling match and pillow fight which usually culminated in Laureen grabbing me and kissing me on the mouth—a big smacker—from which I would then struggle free and run downstairs to report that Laureen was awake and, finally, getting up. So that was one reason to call her Lovey Laureen, the kissing. Laureen's kisses were more interesting than Lou's kisses.

Now and then, Laureen would go for walks with me on Agate Beach. Mornings. Then, in the afternoon, friends of mine would come over and we'd play in the nearby trees. But I'd always have to be within hollering distance of the house.

Mid-afternoon one day, the news came to us. Marge McCormick had heard about it and come running to tell us. She was out of breath and barely understandable. There had been a big logging-truck accident, she said. The truck had been on a dirt road coming down a steep hill. The entire load of logs had broken loose. Then all the logs came forward and sheered off the cab of the truck. The logs also sheered off the head of the driver. "Decapitated" was the word Marge heard from the grownup giving the news in town. It was the first time I'd heard that word. Decapitated! But, as you know, this exact same thing had happened to another guy! Powers!

The time they could only find one tooth!

I remember standing there not wanting to know who it was.

I didn't want to hear.

I hoped that Marge didn't know.

But she did.

"It was Bobby," she said. "Bobby Walker."

I looked back toward the house. I knew the Schaeffers were inside, but that Laureen was at Doyle's having a cherry coke with a friend of hers.

My legs started to shake at the idea of having to go in there and tell Laureen's parents. My mouth went dry and my chest tightened up. It was exactly like the tonsils time in the Bandon hospital when I was forced to take off my clothes in the white room. Horror-struck. Paralyzed. Did I tell you that I knocked over a can of ether in the operating room? Now I had to deal with the news about Bobby. I thought it would take me two full days to creep the 50 or 60 yards back to the Schaeffers' house. Maybe on my hands and knees. That's how scared I was.

I heard a nearby siren. Since Gene White didn't have a siren on his pickup, it could only be the State Police. When something really terrible happened in town, the State Police arrived. Gene White merely kept the lid on things and restrained drunken sailors and fishermen. But when something really bad happened—like when somebody got killed—then the State Police showed up.

The car appeared and the siren slowly wound down and the patrolman went to the door of the house.

Mr. and Mrs. Schaeffer both appeared on the porch.

I was too far away to see the patrolman's lips moving but I could see Mrs. Schaeffer covering her face with her hands at the instant she was told what had happened.

Mr. Schaeffer stood straighter at that moment, as if he was in the Army and had been called to attention.

The other kids immediately started running toward town, as if there was going to be something to see there. Maybe the ambulance or the hearse that would come down from Bandon to take Bobby to wherever they took dead people.

A gruesome thought suddenly crossed my mind: would Bobby's head be with him?

Jesus!

I wanted nothing to do with this. Any of it.

I didn't want to rush into town with the kids because I was afraid that I might run into Laureen. She would know from the look on my face that something truly horrible had happened. And I would have to tell her. And neither did I want to face Laureen's parents back at the house. I didn't want to go home. I didn't want to go to my grandfather's house. I wished I was suddenly with Uncle Harvey and Aunt Hester in Portland buying tickets at the Oriental Theater, getting some popcorn, and then sitting in the dark waiting for a pirate movie to start.

I went through a few back yards and along the side of a hill to avoid people. I walked past our store on my way up to the house where it was my intention to hide in my room for the rest of the day—possibly even the rest of my life.

My mother saw me.

"You heard?"

"Yes," I replied.

"Awful," she said, and went back in the store.

That was it. All of it. The shortest conversation I'd ever had with my mother.

As if I'd been a fortune teller or something, an ambulance appeared and sped down Highway 101—southward, toward the accident. A few people were following it in their cars. I wondered why. I wouldn't have!

I hid in my room. I pulled the blind down.

I was happy that I was not required to go to Laureen's house the next morning. I worried about it half the night, it seemed like. Just like the tonsils.

But the day after that I flipped completely around and wanted to go over there.

It was nothing morbid. I simply felt a need to go over there.

I was told by both of my parents that I couldn't.

Fully expecting this decision, I snuck out and went anyway.

The side door of the house was open and I could see the Mr. & Mrs. Schaeffer through the screen door. They were sitting at the kitchen table.

They waved me in and motioned me to sit down.

I was given a bowl of boysenberries with fresh cream on them.

They had a conversation and I learned that Laureen had locked herself in her room and wouldn't come out. She'd been there since the moment she found out about Bobby. Locked up there in the dull green light that I imagined was the way things looked under several fathoms of water beneath the dock.

They had ruled out knocking down the door. They thought it would only make matters worse.

Laureen's father had an idea.

"Maybe Johnny, here, could take her up some tea or something. A sandwich. An egg." the father said.

They looked at me. I looked back. Then I finally nodded that I would.

"Okay," Mrs. Schaeffer said. "Try it. It's been practically two days."

They decided on two soft-boiled eggs, two pieces of toast, and a pot of tea. They put all of this on a tray along with silverware, a creamer, a small sugar bowl, and a jam pot with some of the boysenberry preserves that I also liked a lot. Boysenberries that I very well might have picked.

"Can you handle it okay?" Mr. Schaeffer asked me.

"Oh, sure," I said, although the tray was a little heavier and harder to manage than I thought.

"Wait a minute," he said.

He added salt and pepper shakers.

It was a lot of stuff to drop.

I started across the kitchen toward the hall.

"Napkin. Napkin. Napkin." Mrs. Schaeffer exclaimed quietly, and fetched one from a drawer.

I went carefully up the stairs, watching each step. I could easily imagine the tray falling over the banister and into the hall below. I could imagine the embarrassment. It felt like one of those impossible tests that a Prince had to perform in order to save a Princess from a nearby kingdom in order to be able to marry her and live happily ever after in one of those castles on a pointy mountain.

I tapped Laureen's door with the tip of my shoe.

There was no light under the door. It was very quiet.

I turned around. Laureen's parents were at the foot of the stairs looking up.

I tapped again, but nothing happened.

I tapped a third time.

Rustling.

I voice I didn't recognize asked:

"Who's there?"

"Me," I said. "It's me, Johnny."

"Please go away," she said.

"Let me in, Laureen," I said. "Please. I've got a tray. I think I'm going to drop it."

Silence.

I continued, knowing intuitively that sometimes you can help people by getting them to help you—to come to your aid.

So I lied.

"Laureen, please let me in, Laureen. If I have to take this tray back downstairs I'll drop it for sure. I'll trip. Everything will break. I could get killed."

Nothing.

"Honest," I added.

Rustling. Movement.

I heard the key in the lock. The skeleton key. Jesus.

She opened the door and I quickly stepped into the dark moss-green light.

Laureen was in a silk dressing gown. She closed the door and locked it again.

I put the tray on an end table.

She pulled up a chair and I saw from her look that I wouldn't have to beg her to eat something.

I sat down, too. In that odd gloom.

Her long hair was messed up and her eyes were puffy.

She opened one of the soft-boiled eggs and spooned the contents onto a piece of toast. She didn't look at me. She ate it in three bites. It disappeared.

She poured a cup of tea and put a spoonful of sugar in it. She put some of the cream in it, started to put the creamer back on the tray, but then put it to her lips and drank it down. All of it. It gave her a white mustache which she must have realized because she looked at me and made a solemn clown face before licking the cream off her upper lip.

She ate the other egg with the spoon.

She put preserves on the other piece of toast and handed it across the table to offer me a bite.

I took it. But with no words. No conversation.

I watched her eat, fearful that she would start to cry and I wouldn't know what to do. Like when my sister and mother had their rain sobs.

But she didn't cry.

She finished the toast and wiped her mouth on the napkin.

She stood up, crossed the room, and sat down on the edge of the bed.

– 217–

She beckoned to me, both arms outstretched. I went to her and she put her arms around me. She opened her dressing gown and pulled my face into her breasts. She was very warm and held me for a long time before she finally stopped and took off the gown altogether and then carefully and systematically unbuttoned all my buttons and untied my shoes and took off my clothes and then held me against her under the covers of the bed. I closed my eyes and the blurry green went away and there was nothing but the dark warmth and smoothness. "Ah, so," as the Japanese would say.

Some skin is like silk.

She ran her hands softly all over me and into my hair and put her fingers in my mouth. She guided my hands to various parts of her body, her breasts especially at first, and then settled on another part where she placed my fingers in motion in a special way that I was encouraged to keep up on my own, without her guidance. So I did, nestled against her, my tongue on the nipple of one of her breasts and her hand resting gently on my closed eyes.

I stopped immediately when she suddenly shuddered and began to moan—a moan that she stifled. I was not alarmed or afraid. Just concerned that I might have done something to hurt her. Which was not the case. Her hand invited me to continue.

The green became darker, I remember, as the sun climbed over the peak of the roof and, after a while, I fell asleep. Laureen was asleep. The house was quiet.

I awoke to whispers. Outside the door.

I was lying side by side—skin-to-skin—with Laureen, who was asleep. I merely resented the whispering at first—a distraction—but then I came fully awake and was instantly afraid. I could hear Gene White shouting SHAME, SHAME! in the empty chicken coop at me and his daughter, Annette. Shame about what? Nothing was wrong. Irregular, maybe. Unusual, yes. I was calmly aware of that. But, on another level, the kid level, I was panicked.

I became panicked in the paralyzed mode. I could not move.

Looking back on it, I would have had plenty of time to get out of bed, put on my clothes, and sit on a chair. That's how they would have found me. A kind boy, that Johnny. Looking out for his friend. Sympathetic. What a true, kind young person. It would have been a cinch.

But I lay there. I hoped that Laureen would wake up and tell me what to do. To take charge. But she was deep asleep and her eyes were no longer puffy and she was dark beautiful and I pressed my lips against her shoulder.

What they did, out in the hall, was to carefully insert another key, push the inside key out of the lock where it fell on the floor, and then unlock the door from the outside.

That's what happened.

I could hear it happening. I knew what was happening. I knew that any second the door would open and I would be . . . what? Caught! I was about to get caught at something. That was the exact feeling. And I was powerless to do anything about it. I just waited for the awful consequences. The shouting. The commotion. The furor. Getting slapped.

Laureen was in the bed between me and the door. She didn't hear her key clatter on the floor or the door open. I was almost hidden from view behind her. I peeked through the valley formed between her shoulder and her head—her neck.

Dr. Baird opened the door. My nemesis. The man who had totally ignored my pain from a firecracker explosion one time and told me to stick my hand in a mud puddle.

I knew I was in for it.

Mrs. Schaeffer saw my clothes scattered on the floor and exclaimed: "Oh, dear."

Mr. Schaeffer said nothing.

Dr. Baird said he would handle this, entered the room, and closed the door behind him. Doctors have the power to seal rooms. Just like that. "Stay out," they say, and people automatically do what they're told and don't go in.

Dr. Baird went to the edge of the bed and looked at Laureen sleeping.

He motioned me out of bed with his index finger. This gesture meant: "Get out of bed, put your clothes on, and let's you and me get out of here. Right now!"

Which I did, and without any embarrassment at being naked. Dr. Baird was one of the few non-parents authorized to see you naked. So that didn't matter. It was the scolding I feared. Once we got out of there.

I got dressed and, in the hallway, Dr. Baird spoke to Laureen's parents in a tone that was calm and absolutely confident:

"She'll be fine, now. Keep the house quiet and leave her alone. Let her sleep. Everything's okay."

Except me, I remember thinking. Everything's okay except me who's going to be taken someplace and given hell, plus most likely beaten up.

Then a truly horrible thought occurred to me. Baird was going to take me to the store and make The Announcement to my parents and, very probably customers! The only thing missing would be Uncle John in his police captain's uniform. Public humiliation! That was it! That's what was called for.

Holy God, what had I gotten myself into?

He invited me outside and into his coupe.

That was it. He would turn the key. Start the engine. Drive to the store. And spill the beans.

I was ruined in that town. Finished.

Before he turned the key, however, he looked at me very carefully and asked:

"Are you all right?"

He asked this in a kind voice that I'd never heard him use before. It was easy for me to answer:

"Yes."

He drove to Doyle's place, the bus stop. It had a lot of deserted tables in it. He picked the one furthest from the counter and the cash register. No one could hear our conversation. He ordered a cup of coffee, black, and I was encouraged to have anything I wanted. I chose a 7-Up float, my new prescription of choice for all physical and some mental afflictions.

Dr. Baird interviewed me with the same solicitude that he'd shown in the car.

As I went through the step-by-step explanation of what had happened, he would nod his head affirmatively and say "Uh-huh," or "Yes," or "I understand." We took it step by step. The things I told him were, he said, perfectly okay, and nothing out of the ordinary. It was as if he'd heard this four or five thousand times before. Ten-year-old kid. Nineteen-year-old girl. In bed. No clothes. Doing things in near darkness. I finished my story and polished off the vanilla ice cream in the bottom of the glass.

"How old are you?" he asked me.

"Ten," I said. "Eleven in October."

"Do me a favor."

He conveyed urgency.

"I would like you to keep quiet about this. It will be our secret. I don't want you to mention this to anybody for, . . . uh, let's see, . . . five years. Talk about it when you're fifteen. Or, if there's anything that starts bothering you about it, come and talk to me. Understand?"

"Yes," I said.

"The thing to know is that what you did was normal."

"Okay," I said.

"But if you talk to other people about it they will likely misunderstand and say something stupid. So don't mention it to anybody. All right?"

"All right."

"And you're fine?" he asked once again.

"Yes," I reassured him.

"Very well. You look fine. In the eyes. That's what counts."

I realized then, and appreciated it a lot more later of course, that this was counseling to avoid a Traumatic Experience—some kind of life-bending event that could happen to a kid and wreck his future sex life. Turn him into a sicko of some kind or an authentic ladies-underwear thief.

We left Doyle's.

Only the movie theater separated Doyle's place from our new store so it was a short walk over there.

My father and mother were with customers. They barely acknowledged me with nods.

I went to my room. I smelled my fingers. 7-Up and vanilla. Citrus. Laureen.

Good.

I remembered Dr. Baird's look of satisfaction as he got in his coupe and drove away. The Healer. The Man Who Understands. He who made everything right.

I kept Baird's secret well beyond the five years he specified.

And I did even better on Laureen's—decades better.

She pledged me to keep the secret forever.

Well, I decided forever was over last week. Maybe actually last Friday, on some unnumbered anniversary of those fine events.

That's why I can tell you this now. Because it's okay.

Questions From Old Lady Beck– Answers From Moran

Old Lady Beck, who knew everything about botany, told me that marigolds are flowers of the sun and great luck-bringers. She also said that roses, in addition to being the symbol of love, also bring luck, and that purple flowers confer financial good fortune. Mimosa is a death bringer. And a flower blooming out of season is an omen of death. She had no explanation for any of this, she said, it was merely the way things were. Like planting parsley on Good Friday, or always making a wish when you see the first robin of spring.

She had also been told as a child that if a seagull brushed against the window of a sailor then he would die. She also said that seagulls were the souls of drowned sailors. Not only that, she believed that if a person knocked a bracelet or a ring on a crystal goblet and made a bell tone, that the ringing must be immediately muffled lest a sailor be drowned.

I stumbled into a conversation about superstition with Moran because we both happened to say the same thing at the same time. He held up his hand and said:

"Make a wish."

When I asked him why, he said that it was a New England superstition that when two people say the same words simultaneously they will have a fulfillment of their desires, provided they wish before another word is spoken.

I asked him about salt being thrown over the left shoulder and told him of my recollection of T.J. doing it. He said that in ancient times to spill salt was an omen of misfortune. Salt, he explained, was used as a preservative. Decay is the enemy of salt. Decay is the Devil. So cast a pinch of salt over the left shoulder and directly into the Devil's face. That was the story.

He went on to explain that 99 percent of people avoid walking under a ladder whether or not they know about the association of the ladder with old-time gallows (a self-standing ladder), or an affront against the Holy Trinity (a ladder leaning against a building and forming a triangle).

He explained a mysterious part of the saying which is used to confer luck on brides: "Something old, something new, something borrowed, something blue." The blue part? Blue, since the time of the ancient Israelites, has always represented purity.

Ladybugs, Moran said, because of their red color were once associated with the ancient gods of fire. This explains the chant of little children: "Ladybug, Ladybug, fly away home. Your house is on fire and your children are gone." Well, it *kind* of helps to explain it.

Also, according to Moran, the word umbrella comes from the Latin *umbra*, shade. It was originally a sunshade. Because of its close association with the sun and its symbolic shape of the solar wheel, it became a sacrilege to open an umbrella in the shade. Hence, the origins of the unluckiness of opening an umbrella indoors.

Clover was used by the Druids to charm away evil spirits and they thought that four-leafed ones were especially lucky.

About parsley he said: parsley was associated in ancient times with the spirit of death and the only way to sidestep the danger was to plant it on a holy day, Good Friday.

In restaurants, he said, 13 people are never seated at the same table. This superstition can be traced back to the Last Supper when Judas Iscariot was looked upon as the thirteenth man.

Moran said that he did not know the origins of the following beliefs:

To touch the hump of a hunchback brings success.

To cross knives on a table will cause an argument in the house.

The foot of the bed should not face the door.

So there you had it. Even Moran, it turned out, didn't know quite everything. Lots, but not all.

Another time, he also talked about words that end in MANCY and have to do with foretelling future events. There were dozens of them, he said, maybe hundreds, but very few were understandable. *Alectoromancy* is a process where you put the alphabet in a big circle on the ground. Then you put a kernel of corn on each letter. Then you turn a rooster loose in the middle of the circle. He, naturally, will start eating the corn. You keep track of the order in which he eats the corn and put the letters together to see if they form words. Or you interpret what the letters mean. Something like that.

Bibliomancy is accomplished by opening a book, such as a Bible, and poking your finger at random; *capnomancy* by observing smoke; and *ceromancy* from figures formed by pouring melted wax in water. *Pyromancy* is divination by means of a flame or fire. Maybe my grandfather was a pyromancer.

The Con Men— and Then There Was Mr. Parker

Two gyp artists came to town at different times over the years. The first Flim-Flam Man, as my grandfather called him, was a fellow with a railroad scheme. It was called the Port Orford, Portland and Orient Railroad (the P. O. P. & O.Railroad).

The guy had pen and ink renderings of the engines, the freight cars, and the train station with Port Orford on the sign. It was guaranteed to make our town a major rail hub in order to transport lumber to the ports to the north. Also fish and crabs.

It would bring major manufacturing to the town and a lot of jobs.

Business would boom. The man wore nice suits and drove an expensive car. He looked for real. He bilked several townspeople of several hundred dollars and was later convicted, but nobody got any money back.

They caught him in California, promoting the Sonoma, San Francisco and Orient Railroad. Same picture of the train station, only this time with Sonoma on the sign. Quite a guy.

The other man showed up one day, equally well dressed, but after Moran had come to town and built his house.

The man went down to the beach for a couple of days and then announced in a quiet voice in the Pastime that there was plenty of gold in the beach sand, if only a man could get it out. He said he knew a way, but that it would take some investment capital for what he called "scientific equipment."

Somebody decided it was a good idea to consult Moran about this idea and Moran was persuaded to come down from his house and ask a few questions. He did, and the man left town immediately.

The story then made the rounds that Moran was secretly a mining engineer or a geologist of some kind. He knew his stuff, no doubt about it.

Speaking of gold, you need to know about Mr. Parker.

Although he wasn't a con man, far from it.

I mentioned Parker before. He talked to Moran when Moran was using surveying instruments and then he worked for quite a few weeks helping to build Moran's house. Well, here's the whole story about Parker. It's not a very long one.

And I was about to report that it wasn't very long because Parker wasn't successful. There was no outcome to his efforts. But a success story could have been short, too, couldn't it? I mean you could have a story that was not much more than a headline. A MAN NAMED PARKER FOUND A SOLID GOLD METEOR! That's a short story for you.

North of town, half way to Silver Springs, and west into the trees was a pond fed by a spring and an old house next to it. It was swampy ground which you could tell because skunk cabbages grew there. Most people didn't like the smell of skunk cabbages, but I didn't mind it at all. It smelled kind of good, actually.

Parker lived in a small house that was very old but hadn't turned into a shack yet. I was always unclear about how a place turned into a shack, and the exact metamorphosis that a house underwent to do it. I asked my sister one time if paint could be stolen, since that could account for the shack color of a place. Or if birds or insects could transform or transmute a house by eating the paint or rubbing it off in some fashion. Just as his house seemed to be decaying into a shack, the man who lived there, Parker, seemed likewise to be deteriorating into a derelict. He looked more and more like a bum or a tramp.

Parker walked as a profession.

He tromped around the hills, the mountains and the forests, looking for something, a bonanza.

He looked for a meteor—a meteor that had fallen, not in the distant past, but practically in people's memory. It had landed, according to Indian accounts, a year or two before Captain William founded the town. It had streaked across the sky and kerplunked inland in the mountains. It is said to have buried itself in the ground. The story also had it that an Indian had found the location and took gold from it. He had broken off a piece and taken it back to his village on Sixes River, Kthukhwuttune, Where Good Grass Is. Old stories said that he wore the glittering piece of gold on a leather strand around his neck. The research into the Indians that the Principal had done only reinforced Parker's belief in the story and the existence of the meteor.

"And even if it's not solid gold, but just had a lot of gold in it, it could still make somebody a fortune."

I overheard my dad tell my mom one time that I was a lot like Parker. That I was always willing to work my butt off trying to avoid real work.

– 225–

Parker was out there six or seven days a week in all weather. Rain and wind didn't even slow him down, let alone stop him. Out he'd be, blazing trails through the brush with a sharp machete.

His experience of getting to know Moran was a useful one. He learned basic surveying skills from Moran and how to create maps of the areas he searched. It became apparent to him that he may have been looking in the same places time after time, jamming an iron rod into the earth trying to hit the solid (gold) meteor. This way he could be more systematic.

Moran went out there with him one time to help have a look around.

Moran was the only person who took Parker at all seriously.

Parker got good enough with his instruments so that one time a lumber company hired him to do some work in a pinch. The next thing you know, he was working more or less regularly and finally made enough money to get out of that shack and live somewhere halfway decent.

It didn't break his habit of looking for the meteor, though. We moved away in 1943 and I don't know how much longer he kept looking. We moved inland only to Grants Pass, so if Parker had ever found gold (especially a gold meteor!) I'm sure the news would have gotten to us.

Parker had confidence. Confidence comes from conviction. And conviction stems from an abiding faith.

Can you imagine embarking upon an outdoor search in every kind of weather, day in and day out, for years?

Teeth and History

My teeth were terrible. Port Orford water was awful. My dental hygiene was appalling; nobody taught me how to brush and nobody flossed. The upshot was that I went to Portland at least once a year and suffered terribly under the hands of the family dentist, Old Doctor Woods, who would repeatedly needlize my gums and drill awesome holes in my teeth.

I would reward myself after these ordeals by taking a ride on the Council Crest streetcar to get over the shock and recover feeling in my lips after the Novacaine. The Council Crest streetcar was a truly magic experience and I realized it at the time. I went through a residential neighborhood and then suddenly went into a forest and up a slope, bending and curling along a hill through the trees and bushes. It went past the Portland Zoo where I could see jungle animals. It finally came to the crest and there was a nice view of the city, the Willamette River, and the Columbia River. I could see the State of Washington in the distance and knew that Battleground Lake was up there to the north somewhere.

Very few people ever rode all the way to the top so I was frequently the only passenger in the yellow streetcar. For a long time I thought the motorman deliberately took his time so that I could enjoy the ride through the trees and recover from damage incurred in the torture chamber of Doctor Woods. I realized later that the slowness was because of the grade and that the streetcar couldn't have gone any faster even if the motorman had wanted to. Always, by the time the streetcar reached the top, I had put enough time and space between me and the hurt and I felt pretty much okay.

One can also be made to feel pretty much okay by the appropriate application of remembered amulets. It converts shock to silence.

It was because of the trips to Portland to see Dr. Woods that I would learn more history from my grandmother. She had looked at the records and knew more about Captain William Tichenor than my grandfather seemed to know.

For example:

Captain William Tichenor was twice elected to the territorial legislature and later to the State Senate from the counties of Coos, Curry, and Umpqua. When Curry County was created in 1855, members of the legislature favored calling it Tichenor County. William declined the honor, suggesting the county be named in honor of Territorial Governor Curry.

My Grandfather Frank would have jumped at the chance.

He might have killed for it.

When the Rebellion broke out (the Civil War), Captain William offered his services to the government but, on account of rheumatism and various other complaints brought about by two years in the mountains tracking down Indians, the physician advised him to stay home. He was appointed the Collector of Customs at Port Orford. His son, Jacob (my great-grandfather), served in the Union Army instead. First Oregon Volunteers. Company K.

In 1864 there was a dispute about the ownership of property in Port Orford. Captain Tichenor took on the government and lost. After throwing an official out of a building he claimed was his, he was arrested by military authorities and imprisoned for several weeks at Fort Alcatraz, later a federal prison.

He was released on the promise that he would not interfere with or in any manner lay claim to the said property. The government then sued Tichenor in an effort to gain possession of the tract.

The court ruled in favor of Tichenor.

The court then ruled that Tichenor's promise not to claim the land (in return for being released from prison) was not valid because his arrest was without due process of law and any promise extorted from him was void.

The Captain was vindicated.

In 1868, he built the schooner, *Alaska*, in Port Orford.

He sailed other ships.

Captain William's first wife died December 18, 1880. He married another woman (from England) named Elizabeth, and she kicked the bucket on July 25, 1883. He married a third time in San Francisco in January 1884 (a woman named Arrietta). He died in San Francisco on July 17, 1887, at the age of 74, and was buried in the Tichenor Family Cemetery in Port Orford.

The part about "tracking down Indians" interested me, but my grandmother advised me to ask Frank about it. Later I did.

He had no comment.

Barnie Winslow's Christmas

Since my father was a storekeeper, we were pretty well off as compared with the fishermen and the people who worked in the lumbermill. As one particular Christmas got closer, I knew it was going to be a big event. A whole bunch of out-of-town relatives had been invited, including the French-kissers and waffle-tossers, and it looked like there would be some money to be spent. Also, relatives meant big, noisy meals, and jokes, and walking in big groups on the beach.

Two things happened that stood out that Christmas.

First, I was crawling around under the tree and accidentally worked the paper loose on a large present with my name on it. The paper came loose sufficiently for me to see the end of the box, and to learn that it contained a large, wind-up caterpillar tractor.

Once you wound up the spring motor on such a toy tractor, it could climb over books and other obstacles with its large rubber tracks. Richard (The Bully) Pugh owned just such a caterpillar tractor and it was the envy of every kid in town. This highly desirable item was featured in the window of Doyle's store, and my friend Barnie Winslow and I had talked about the tractor on many occasions, standing idly in front of the store window for as much as half an hour at a time.

I was wildly elated as I patched up the end of my present and pushed it against the wall. I walked around the empty house for 15 minutes and had a glass of milk. The elation was replaced by thoughts of Barnie Winslow.

If I was one of the town's "Haves," then Barnie was certainly one of the "Have Nots."

He and his folks lived in what they called a "cabin" a block or two north of town on the edge of a swamp. They called it that, but it was a shack when they started: a shack with a big hole in the roof and most of the windows broken. It was still shack colored, but the roof was fixed with tin sheets, it had makeshift curtains in the windows, and pie smells coming off the back porch.

As one of the town's leading frog hunters I knew the shack and the swamp very well. I had never known anybody to live in the place, but I was walking past it one day and saw people were fixing it up and moving in. It was the Winslows and Barnie was in my same grade. His dad had come to town to work in the mill but he limped real bad and couldn't get one of the better-paying jobs. So they were, by anybody's standards, poor.

In the few months they were there, Barnie was my best friend. This happened partly because my other friends became interested in sports that summer and neither Barnie nor I had much talent at baseball—you've heard my story. We were more interested in airplanes and war movies.

It occurred to me that the tractor was going to be too much of a good thing. I shared my other toys with Barnie, but they were mostly broken and used up. Here was going to be a brand-new wind-up tractor: red with yellow trim, and strong black rubber treads. No matter how much you let somebody else play with it, it was going to cause problems, because Barnie wanted this thing as much as I did, and yearned for it more desperately than I had. It was going to be like the two of us walking along the beach and me finding a big diamond or something and him not. It would put a distance between us, a bigger gap. The tractor would be a symbol, somehow, of the difference between our families.

I knew that Barnie would deny anything of the kind, but I also knew that it would nearly kill him. In some important way it was going to hurt real bad.

It was still six days before Christmas and I decided to do something about it. I was not known then (or any time later) as a particularly "generous" person. I'm not that eager to share my things with people who have less than I do or have nothing at all. I pretend that Bangladesh is on a different planet, not on the other side of this one. The impoverished are simply not in my jurisdiction—they are not my problem.

But I had the feeling that my friend Barnie was. And that I had to get him a tractor. First I thought of trying to trade Richard out of his tractor, but then decided that this wasn't the answer. It would be a used tractor that way, and Barnie needed a new one. I was convinced of that. I had two dollars and sixty cents at the time, a minor fortune for a kid in those days. The tractor at Doyle's store was $4.00, a Big Ticket Item, indeed. I made up the difference by stacking two truckloads of wood (which took an entire weekend) and selling my double-barreled pirate cap pistol to the mayor's son for seventy cents. When I had the money, Eve Doyle gift-wrapped the package for me and then put it in a large brown paper bag. I hid Barnie's present in the woodshed and then got back to feeling elated about my tractor. No guilt now. (As my sister will tell you, I've been trying to buy my way out of responsibility for several decades.)

Days passed. Aunts and uncles and cousins started coming into town and filling up our house and a good part of Spence's Tourist Court. Anna and Marianne were there, the twins, and Aunt Margaret, whom I still call Aunty Marnie. Skippy (cousin Charles who got Bruno) seemed to be in Goof-Ball Remission and fun to be around.

Because of all the activity and confusion, I was busy all day on the day before Christmas; I didn't see Barnie and he didn't come over. I've talked to you about how we always opened presents on the night before Christmas, not the morning of Christmas Day. So we got busy opening presents and it was very dark by the time I could slip away and take Barnie's tractor over to his place. It was only a half a mile or so, but it was raining and I rode my bike over as fast as I could. The place was dark when I got there, so I left the present on the front porch next to the door and pedaled silently away. That was the best way for Barnie to get the present anyway—suddenly and unexpectedly on Christmas Day.

The next morning there was the usual uproar of people eating the big Christmas breakfast, finding things in stockings, trying on new sweaters, and playing with toys. I left my "big" present under the tree, figuring I'd play with it later over at Barnie's.

Christmas morning had broken clear. The wind off the ocean was stiff and fairly cold, but there wasn't any rain. At about 10:30, I rode over to Barnie's with my tractor. As I coasted up to the porch I saw that Barnie's present was still by the door where I'd left it. I looked at it for a long moment and then noticed that the curtains were gone from the windows and that no smoke was coming from the chimney. I couldn't believe it.

I knocked on the door, hoping for the best, and then finally looked through a window. The place was empty. I hooked both presents on my handlebars and rode back home.

My sister handed me an envelope when I walked back in the house. She said that Dad had found it slipped under the front door of the store. I sat down next to the fireplace and opened it.

Inside was a piece of tablet paper with faint blue lines on it. It was folded to look like a Christmas card, and had a green tree with red and yellow ornaments drawn in crayon on the front. Inside, in pencil, was a message from Barnie.

"Dear John," it said. "Things didn't work out here for my father. And so we are going down the coast to where things might be better. We all figured that since there wasn't going to be a tree and stuff that we might as well get going and Christmas wouldn't make much difference one way or the other. I'll write you a letter from where we go and I hope that you will write back. I am glad that you were my friend. Your friend, Barnie."

This was worse than Grandpa Frank's nearly dying the year before by choking on a rock fish bone. And twice as bad as having a promising cat run over by a logging truck or the Greyhound. It didn't seem fair that the sun was shining.

– 231–

I put the two presents in the back of my closet for a few days and placed the letter in a book of Kipling stories. I didn't know what to do about the way I felt. Years later I learned how to cry a little bit about it, always at Christmas. Because, to make things worse, Barnie didn't write and I never got the loop closed, or the feelings talked about, or the tractors really played with. It just didn't happen.

So the only thing that comes out of it, really, is the good fact that I have never had a Barnie Winslow Christmas. Things have never been that gloomy or bad. I have never been on the road in a beat-up car on that day, or in a cold room, or without best wishes of some kind from somebody. I have never been in a spot where "Christmas," as Barnie said, "wouldn't make much difference one way or the other."

The tractors are gone, of course, but I still have Barnie Winslow's card and its own odd way of saying Merry Christmas.

The New Mrs. Grant

I went into the fourth grade classroom the first day and there, along with the incendiary-bomb extinguishing supplies was Mrs. Grant. I swear to God that I momentarily lost the ability to read and write. Just for one second. Flashback to Grade One Dummyhood.

A girl asked what Mrs. Grant was doing there.

Mrs. Grant explained that she was now teaching the fourth grade and not the first grade any more. Nobody knew that such a thing was possible! We thought that being a particular-grade teacher was immutable, like always having red hair like the Irish kid or being born a Filipino. We also thought that the fourth grade would, therefore, be a cinch. It was Mrs. Grant, wasn't it? Her First-Gradedness would have inelibly inked her, wouldn't it? Made her simple?

No. On the contrary. She worked our tails off. To prove a point, probably.

Thinking of her earlier classroom, I just remembered that the first thing we did in the first grade each morning was to salute the flag. We would stand next to our desks, extend our arms (hands down) toward the flag and recite the Pledge of Allegiance. There was no "under God" part in those days. We saluted, I was told, in the way the Romans saluted Caesar, arms outstretched. Since this was also the way the European fascists were saluting Hitler and Mussolini, Americans were told to knock it off. Somewhere between Mrs. Grant in Grade #1 and Mrs. Grant in Grade #4, we adopted the new sissy hand-on-heart method.

On Friday afternoons Mrs. Grant would allow creative activity, including shadow plays. The blinds would be drawn, a strong light would be placed in a corner, and a sheet would be strung up. Kids could then do things in silhouette behind the sheet, usually just random flapping and waving. I conceived the idea of a surgical operation in which Pat Masterson would lie on a table and I would operate with the tools common to any tool box. Pliers. Tin snips. Hack saws. Chisels. The works. It was sort of an Orson Welles deal that I worked up. Pat had no lines because he was anesthetized. My nurse assistants had few lines. All they did was repeat my one-word commands as Chief Surgeon. "SAW!" "Saw." "PLIERS!" "Pliers." The highlight was when I removed a green balloon from the gaping incision in Pat. So I wrote, directed, produced, and starred in this piece which was a big hit, but which inspired Mrs. Grant to make her now-famous "Do you know what you are? You are self-important" remark. I thought it was a compliment. My sister assured me that it wasn't. And she added another two bits worth of her own to the effect that I was getting a little too big for my britches. I told her that she sounded like our grandmother in Portland. Too big for my britches, indeed.

But Mrs. Grant's sentence has stuck with me.

At the time, my grandfather and Mrs. Lacey clucked at this pronouncement. My mother wholeheartedly agreed.

Moran stuck up for me by suggesting that if I didn't think I was important, then surely nobody else would, and T.J. Collins said: "Ah, piss on her."

Speaking of Show Business, here are a few of the movie slang terms of the Thirties: "Hey, take it easy, you Big Lug!" "Gee, you're swell, Irene!" "You'll never take me alive, Copper!" "You slay me!" and "Take a Powder."

" Turd" McCormick: Wagonmaster

What happened was this. The McCormick family lived in the house with the cedar trees, the berries of which would knock you dead on the spot if you ate even one of them. That was the story: eat a berry, drop dead, then fall out of the tree onto the ground. (I warned you about this earlier, but it doesn't hurt to remind you again. As T.J. would say: "This is not just a bunch of Old Wives' Bullshit!")

There were numerous children in the McCormick family, the first three of whom were older and not playmates. The youngest one, Marge, was too young to play with. Matt was our age. His brother "Perk" was one year younger, but a frequent playmate despite this age discrepancy. "Perk" was so-called because he was perky or something. I never knew. The nickname didn't stick with him after the submarine incident anyway.

I had been given a wind-up submarine as a present. It was maybe a foot long and enameled blue and white. There was a cork in the bottom that enabled you to put water in it to act as ballast. The trick was to get the sub to float, but just barely, then wind it up and adjust the bow planes to make it submerge. As long as the wind-up motor was running, the propeller would keep the submarine below the surface of the water. When this energy was expended, the sub, on its own, would resurface for another wind-up.

Matt McCormick, Pat Masterson, Perk, and I took the submarine for a test in an abandoned water tank that was still full of water. The tank was maybe twenty feet high and had a ladder going to the top and a platform to stand on once you got there. Masterson said we should have taken it to the dock at Garrison Lake, even though it was a mile farther away. He was correct.

Perk created a scene in which he used his frequent excuse: "I never get to do anything because I'm the smallest." This was true. He didn't and he was. So he whined himself into the responsibility of putting the right amount of water in the submarine. He put in too much. He wound up the submarine, put it in the water, and it crashed-dived to the murky bottom of the tank. So Long, Submarine.

Matt, his brother, said:

"Nice work, . . . Turd!"

I lost a sub.

Perk got a new nickname.

He was thenceforth "Turd" McCormick. Every time I looked at him for the week or so after I'd think of the lost submarine and call him TURD with a special intensity.

Perk didn't think it was funny at first, but Pat Masterson persuaded him that "Turd" was a much more manly nickname than "Perk." Pat asked him to imagine a United States Marine called "Perk" or "Perky." Then he asked him to imagine a big, burly Marine with anchors and naked women tattooed on his arms. Pat then said, in a deep voice: "I'd like you to meet my friend United States Marine Sergeant 'Turd' McCormick!"

Masterson was good at that kind of stuff, getting people to believe what T.J. Collins called "the Rankest Horseshit."

After the loss of the sub I happened to pass Moran on the boardwalk near Bennet's and he asked me why I had such a long face.

"I lost my submarine."

He asked for the details and I told him what happened.

"Negative buoyancy," he summed it up, and then lectured that maybe Perk hadn't exactly overfilled the ballast tanks, but cut the margin so close that once the submarine encountered the increased pressure at depth it couldn't surface but continued to descend. Something like that. Moran seemed to know something interesting about any subject you could come up with.

"In general," he said, "it's a good idea to do what trapeze artists do."

"Trapeze artists?" I asked him. "What do they do?" (And silently to myself: what do they have to do with it?)

"Well," he explained, "trapeze artists in circuses use a special technique. When they learn a new routine, they wear a safety harness that's attached to a rope high up in the tent. This way, if they make a mistake, they won't fall and hurt themselves. They get back up and try it again."

He waited.

Usually when he waited like that in a conversation, it was a cue for his listener, me, to make a connection.

"Ah," I said, "I should have put a string or something on the submarine when we started our tests. That way if it got lost, we could pull it back up."

"Good idea!" Moran said, as if I'd made a discovery without any help.

Regular adults like my parents would be more apt to lambaste you with an idea, as if they were whacking you with a yardstick for your stupidity.

"You shoulda put a string on it," they would have said in a snotty know-it-all tone of voice. "That way if it sank you could pull it back up." Perfect Adult After-The-Fact Reasoning. They look smart. You look like a dummy—Mortimer Snerd, the idiot on the Charley McCarthy radio show.

Moran would always find a way to get you to come up with the idea on your own. This way you'd probably remember the Principle for the rest of your life. (In my personal planning, for example, I seldom embark on important experiments without wondering if I should employ a "Sub String" of some kind. It has saved my life at least once. By forgetting it, another time, it cost me a lot of dough. A legally sound premarital agreement can be a "Sub String" of sorts.)

Back to the McCormick family.

The younger kids got a "group" present for Christmas. A wagon.

This wagon was the envy of every kid in town.

Most wagons were for babies—little red deals that were pretty flimsy when you got right down to it.

The McCormick Wagon was a well-built device that was about three times bigger than any wagon I'd ever seen, and it had stake sides that would lift in and out. You'd leave them in if you were pulling a load of something, but take them out if you wanted to put four kids on it and steer it down a small hill. There was just such a small hill up from Bob Forty's place. It made for an exciting ride. A little bit like the third downhill part of the roller-coaster up at Jantzen Beach.

The hill got boring.

"What," Matt McCormick asked, "if we took it down that big hill on the highway south of town?"

The other three of us (Pat Masterson, Turd, and me) looked at him as if he was crazy. We all agreed that it would be very dangerous because of the traffic on the two-lane, twisting highway. The Main Highway. The only highway. Highway 101.

"There's a place on the hill where we can look all the way into town and see if there's a bus or a big truck coming," he explained.

"But what about traffic behind us?"

"We'll be going almost as fast," Matt assured us.

That's all the persuasion it took. Talk about a long walk up Fool's Hill, we embarked upon it that very moment, pulling the wagon behind us. It took us a half an hour to reach the site which Matt had described. One could, indeed, see all the way to the Red Fire Gong in town, and I wished I was down there still talking with Winnie Lacey, magically restored to life. Instead, I was poised at the brink of a precipice getting ready to extinguish my own life.

It was a summer morning and there was hardly any traffic, so we decided to expand our delusion by going even farther up the hill.

There were lots of curves up there to make the ride more fun.

Fun.

I didn't want to do it, but was afraid to say anything. I didn't want the nickname CHICKEN SHIT or YELLOW BELLY screamed at me from a half mile away.

Turd, as it had turned out, was an accomplished wagon-steerer. Since he was smaller he could maneuver the handle better when it was folded back into the wagon for steering. So he was first, Pat Masterson was second, I was third, and Matt was next, in the very back of the wagon. We arranged our legs around the person in front like people do on a toboggan. We had seen only newsreel pictures of toboggans, by the way, since it never snowed in Port Orford.

Turd looked down the hill toward the first curve.

"I don't know," he said.

I was relieved. I thought the adventure was going to get called off—and it wouldn't be my fault for suggesting it. Pat Masterson's legs relaxed so I figured he felt the same way.

"Nothing to it!" Matt McCormick said from behind me. "Let's GO!"

Nothing to it.

The younger brother in front obeyed the older brother in back and we were off.

We were launched.

We started down the highway toward the first curve. The wagon accelerated toward it and Turd made an observation that made us all realize that we should have had a "Sub-String" discussion about how to stop the wagon if it started going too fast. The wagon never went too fast on the short hill by Forty's. The ride went rapidly, all right, but then the hill ended and you didn't have to worry about slowing down. It was automatic. This downhill highway situation was quickly shaping up into something very different.

"We're going too fast!" Turd yelled.

Wagons do not have brakes. In order to make the curve, Turd had to veer into the uphill lane. Luckily, there was nothing coming in that direction. He made the curve and headed into a short straightaway.

"We'd better stop!" Matt McCormick shouted from the back.

His brother summed up our situation in one word:

"*CAN'T!*" and we gained more speed in the straightaway.

"Everybody!" Matt yelled, "stick out your feet!"

We were going too fast. You don't stick your feet straight in front of you at 35 or 40 miles an hour. You'll break your leg in twelve places.

Pat Masterson made an observation that seemed very calm and controlled under the circumstances.

"The three of us behind Turd should have been sitting backwards in the wagon. That way we could have dragged our heels and slowed down."

True. But futile. Too late.

To make the next curve, the driver had to go into the loose gravel at the side of the road. The wagon threw up a tremendous cloud of dust, and stones banged into the metal bottom of the wagon. Turd, to his credit, retained control.

"STAY IN THE GRAVEL!" Matt ordered. "IT'LL SLOW US DOWN!"

"CAN'T," Turd screamed, once again. "*I CAN'T STEER IN IT!*"

We barely missed a guard rail on our side of the highway.

There are moments of calm in the eye of a storm. Also clarity. It became apparent that we were doomed. We were going to get hit by an oncoming car or truck. Or, more likely, the wagon was going to flip us onto the blacktop. Or the wagon was going to disintegrate. Failing any of these three, it was highly likely that we'd go off the road in one of the places where there wasn't a guard rail. The guard rails protected people from straight drops of 50, 60, or 100 feet. The unguarded portions were steep slopes with lots of bushes and trees—easily survivable in a car or a pickup, but doubtful in a runaway wagon.

On the next curve, still accelerating, the wagon cornered on two wheels.

"LEAN! *LEAN!*" Turd commanded. So we all leaned like sailors on the sailboats we had only experienced in the movie theater.

Then we saw it!

It was a guy named Merkle at the wheel of a State Highway Department truck toiling slowly up the hill toward us. We must have been going three times faster downhill than the truck was coming uphill.

Merkle, despite a big case of White Eyes, made a smart decision. Since it was obvious that we were barely in control, he drove to the center of the highway. That way we could pass to either the left or the right of the truck—whichever seemed the most likely to succeed. It was smart because, as it turned out, Turd couldn't make it to the right. Even as it was, we went into the gravel at the left-hand side of the highway. If there'd been another truck behind Merkle, we would have been finished. As I learned to say much later in Japan, it would have been: "*Sayonara, Boysan!*"

After that curve there was a long downward straightaway the rest of the distance into town. There was a gradual curve at the end of the straightaway but it appeared to be negotiable. If Turd could only hang on and maintain control for another few hundred yards, it looked like we might pull through. We might actually make it. I made a solemn pledge to myself to never ride in a wagon again. I think the others did the same.

Two things happened next. There is a perfectly focused freeze-frame in my mind of a pickup (with a lot of rust and an oxidized green paint job) speeding uphill from the gentle curve. Next to it was a late-model maroon-colored Buick sedan with California plates WHICH WAS TRYING TO PASS THE PICKUP!

Because of the concentration of the drivers in this latest in an ongoing series of Oregon-California Racing Contests, the people didn't recognize us immediately. All drivers teach themselves to recognize large items like cars, but not necessarily low-slung wagons with short fools in them.

The two vehicles sped at us, completely filling the highway from left to right.

There was a solid rock face to our left.

There was a steep hill to our right.

Mr. Turd McCormick, Wagonmaster, had no choice.

He steered us off the road to the right, careening through gravel again and throwing up dust.

And then suddenly the vibration of the speeding wagon stopped, the rattling and the noise of the rubber wheels—it all ceased. There was an eerie quiet. Nobody screamed. None of us shut our eyes. We simply flew. Like the boy on the Flying Carpet in the movie about Sinbad. Only

– 239–

this was McCormick's New Wagon. We didn't roll or tilt. We were in Correct Flying Attitude for a controlled approach (had we been a light airplane, that is). But we weren't in an airplane; we were in a wagon. Wagons do not have wings. Wagons do not, therefore, have good glide ratios. Single-engine airplanes, with their engines off, may have a 15-to-one glide ratio, which means that for every foot of altitude they lose, they go 15 feet forward. My retrospective calculation of the McCormick wagon suggests a glide ratio of 1 to .5. In other words, for every foot we dropped, we went six inches forward. In a ballistic curve, no less.

We looked good, though. The picture was good. The driver was looking bravely forward. The rest of us were likewise alert and erect. Pat Masterson's hands were on Turd's shoulders. Mine were on Masterson's. Matt's hands were on mine. The wagon flew, as I said, straight and level. No cart wheeling. No hopeless tangle of arms and legs like in movie cartoon cat-dog fights in clouds of dust. No screaming. Just like the song says: we "flew through the air with the greatest of ease!"

And, as the old joke goes: it wasn't the fall that did us any harm, it was the sudden stop!

Actually, nobody was killed.

The same kindly Spirits who gave me Two Home Runs had thoughtfully provided one of the biggest blackberry brambles in the history of Southern Oregon for the wagon to land on and in. The three-point (four-point) landing was cushioned by the vines and leaves.

Nobody was maimed.

Nothing was broken.

We sat on the ground in exactly the same attitude as our flight, each of us still in a row, hands on the shoulders of the person in front.

But we couldn't move. Millions of blackberry vine stickers held us captive.

Merkle stopped his truck and came back to look for us, fearing the absolute worst. The pickup and the Buick had stopped at the side of the highway.

The people looked down the hill in amazement because we had disappeared.

"Where ARE you?" a lady from the Buick hollered.

"Down here!" our muffled voices replied.

But they couldn't see us.

Merkle reached the blackberry thicket first and could barely see us deep in the vines.

"Don't move," he cautioned (as if we could move if we wanted to). "Don't move or you'll cut yourselves to ribbons."

From the taste of blood trickling into my mouth I could tell that I'd already cut myself into at least one ribbon.

My companions soon reported similar developments on their faces, hands, and arms. It hurt a little, but any pain was dimmed by our relief at not having been killed outright. Had we landed in rocks, there's a good chance we would have been.

"We're going to catch hell for what we've done to this wagon," Matt observed to his brother. Reality was starting to catch up with us.

"Boys," Merkle advised us. "Don't do anything, . . . you hear me?"

"Yes, we hear you."

"I've got to go to town for some cutters to get you out of there."

We said okay.

"Stay right where you are," he commanded.

Pat Masterson whispered just loud enough for us to hear: "Right, Merkle, you asshole. Like we have a choice."

Four other Highway Department guys and at least three towns-people came back with rakes and shrubbery cutters.

A State Patrolman showed up (but wouldn't approach too close to the blackberry bramble for fear of scratching his shiny black boots. He "supervised" from a distance.)

Gene White was there as well, naturally. We could hear his voice but couldn't see him. Turd wondered if we were going to be arrested. The consensus was that yes, we would be arrested. But that would only be the start of it. The rest of it was that we would all go to Reform School, the dreaded penitentiary for kids.

It took all the grown people nearly twenty minutes to carve their way in to us and cut us loose. Other volunteers with gloves pulled the vines out of the way as each one was cut. The final work had to be done very carefully to avoid scratching us up any further.

There was no whimpering or whining from any of us. The thrill of being alive was still there. Not only that, but the growing dread of a criminal trial and the sentence of nine years in Reform School. No more forts. No more swimming. No music listening at Moran's.

Dr. Baird was in the crowd with his medical bag open. As each of us was freed, from the back to the front, Dr. Baird silently put merthiolate and Band-Aids on our superficial wounds, a far cry from his Belleau Wood, but not ours.

Pat Masterson's mom was in the crowd. She took Pat's hand and they walked back into town.

The Highway Boys then freed the wagon and looked at it in amazement.

The paint wasn't even scratched. Nothing was bent or otherwise damaged. The wheels looked okay. The steering/towing handle worked. It was a little dusty, but that was it.

They put the wagon in the back of Merkle's truck and he drove the two McCormick boys to their house at the north end of town.

Dr. Baird dropped me off at the store.

I mentioned earlier that there is a silence after any calamity. A catastrophe can be violent, loud, and bloody, but immediately afterward, when things are sorted out and picked up and under control, there is a peculiar quiet.

There is no shouting.

Blame is not placed.

Retribution is not threatened.

No incriminating words are spoken.

It is merely silent.

I received a visual inspection from my parents. I had not been blinded or disfigured, merely scratched. So they went back to their store activities without a word.

I went to my room.

Somebody called my name. They said it was the phone.

It was Pat Masterson. He said it was only right that we should go Face the Music with the McCormicks.

We rode over on our bikes.

The McCormick boys were in the back yard sitting on a fence. Their mother was on a screened-in back porch doing a wash in the washing machine.

All boys whisper after a catastrophe.

They also whisper after they have gotten themselves into trouble. So this was double whispering. We did not wish to attract the attention of either Gods or Grownups. We wished to be very quiet and invisible.

For several minutes we simply waited. We didn't even whisper. We waited for Gene White and the siren of the Patrol Car. We waited for parents with switches and belts.

Finally, Matt said:

"We should take my brother, here, to Doyle's and buy him a coke or something."

Masterson and I agreed. Turd had clearly won his wings that day.

Jubilation usually attended such an event at Doyle's. Merriment. Horseplay. Loudness. A demand from a part-time waitress to "Hush." But the disaster was still too near; too proximate. Our miraculous delivery was too fresh.

We sat at a corner table like a bomber crew that had just returned from its first mission over Germany—having encountered skies full of ME-109s, flak, and terror. For the moment, at least, we were young kids with the eyes of men.

No adults ever said a word about the stupidity and dangerousness of what we'd done. We never got smacked, tried, convicted, or sentenced.

It was a subject that our little group (the Fool's Hill Survivors Association) discussed on numerous other occasions, however—in the mornings throwing jackknives at trees, over sandwiches at lunch, in the afternoons playing on the beach, or standing around after playing Kick-the-Can at twilight.

We always reached the same conclusion the one our parents would have wished.

It was a dumb-shit stunt.

Really and truly.

4ths of July

4ths of July were as memorable as Christmases or birthdays.

The 4th was a day for everybody in town to be outside and together.

Sunny skies. Not much wind. People together talking and laughing.

In the back of the volunteer fire station was a huge iron kettle like the ones you always see in cartoons about cannibals where the explorer is sitting in the pot with broth and carrots.

This kettle would be hauled to the beach by a gang of kids who looked as if they were playing Tug-of-War against it. We'd ease it down the grass slide into the driftwood and then position it on a fire pit near Battle Rock.

Once it was there, people (including Cliff who had once been a chef in a hotel) would fill the kettle with potatoes and onions, spices and clams and, in the course of an entire afternoon, would cook up the finest clam chowder in world history.

There were races and games on the beach and the launch of daytime rockets that would explode in loud bangs and huge black clouds of smoke in the sky.

Doc Pugh would swim around Battle Rock. It never failed to astonish everybody. He was Port Orford's own version of Clark Kent. One day a year he would reveal his True Power.

Then people would eat clam chowder until they fell down in the sand. Plus there were pies and cakes and washtubs filled with ice under which bottles of soda pop and beer were submerged.

It was Pat Masterson who figured out how to take a Hires Root Beer bottle (which was made of dark brown glass so that grownups couldn't really tell what was in it), dump out all the root beer, and then refill the container with a bottle of Blitz, Oregon's Finest Beer. Before the afternoon was over, several of us would be overcome with a need to take a nap right there on the beach, zonked.

In the evening, a fortune in fireworks would be shot off the top of Battle Rock.

This was great—the zooms and the roars, cascading showers of colored sparks, the rockets and other beautiful things that would arch up through the night and reflect in the water as they came back down and were suddenly extinguished in the ocean.

When the fireworks were all used up, the women and children would go home.

The men would stay for awhile and drink beer and whiskey around a fire.

I stayed for a while longer one time to watch my grandfather organize a bonfire. With dozens of grown men to carry logs, my grandfather's imagination went haywire.

It set a record. Four different ships radioed the Coast Guard station to see if there was a new forest fire or if a town was burning down. Although we were far over the horizon, they had seen the orange light reflected in the clouds.

Then the war came and the fires stopped. The fireworks stopped, too. Automobiles and trucks drove with their parking lights instead of headlights. Some had blue filters. Blackout curtains covered all the windows in town. And the beach became off limits at night. Later, there were Coast Guardsmen with police dogs and guns patrolling down there. As if the Japs would ever be close.

It was Grandpa Frank's last Night Bonfire.

"Bonfires are ten times better at night!" he would emphasize. He would then tack on another thought:

"The Nipponese Sons of Bitches!"

It was their fault and it made him sick.

Happy Days Are Here Again: Played Live

Everybody saw plenty of movies. A new one came almost every week to the little movie theater which was open Friday night and the weekend, with a matinee and evening show on both Saturday and Sunday. Friday was sometimes Bank Night and it was important to save your ticket stub because you might win dishes or something. A movie was really a movie in those days. As the sign outdoors said, there was a feature movie and Selected Short Subjects. The latter were very entertaining. There was always a cartoon and the latest Movietone Newsreel in which you could actually see some of the things that had been happening that you'd heard about on the radio but were having trouble imagining. The Blitz in London was one of them. You could hear all about it, but it wasn't until you saw the enormous fires with whole buildings ablaze and the firemen with their trucks and hoses that it became real. And the aerial pictures of the bomb damage. I really felt sorry for the children who were bundled up and taken away from their homes and parents to live in the English countryside. I worried that something like that could happen to me. There were also travelogues as part of the movie program. Or short, humorous pieces by Robert Benchley and another guy named Smith. And there were also Follow-the-Bouncing-Ball sing-alongs where everybody in the theater would sing out loud from the words on the screen. You really felt like you'd been somewhere after such a performance—one that featured a movie and maybe four or five different kinds of short subjects.

There was still a complete separation between what you saw on the screen and what happened in real life. Especially when it came to huge homes where there was an entryway and a big spiral staircase going up above and a butler to meet you at the door. There were no maids or butlers in our town. There were no chandeliers and no cars where the driver in a uniform sat on the other side of a piece of glass from the passengers. There were no fashionable night clubs with orchestras (with band members all in the same uniforms). Caviar was unknown. Champagne was known but rare, being restricted to a couple of bottles at a really important wedding. There were few real jewels on the hands or the throats of the town's women, rhinestones mostly. There were no tuxedos. So, when you saw these things you might recognize them but you knew they didn't exist. They *couldn't* exist. Who could afford that stuff? It was just a movie. Nobody had it that good. And all that clowning around between Nick and Nora Charles in *The Thin Man* movies, the joking and kissing and hugging, the affection? Unbelievable as a troll under a bridge.

Then, late in the summer of 1941, a yacht anchored in the harbor.

It was only 75 yards or so from the dock, so you could see aboard. You could see the decks and the white deck chairs. The main salon. This was not a trivial little boat. It was a ship. It was more than 200 feet long; maybe 250. It had several decks. It had a captain and a crew who stayed in uniform when they came ashore. My father sold them a lot of steaks and fresh fruit. They also requested flowers and my father didn't know what to say. He merely pointed toward the hills. No, no, they said. A florist's shop. These were as rare as chop suey joints between Bandon and Portland. Which is to say as rare as hens' teeth. The first night the ship was there nobody came ashore and live musicians played in the salon. Men in dinner jackets and women in long dresses danced to the music. A bunch of us sneaked down there and watched them with binoculars.

It was a scene that was exactly from the movies! Exactly! So it wasn't made up after all! There were people somewhere who actually lived that way. And that luxuriously. Here was proof. Before our very eyes! A white ship with strands of little white lights strung all over it, lights whose reflections twinkled in the calm waters of the harbor. Music which drifted up to the tops of the cliff. Handsome men and beautiful women. Dancing. Lordy-Lord!

The next day some of these people, in more casual clothes of course, walked up the hill and into town. They laughed. Real diamonds sparkled on the fingers of the women. The men wore gold wrist watches. Mrs. Studley, who had once been a manicurist, observed that some of the men were wearing clear fingernail polish! Unbelievable! These men smoked fragrant cigars, one of the half-smoked butts of which was discarded and snagged by Zoom Zumquist. The greatest smoke of his life, he reported later.

As these aristocrats were drifting around town, Moran happened to walk down to my father's store from his house. He had just ordered a dozen eggs when one of the men from the yacht entered the store to buy cigarettes or something.

The man froze for a second and then said, quite loudly:

"MORAN! My God, is that you?"

Moran tried to pretend he was somebody else, but the man laughed and slapped Moran's back.

"It really is you. How terrific!"

The man ran from the store and called one of his friends.

"Look who I've found! It's MORAN!"

The person hurried in. Two or three other people obviously knew Moran and were very glad to see him. They hadn't known what had happened to him. They were afraid he'd been caught when the Germans occupied Paris. Or lost in Africa. Or bombed in the Blitz. They invited him to dinner. Then they resumed their walk.

Moran seemed embarrassed. Nobody else was. We were pleased at his ever-increasing celebrity status. His notoriety.

Henri came in the store.

Moran said something to him in French which made Henri laugh.

Then he said, for all of us to hear:

"Henri, I will be happy to give you five dollars if you will be kind enough to unlock your garage later tonight, take out the Prum-Yay, and drive me down to the dock so that I can have dinner with some of my friends."

"A pleasure," Henri said, "but the five dollars is not necessary."

"I will haggle with you later," Moran said. "Shall we say seven o'clock?"

"Agreed."

"Ah Byahn Toe," I think they said, and left.

Later, at the appointed time, Henri (dressed in his best black Sunday Suit, because he would never dream of driving the perfect automobile in anything less a perfect costume) drove to Moran's house and picked him up. Half the town was on hand. Dozens of people lined the road down to the dock. It looked as if President Roosevelt himself might be making a special visit.

Moran, for the benefit of the crowd, asked Henri if they could put the top down. Henri obliged. Then Moran stood up in the back of the car and gestured grandly at the crowd. He was dressed like one of those guys in the movies—one of the heroes. He wore a white dinner jacket and tuxedo pants. He wore a cummerbund, probably the only one in the county. He looked like a movie star. He acted like a movie star.

The crowd cheered him as he went past.

They didn't hide behind windows in envy. They lined the way. They got a big kick out of it. They enjoyed it, his being dressed that way and going down to a big yacht in the Prum-Yay. Who else in town could carry that off? Who else could go down to that ritzy yacht and look and act like those people? Only Moran. So nobody envied him.

Like I said, they actually cheered.

And the people on the yacht had fun with it, too. As the magnificent Prum-Yay came down the road to the dock, they all went EW and AH and murmured at its strange beauty. They were as amazed by the car as we had been amazed by the yacht the day before.

When they recognized Moran standing in the back with his arms outstretched in greeting, they, too, cheered. They applauded.

The musicians came on deck with their instruments and played "Happy Days Are Here Again!" with a lot of oom-pahs and trombone slides, up-tempo. It was better than a scene from a movie!

The light was perfect. No longer bright daylight, but not dark either. All the colors of the car were jewel-like and astonishing. A part of a moon was out. There was no wind. It was calm as you please. Picture it: twinkly lights on the ship and nicely dressed people in movie clothes.

A little launch then motored over to pick up Moran from the bottom of the ladder.

The people along the road to the dock and those of us actually on the dock applauded the scene. The people on the yacht applauded back. They applauded Henri and the Prum-Yay, they applauded the people, and they applauded the town and the weather and the darkening night.

Moran went aboard and the musicians returned to the main salon and played "The Anniversary Waltz." You could have cried for the beauty of it all. Old Lady Betts did.

We walked back up the hill.

My mother said:

"You know something? We ought to move to San Francisco or someplace. We ought to get out of here."

I suppose some other people felt the same way.

But they didn't leave.

Moran stayed aboard the yacht that night and didn't go home until the next afternoon.

After Pearl Harbor, Moran paid somebody to look after his place and disappeared. But he was back in a couple of months wearing a Navy Lt. Commander's uniform with the twisty-snake insignia on it—the symbol of a doctor. It turned out that Moran was a well-known Boston surgeon who had also studied engineering.

I was not surprised. Dr. Baird and Doc Pugh were not surprised.

Everybody else was surprised.

Debacle #2— The Rifle

Debacle Number Two followed roughly the same pattern as the earlier one.

I tried to do something against my own better judgment.

My grandfather had made a statement that any time I thought I was big enough and strong enough to perform a particular test I could have his Spanish-American War rifle. My grandfather had taught me how to stand at Attention and how to stand At Ease. He had given me marching instructions and would call cadence as I marched around his back yard with a broom as a rifle. I was taught to perform the Manual of Arms. I would, however, Present Broom! at that command. I learned Column Left, Column Right, and Double Time.

The deal was this: any time I thought I was ready to shoulder the rifle and march in a correct military fashion the complete distance from my grandfather's house across town to my father's store, the rifle was mine the moment I completed the journey.

The rifle was very heavy. About once a week I would ask for it to be taken from the rifle cabinet so I could put it on my shoulder. It hurt. I would march around the house with it and wonder if I was ready. Could I bear the suffering that day? The answer was always no. I knew I couldn't. I would only humiliate myself by trying and failing.

One morning I had said something out of line and my mother (yet again) slapped my face. This happened frequently when she'd lose her temper. I hated it. And I hated her for it. I hated it especially because I couldn't do anything about it. I couldn't slap her back. She'd have killed me. At least that's what I thought.

This particular day I was feeling frustrated by this treatment and decided I could take it out on the rifle! I could carry the goddamned thing across town in my wrath.

I went to my grandfather's house and said I was ready.

I was not ready.

But I said I was ready and he couldn't tell the difference between Real Ready and Slapped Angry.

He gave me the rifle and I marched away.

I marched out to the main street. I didn't look back to see if my grandfather was watching me. I knew he would be. Because the deal was that I had to march like a soldier all the way—Hut, two, three, four; Hut, two, three, four! All the way home. His cadence rang in my mind. I marched to it.

People saw me.

I hoped nobody would be around, but they were.

Two men standing in front of the Pastime yelled in to their buddies. The men came outside to see.

Somebody started whistling: "When Johnny Comes Marching Home."

All the others picked it up.

It helped for quite a number of paces. Maybe fifty. Maybe sixty.

I pressed ahead. The rifle was killing me. It was eating my shoulder, biting it, gnawing into it. The muscle was starting to cramp. But I kept the pace. Then the realization came to me. I was beyond the Point of No Return. I was more than half way. It would have been honorable to have gone a third of the way and then marched back. That would have been acceptable. It would have been honorable. It would have been regarded as a free trial. It could have been reckoned as a test in preparation for the real event.

Now I was committed. But I knew it couldn't be done. The rules forbade my shifting the rifle to my other shoulder. It had to be accomplished in a Military Manner. I was sick at the thought of the defeat I had brought on myself.

The whistling continued. It was also coming from the other side of the highway. Other bystanders had picked it up. I was starting to falter.

A thought came to me!

The Wood Hauling Trick! If I closed my eyes, I could rest!

I drew a careful bead on my target, the store about two city blocks away, then closed my eyes and kept moving. I had found a new source of energy. I sprang forward. The onlookers saw this and recognized it. They were encouraged. A couple of people clapped. A lady cheered.

It helped. I flicked my eyes open for a tenth of a second, just like a camera shutter, to verify my bearings. Then I shut them again, against the reality and against the pain. I was okay in the dark. It was like bed at night. It was like rest. I was proceeding as a robot. Few instructions. Only walk. Walk in a straight line. Keep walking. Rest and keep going. Nearly there. Nearly there. It can be done after all. Ground is being covered even in the dark, even during the Rest.

"When Johnny Comes Marching Home Again, Hoo-Rah, Hoo-Rah," the whistling continued even louder. They tell me a couple of cars stopped. During an interval when my eyes were closed tight. They stopped mostly to avoid hitting me, but also to observe. I was heading in a correct bee-line. Every twenty paces or so I would blink and snap another frame of reality, I would expose another crucial piece of Mind Film as I pressed ahead and rapidly ran out of heart and energy for the task.

The last snapshot failed to take note of a tin can that had been used in a Kick-the-Can session the night before. It was an oversized juice can. It was in my path. A murmur rose from my audience two or three steps before I stumbled over it.

They must have realized that my eyes were clamped shut.

I fell over it. I fell forward. I went sprawling into the gravel. I saved the rifle from harm by turning as I fell and landing on my side. The fall was noisy. The aftermath was very quiet. I was cut in several places from the fall. Cut and bruised.

Grownups ran over to retrieve the rifle and inspect me for damage. But they didn't say anything.

I glanced toward the store and saw my father standing there.

T.J. Collins helped me up and picked some of the gravel from my arm.

My grandfather arrived. He retrieved the rifle and went back home with it. That was the rule. There was no payoff for anything less than complete success. That was the first rule in the Tichenor Book of Rules.

The bystanders evaporated without a word. The town was silent. My father stood with his arms folded, looking at me with the stern, judgmental look that I had seen before when I failed to live up to expectations. I also think he took this personally as yet another defeat at the hands of the Tichenors. Another Quick had been discredited.

As with the other Debacle, I didn't cry. It was too overwhelming and shocking an event to be wept at. I was hurt. My shoulder was cramped. I had inadvertently created a spectacle. I was a loser.

T. J. asked me:

"You want me to walk back home with you? You need any help?"

"No," I said, "no, thanks."

And then he said in a low voice, practically a whisper, that nobody else could have heard:

"Fuck it," he hissed.

I looked up at him and he continued.

"That's right. Fuck it. Piss on it! It's not worth it. That rifle's not worth a shit anyway. It'd knock me down if I tried to shoot it. It's five times heavier than it needs to be."

I kept listening and he kept talking.

"I've got a 30-30 Winchester carbine that I'll bet you could have marched all the way to Silver Springs with. So just fuck it and don't worry about it."

It was some help, but not enough.

I limped back home for the traditional Loser's Welcome: silence and indifference.

As with the earlier calamity with the beach ball, no mention was ever made of the incident.

No words were ever spoken.

Just looks.

Just those looks.

1942

In January, we stuck a Japanese flag on the Dutch East Indies. The bazooka antitank weapon was developed and so was napalm.

Singapore got a pin in February and the Japanese expanded to the Solomon Islands in March. Bataan surrendered. There was a big morale-lifter in April when Jimmy Doolittle bombed Tokyo with a bunch of B-25 Mitchell bombers.

Grandpa Frank was saddened when a lot of West Coast Japanese Americans were rounded up and sent to concentration camps. Said it wasn't right. Other people disagreed and smashed their Noritake china.

Burma fell to the Japanese in May and, one afternoon after school, I was listening to radio Tokyo and they announced that the aircraft carrier *Lexington* was sunk by Japanese aircraft. I reported this as hot news and was told it was Japanese propaganda. It turned out to be true, however. The war seemed to be taking a lot out of my grandfather. He was slowing down a great deal and acting weak.

I took over the maps and the flags after June 6th. My first duty, on June 7th, was to place Japanese flags on Attu and Kiska in the Aleutian Islands. It scared us plenty to know that Japanese soldiers were in a part of Alaska. On June 21, I placed Nazi flags in Libya and El Alamein in North Africa.

Women who went into the Army were called WAACS (Women's Auxiliary Army Corps) and the one who went into the Navy were called WAVES (Women Accepted for Voluntary Services).

Later in the year U.S. flags could be placed in Casablanca, Oran, and Algiers. It was the first hint of some kind of a swing.

The Office of Economic Stabilization started and salaries were limited to $25,000 a year. Zoom Zumquist said he would jump off the dock every day for 25 grand a year—off the far end and swim all the way back to the ladder. Even though it would cut into his drinking somewhat. And even though he lacked Doc Pugh's *magique* (Frenchie's word, but we all knew what it meant.)

Tire rationing started. White pennies were minted, zinc-coated steel ones. For 1942 only. I saved a zillion and then figured everybody else saved a zillion, too. I quit. Now try to find just one.

Gasoline was rationed. You had to have a letter pasted on the inside of your windshield. X = unlimited gasoline. A = 4 gallons per week.

B and C were a lot less. T = truckers who got all the fuel they wanted. A 35-mile-per-hour speed limit was imposed for highways.

Movies: I remember *Casablanca, Bambi,* and *Mrs. Miniver* most clearly, but there were also *The Magnificent Ambersons, The Postman Always Rings Twice, This Gun for Hire, The Palm Beach Story, Wake Island, The Road to Morocco,* and *The Fleet's In.* It was the year of the movie *Holiday Inn,* in which Bing Crosby first sang "White Christmas."

Other popular songs: "That Old Black Magic," "Tangerine," "Springtime in the Rockies," "I Had the Craziest Dream," "I Left My Heart at the Stagedoor Canteen," "Don't Get Around Much Anymore," "My Devotion," "Serenade in Blue," "One Dozen Roses," "(I've Got Spurs that) Jingle Jangle Jingle," "Perdido," "Paper Doll," "This is the Army, Mr. Jones," "When the Lights Come on Again (All Over the World)," and "You'd Be So Nice to Come Home To."

Some guys over at RCA-Victor took a record of Glenn Miller's "Chattanooga Choo Choo" from the year before and sprayed gold paint on it. They presented it to him in recognition of One Million records having been sold. So that's where that idea came from.

The Red Skelton Show started on radio, sponsored by Raleigh cigarettes. So did Johnny Presents (Philip Morris) in which Johnny, the Bellhop, runs all over the place shouting (Caaaalllll for Philllllllip Moooooriiiiis!) which a lot of people found a little irritating. Also new was The Great Gildersleeve (Kraft Cheese), Ellery Queen (O! Henry candy bars), and The Thin Man (Woodbury Soap).

492 people died in Boston's Coconut Grove nightclub fire.

Speaking of death, Fletcher either fell off or jumped off the cliff above the dock and landed in the rocks of Nelly's Cove. Women and ardent Christians believed that he must have accidentally fallen. Fishermen postulated that he not only jumped but took a running start. Both opinions were based on faith, Frank said, not facts. No note was found.

"Victory Gardens" became a big deal in the U.S., while British people called their program "Dig for Victory," and planted vegetables in their back yards.

K rations were packed for the military by the Wrigley Company. Uncle (Corporal) Harvey said that K rations contained "defense" biscuits, compressed Graham crackers, canned meat (Spam), tablets of sugar, four cigarettes, a fruit bar, a packet of lemon-juice powder, a stick of Wrigley chewing gum, soluble coffee, bouillon powder, chocolate, and some other stuff. (My dad learned after the War that Instant Maxwell

House had its beginnings in that soluble coffee for K rations.) The joke was that if you got drafted then you never got a job remotely like the one you had when you were a civilian. Do you remember what my Uncle Harvey did in Portland? Right. A taxicab driver. So did they make him a driver in the Army? No. They sent him to Cooking School. "Hooray," said my Aunt Hester, but she later changed her tune. She said he didn't learn to cook anything worth having. Besides, all the recipes were for 200 people.

Kellogg's Raisin Bran was introduced by the Kellogg Company. It was 10.6 percent sugar.

Sunbeam bread was introduced with the "Miss Sunbeam" trademark.

(My friend Bill Kurchak said that when he was growing up in Ontario, Canadian boys believed that enriched white breads, from any manufacturer, would turn you queer. The chemicals caused it. That was the word.)

Which reminds me of the chemistry set I received about that time. Nothing blew up, but I made an absolutely permanent black ink that got all over everything and, being indelible and eternal, would not come out under any circumstances.

The Flag & the Rose

In the last week of May 1942, my grandfather became very sick and went to the Veterans Hospital in Portland. I took the bus to Portland with my mother and we stayed at Aunt Anna's place. Her husband (my Uncle Bob) was by then an Army Air Corps Captain far away in England. It was their young son Charles ("Skippy," like our dog) to whom my parents had given Bruno, the odious Bear. But you knew that.

I went to the hospital a couple of times with my mother and all my aunts were present: Anna, Margaret, and Marianne. It was one of the two places upon which I based my dislike of all hospitals. It and Bandon. The smell was so pronounced. All the men I saw were so painfully sick that it was distressing.

As you know, there is uphill sick when people can start sitting up straight in bed and smile, however weakly. Then there is downhill sick when people are lying down flat, moaning and wheezing. There were lots of moaners and wheezers at the Veterans Hospital on the days I was there. It was quiet and there weren't any flowers, as if they weren't manly things to have. The doctors and nurses were stiff and abrupt, hurrying from one place to another without apparent enthusiasm, just hurrying. Like hurrying around until quitting time and then streaking home. Grandpa Frank was going downhill. The women kept saying how great he looked and muttered things like:

"You're looking a lot stronger today, Dad."

"Your color's a lot better today, Dad."

He knew he looked like shit. He was yellow. And he got yellower and yellower each time I saw him. How could my mother and my aunts look at him with a straight face and say his color was better. It was better than green maybe, but that was about all you could say for it.

And also, every day, he was scrunched deeper into the bed and farther down on his pillows. It was no longer the semblance of sitting up in bed (which he tried to do on the first day), he was now lying on it. He was literally sinking—into the bed, nearly out of sight, as if pulled down by an invisible shark.

Sunday was worse than Saturday. Monday was worse than Sunday, and so forth.

The women acted like agitated birds, as if their vitality and chirpiness would rub off on the room or infuse their father. It was the appearance of life. A comic dance.

But the magic wasn't working. It was weak medicine. Insufficient voodoo.

On Tuesday he was almost out of sight. The deeper he sank during those days I visited, the farther away from him I stood. Finally, I was in a corner trying not to look at him at all. The women flapped around, various of them sitting on chairs, perching on the edge of his bed, standing up all of a sudden. Getting new positive ideas. Saying them. Getting agreement from the others.

"When you're well, dad, we'll do this . . ."

"When you're well, dad, we'll do that . . ." This and that.

He looked at them with his motionless yellow face and his yellow eyes.

He still had his voice. Not like the old days. Nothing like loud or booming. It was soft. Quiet.

"Please," he said politely.

"Yes. Yes. Yes. Yes." each different one said, eager to please.

"Go away for a little bit."

Clucking. Clucking. In-throat noises from all four of them. Red Chicken noises. Sitting-on-eggs murmurs from them. Reluctance.

We all started to leave.

"Not you, Johnny," he said. "I want to talk to you."

The women paused, their wings at their sides.

"Shoo," he told them and they left.

From his eyes I knew I was supposed to come closer. So I went closer.

I was next to his bed.

"You may sit down, if you like," he said.

I leaned against the bed. I realized that he was easier to be with if I was closer. I had been afraid across the room, but the fear went away when I got close enough to realize that this was the same person with the short-wave radio and the maps and the flags. He was still the Justice of the Peace and the performer of marriages. He could sentence people to jail or prison. He was entitled to the use of two coats of arms on his stationery. He was the guy who had been made a United States Marshal during World War One and arrested the pro-German guy, Albers, of Albers Milling.

Frank. Bonfire producer. Fisherman in Hubbard Creek. Town leader.

"I am going to be operated on tomorrow," he said. "I haven't told your mother or the girls yet because they'll go into a tizzy."

He looked at me carefully. Probably to see if I was going into a tizzy. I wasn't.

He continued:

"Did they give you ether when you had your tonsils out in Bandon?"

"Yes, they did."

"Do you remember going to sleep?"

"Yes. The ether smelled awful and they poured it on a mask-like thing."

"But you finally drifted off to sleep, right?"

"Yes."

It came back to me. The point at which I had quit struggling. When the ether captured me. It took over my chest and my stomach and I got very dizzy. I grayed out and got tingly. Then I blacked out.

"It will be very easy," he said. "To go to sleep under the anesthesia. But I'm going to tell you something."

I looked at him. I listened for him to tell me something.

"I'm not going to wake up."

This remark didn't alarm me. I had been watching the decline and so what he said was not solemn. It seemed to be a logical assessment.

"I am going to God's Country."

This startled me. Not because of its reference, but because this was always the way he described his home town, Port Orford, to tourists and other visitors to the place.

He would hook his thumbs in his vest, stand very erect, and say that to them with all seriousness.

"Yes," he would say, looking toward the ocean and the distant mountains rising in the south. "This is truly God's Country."

Now he was lying very flat and quiet and saying the same thing, but meaning something else—perhaps the heaven directly above Port Orford, above the dock and the cannery, where the smoke rose skyward from the Indian's burial place.

"Don't worry about this, will you?" he asked.

I was silent.

"Try not to let it bother you. These things happen. It won't be so bad at all. I can think of lots worse things, can't you?"

I could think of freezing to death in Leningrad and eating Wallet Soup and one of Mrs. Bennett's birds. I could visualize falling off a cliff. I could imagine getting my head knocked off with a load of logs. I could imagine being the 14th person in that stack of 20 enemies that Mr. Fletcher's war arrow went straight through.

He kept talking.

"Do me a favor, will you?"

"Sure."

"If I'm right—and I'm positive I am—there will be a ceremony in a few days in which you will be asked to throw a rose and accept a flag. That's all I want you to do. Do you remember about standing At Attention?"

"Of course."

"Please show me."

Stomach in. Chest out. Heels together. Hands clamped to my sides. Chin back and eyes straight ahead. He had taught me this in case I would ever have to be in the Army.

"Perfect," he said. "That's all you have to do. You will look just fine. Just the way I would like you to look. At Ease."

Feet apart. Hands behind back. I relaxed.

"Ten-*HUT!*" he said, suddenly, catching me off guard.

I snapped back to attention.

He smiled.

"You've got it perfectly. Do that for the flag part. Right up to where they hand you the flag."

"On a stick?" I asked him, reverting back to At Ease.

"No. Folded. Folded a special way. A military way. It will look like a triangle. Like a triangular pillow. So you accept the flag, tuck it under your left arm, and then salute. Try it."

I stood at attention once again, pretended to tuck something under my left arm, and saluted.

"Very good," he said. "Do it exactly that way."

I looked at him and remembered the time I had let him down. The time I tried to carry the rifle across town from his place to the store, marching correctly with the rifle on my shoulder, and didn't make it. The rifle had defeated me and its weight had collapsed me. I feared another similar disgrace. A public disgrace. Humiliation.

He must not have noticed my look of sadness and defeat.

"They're going to shoo the visitors out in a few minutes," he continued. "Have the girls come back in and then you wait outside. Okay? Don't come back in. We'll just say our good-byes right now and that will be that. All right?"

He had become brisk and efficient.

He stuck a hand out from under the cover and I took it. I shook his hand and we said good-bye. I immediately left the room and did not look back.

– 259–

I sent the women inside and sat in the hall.

I could hear the noises of protest and unbelieving, the no, no, no's.

Visiting hours were over.

We were ushered off the floor by a nurse.

The next day was Wednesday, June 3rd. Everybody was ready to scurry to the hospital and sit in the waiting room during the operation. I begged off and was allowed to stay at Anna's house with her son's sitter, a next-door-neighbor lady.

"I'm sure your grandfather will be all right," she said.

We were standing in the kitchen where she'd come in through the back door.

It was just something people said. Everybody was trained to say things like that.

If she'd had the chance to take one look at him, however, as I had the day before, her tune wouldn't have been quite so cheerful.

"He's a goner," I said to her, matter-of-factly.

"What?" she exclaimed, thinking I was being callous or indifferent, or maybe just impertinent.

"He's what Dr. Pugh in our town described one time as A Gone Goose," I explained. "My grandfather and I had a talk last night. He knows it."

She busied herself by cleaning up the breakfast dishes in the sink.

"He's going to God's Country, that's what he said."

Knives and forks clattered out of her hands.

He died at 10:30 that morning. On the operating table. Like he said.

We went back on the bus the next morning, Thursday, and my mother said nothing the whole trip. Just looked out the window mostly.

Saturday was to be the day.

There were flowers in the church.

There were solemn men from out of town. Men with whom he'd served as a U.S. Marshal during the Wilson administration. People from the capital where he had been a state representative in the legislature. Officials from the Woodmen of the World, with whom he'd been an important organizer.

Words were spoken, not a single one of which I remember. I was numbed by the sight of my mother sobbing. I had never seen it before. Sniffles about rain, of course, but not sobbing. And I never saw it again. The one cry. And it was one of those open-casket deals and I had never seen a dead person before, let alone my grandfather. I could tell from the very back of the church that they had done something to his yellow skin.

Makeup. Now he looked like a stone man. Once I realized that fact, I was more relaxed. Yes, I would have to walk past the casket (this had already been explained to me as part of the drill), I would have to walk past, but could pretend that it wasn't a person lying there, but a statue, a white statue with one of my grandfather's blue suits on it. With his best tie and vest and with the key chain draped across with that evil tooth on it. (But the gold watch was not connected to the end and hidden in the watch pocket of the vest. It wasn't there because he had willed it to me and it was mine to keep.) That's how I survived it, by thinking of stone. It also helped me to endure the kisses pressed on its face by my mother and my aunts.

I was never so relieved as when they closed the lid and eight men carried the casket to a hearse.

Only the hearse and its cargo went to the top of the steep road to the family cemetery because there is no parking at the top. Other people, including my father, parked down below in a field next to the road to the Coast Guard Station.

What a day! It was gloriously clear and sunny, with blue skies and only a little wind. By the time we climbed the hill, the arrangements had been made at the site. The casket was in place above the grave and was ready to be lowered. It was covered with a United States flag, its colors brilliant in the sunlight. A firing party of Coast Guardsmen and their officer (a Lieutenant Senior Grade—two wide gold stripes) stood next to some trees. The minister mumbled something that nobody heard. I was in the very front, closer than anybody, and should have heard him.

"Ready, Aim, *Fire!*" the officer then commanded.

The volley of rifle shots was very loud and echoed in the distance. Off the cliffs probably. Above the sea. I remembered the happy day of Major Bentley's make-believe funeral and the pistol shots in the woods.

Again.

The command was repeated.

The rifles fired.

And again.

Three volleys. Then a bugler, luckily an expert at it, played "Taps." It was well done.

The Lieutenant and one of the men then removed the flag from the coffin and folded it in military fashion, moving back and forth from one another to get it just so, in a neat triangle.

The Lieutenant approached me with an apprehensive look. As if maybe I would collapse under the weight of an imaginary rifle. Or cry or something.

I snapped to attention. To his relief.

I accepted the flag. He took one step back and stood at attention.

I saluted smartly.

He returned the salute.

The hearse man in the black suit released the tension on the straps beneath the casket and it dropped noiselessly to the bottom of the grave.

My mother handed me a red rose and indicated without words that it was to be thrown into the grave.

I tossed it and it landed on the top of the casket.

I could then relax. Only then. I had accepted the flag without a screw-up. I had scored a direct hit with the rose. A lot could have gone wrong, I realized. My hand could have sailed over my head on the salute. I could have tried to stand at attention and fallen down instead. I could have dropped the flag on the ground and ruined everything. But it panned out and I was not an embarrassment to myself and the others. I was not an embarrassment to my grandfather. The sun was now all the brighter for this success. The holly tree was greener. The distant ocean was as blue as blue was ever likely to get and the breakers couldn't have been whiter or more perfect as they formed, crested, broke, and fanned out on Agate Beach.

I was smiling. This was as perfect as Mrs. Lenieve's leaving money for people to have a drink and something to eat.

It was a God's-Country kind of day that my grandfather would have hoped for and wished that more people besides me could have smiled about.

In those days, the road up the hill to the cemetery was covered by a canopy of dense evergreen limbs which formed a shadowy tunnel in which you always became aware of the dampness of the earth and the air and could smell the trees. There was a pronounced ocean smell in there, out of the sun, and you knew you were on the coast. Coming back from the graveside service, a lot of the adults started to cry in there. As if it afforded them privacy to do that. Secrecy.

They cried and dabbed their eyes and I sprang past them, not to be dragged down by it.

I shot down the path, onto the road and into the light, past the cars, and the edge of the field. Going. Flying.

I didn't pause.

I knew that I wouldn't stop and wait for the slow column of mourners. My mourning was essentially over.

Grandfather's yellow downward slide had been checked and, as he'd said, he had gone to sleep.

They had buried his statue and thrown in the first handfuls of dirt and I, luckily, was speeding away from all of it and them, the flag clutched to me, and running toward town, running like the wind, running like an Indian, running like I used to run with Winnie. Alive I went. Hurtling at an angle, but in control. Breathing all that good air in and out, tearing around the corner at the bottom of the hill so fast that I raised dust just like McCormick's wagon the day we could have been killed but weren't.

It was the best part of the funeral. The running with the flag. And I ran all the way back to my room.

Fletcher had fallen downward like a stone from the cliff. Frank was raised upward like wind above the hill.

The Very Near Passing of the Prum-Yay

Henri came into my father's store with an amazing announcement.

"I am giving you the Prum-Yay."

My father placed his hands on the counter next to the cash register.

"You're what?" my father asked.

Try to imagine a strong French accent.

"You have given me a lot of credit," Henri continued. "I owe you a lot of money. I can't pay you the money. So I must give you the Prum-Yay. The Automobile."

A couple of other customers gasped at this idea. The *Automobile!*

"I can't take your good car. You don't owe me that much money. I couldn't accept it. It wouldn't be fair."

"You must," Henri said. "I don't know what else to do. I owe you the money and I must pay you."

– 263–

"You can wait," my father said. "You can wait until things are better. Or you can give me the other car, the what-do-you-call-it."

"The Dooz-Yem."

"Correct."

"Well, I can't. It has blown up. Exploded."

"It can be fixed," my father said.

"Never," Henri said. "It is destroyed."

(When Henri said "Never," it came out "Nev-Air," which always sounded to me like the name of a fancy resort or a type of sailboat.)

"You are a kind friend to say this to everybody, that things will get better. Then we can all pay you back. But I must leave. I must return to Nova Scotia. My mother is very sick and there is nobody to care for her but a cousin. Who is also old."

Henri looked very pitiful.

I happened to be standing in the corner, next to the egg crates.

I knew about Henri's car. Who didn't? It was possibly the greatest treasure on the Oregon coast!

Hey! Wait!

I never told you what it looked like, did I?

Jesus. It was a 1934 Pierce Arrow roadster with a special paint job that had been executed by an automobile-painting wizard in Portland. It had a great number of colors, not just one or two. Some were the colors of jewels. Deep colors. Many coats of lacquer. Colors you could fall into. Body panels of dark topaz. Doors of sapphire. Front fenders of emerald. Two ruby doors. It was kept in a special garage. It never had a speck of dust on it. As I said, Henri would drive it only on Sundays, but never far and not for long. It had ornamental trim paint. Pinstriping. Curlicues. It was a thing of great and masterful beauty. There was brasswork on the car, and chrome, yellow wheels, and two colors of leather in the seats. It was always absolutely dustless and methodically waxed. It was perfect. It was guarded and protected like the last of an exotic species of parrot (which it resembled, at least in the colors).

The story was that he would return to a small town in Nova Scotia with great fanfare in this gorgeous automobile and marry the town belle. I mean, who could resist such a man with such a car? And then use the car for feast days and special events.

The car was legendary.

It was a museum piece. It brightened the Sunday of every townsperson who watched it murmuring past. Crawford Smith commented one day that it was almost like a circus, all by itself, especially with Frenchie, all dressed up, driving it.

Now you can understand better why it was such a big deal for Moran to ride down to the dock in it to see those friends of his on the yacht.

Henri went back to an apartment he rented from my father to wring his hands and wonder what to do.

A telegram arrived. His mother had miraculously recovered so he didn't need to return. And Lou Monescu fixed the Dooz-Yem for $18.00. It hadn't blown up after all. And, after several excellent catches in a row, Henri paid back my father.

Lou Monescu— Love, Grease, and the Enemy Plane

Louise was stocky and sort of ape-like and maybe 5' 5" in her heavy work shoes. Her eyebrows grew together like a thick black mustache above her eyes and that eyebrow nearly reached her hairline. Her thick curly hair (like pubic hair, Crawford remarked) was cut short like a man's. She went to the same barber shop as the men, not Thelma's little beauty parlor. Her features were coarse and heavy and her teeth were yellowish. She ran the Liberty Garage and directed two other mechanics, skinny sullen little men who, after years of being shouted at in Romanian, finally caught on to some of the meanings, most of which had to do with hurrying up. All three of them wore blackened overalls and worked in one or the other of the grease pits in the garage. Nobody ever saw Louise in a dress. She may not have owned a dress. She talked dirtier than anybody else in town. This was because her command of English swear words was complete and could also be augmented with foreign words that nobody else could understand, but sounded wonderfully dirty and sinister.

Phil Beakman didn't want to pay his garage bill one time and was called a "Two-bit Cheep Nozdraknian Cack-zucker!" whom she, incidentally, intended to kill with a tire iron before "sun goes down today." He paid with two twenties that he fished out of his shoe.

She was also more creative than anybody else in suggesting impossible sexual things for people to do with their carburetors and their transmissions, often in combinations with farm animals or their own pet dogs. It was frequently enough to reduce a sailor or a tough mill worker to respectful silence. She would also invoke God and certain saints to somehow piss into her enemy's blood and turn their brains to shit.

Lou swore better than men, worked with men, and drank with them in the Pastime which was the noisiest tavern in town and the most prone to scuffles. If I was going down to Pugh's drugstore it was necessary for me to walk (or run) past the garage. I would never go across the street to avoid the place, of course, because I took a perverse pleasure in being caught by her. Louise loved me. Not kids in general, just me. To death, she said. She would wipe her hands on a rag and touch my snowy blonde hair as if she'd never seen anything like it—like I was something religious that stepped out of a painting in a cathedral. She would hold my face in her hands and declare that I had to be an Angel from Heaven. She smelled of grease and kerosene and gasket sealant. On the one hand these encounters frightened me because of their intensity. It was like having a zoo animal (an Ontz, perhaps) sneak out of its cage and grab you unexpectedly and act like it might eat you or bite you. This fear was offset, however, by the tenderness of the woman. Her voice changed altogether (to a girl's voice, some people said) and she would coo and sing a lullaby to me—a lullaby in a foreign language about a bird in a summer tree. I was the only person in town to stimulate this soft-heartedness, this affection. She would wail that she wished I was her son. She would kneel and hug me and kiss my face. Her brown eyes would fill up with tears and then overflow onto me and her overalls. It was terribly spooky but a lot of fun, exotic you might say. It was why I would never cross the street to avoid her. More than once, I remember, I would pause long enough for her to turn around and spot me and then I would always stumble and linger just long enough to get caught and hear her say "I *Loff* You," and go through the rest of the routine in which I would be likened to pots of syrup and the yellow flowers in the church-yard of her unpronounceable village somewhere.

It struck me even then as odd that Lou belonged to the place and was a part of it and a fixture in it and that my mother, whose ancestors had founded the place, was not a part of it even though she had grown up there. Louise came from someplace in Europe with dark forests and other intense short people who played violins and drank wine from jugs. Yet she "fit." My mother didn't. My mother and Eve Doyle were the town beauties. They would dress up and pose for one another in Eve's posh apartment living room.

My sister summed them up the best when she asked me one time: "Do you remember how once a year mom and Eve would get all gussied up in fashionable black dresses with pearls, or dove gray dresses with violet corsages, gun-metal silk hose, hats with veils, false eyelashes, and take the bus to San Francisco and be Real People for a few days? Oh, yes, with their silver fox fur scarves. You loved the feel of the fur, but not the sight of the ugly little faces of the foxes. Do you remember?"

Well, sure. More than that, I remember precisely where the little foxes lived in a white box with tissue paper in it on a closet shelf in my parent's bedroom. I would sneak in there and open the box and then either close my eyes and pet the fur or put my hand over the glass eyes of the faces in order to avoid their dead stares while I stroked the rest of their soft bodies.

My mother could not be hugged because it would muss her costume. She could not hug others for the same reason. She could not be kissed because it would mess up her makeup. She would, now and then, offer her cheek to be pecked but only if you stayed as far away as possible and made it quick. She was, as far as I could tell, emotionally unapproachable.

Lou and my mother were, therefore, as different as any two people could be, not just in Port Orford, but anyplace you could think of. My mother never once stepped into a tavern in that town, let alone talked to anybody in one. She didn't curse. She didn't joke with men. She wouldn't be caught dead in such shoes as Lou's or with such grime on her skin or under her nails. She would never betray such naked emotion, let alone raise her voice in doing so. You talk about two different people. Wow.

I went into the drugstore one time looking for Richard (who was either a good friend of mine and a lot of fun or a bully who beat me up and ridiculed me, depending upon our moods, the weather, Indian Spirits, or whatever else controlled such circumstances).

Mrs. Pugh was standing next to the massive and miraculous bronze cash register when I inquired about her son's whereabouts.

"I see that Lou nabbed you," Mrs. Pugh said.

"What?" I responded.

"You have tears and grease on your face," she said. "Here, look in the mirror."

There was a mirror next to one of the display shelves.

She was right. There were tears and grease on my face. I smiled as I wiped Lou's tears away with my hand. The other marks remained and I didn't worry about them.

"Goodness," she remarked and then went into the back to find Richard.

As she passed Doc's dental office I heard her say something that I didn't understand for a long time.

"Johnny's out in front," she said to him. "He just got waylaid at the garage. Grease and stuff all over his face. But he's smiling. So she's not hurting him."

And I heard Doc say:

"Hurting him! Hah! She loves him. He should be so lucky as to find somebody like Lou when he gets big—somebody with that much affection to display. Not like his mom. The Iceberg."

Then he sang a few bars of "Frankie and Johnny are Sweethearts," only he sang "Louie" and "Johnny" as the two names.

Once in awhile Lou would drive her tow truck deep into the woods to be alone and drink whiskey in the dark. She'd take dirt side roads, logging roads actually, and be alone with the deer and the noise of frogs. It was her Night Church, she would say, and everybody would shrug, trying to imagine looking up at the stars from the open window of a truck out there in the damp brush at two in the morning. Liquored up, to boot. She drank whiskey straight from pint bottles.

"Good brands, though," Crawford would say. "I'll give her credit for that."

Sometimes she would fall asleep in the tow truck and not waken until the sun came up. One time she reported seeing the face of her dead grandfather in the dawn clouds, her dead grandfather with a crown on his head like a heavenly emperor or at least a saint.

Nobody forgot this event and people were just as fast to discount her next description when, once again, she had fallen asleep in her truck and was awakened by the Enemy.

"I was woke up by airplane!" she announced. (She said this in Margie's Diner. It was the beginning of the second week in September

1942, the 9th if you'd like to be really precise. How do I know? You'll find out some day.)

"It was putty-putty-putty little weak engine! I wake up. Jump out! Look up. It is airplane! JAP!"

"Jap? " Cliff asked. "Whattaya mean, Jap?"

"Was Jap! Jap airplane. Bluey-greeny color. And she had big red dots!"

"Where dots?" he asked. (This could happen to you. You could suddenly start talking like Lou.)

"Where *dots?*" Lou said. "I tell you where dots. Under wings. On side!"

"Fuselage," he said.

"Fuselage," she repeated.

"So what kind of plane?" a logger asked. "Big plane? Little plane?"

"Little plane!" she said. "Bitty plane."

"Wheels?" the logger continued. "Or no wheels? Retracted wheels?"

"No wheels," she said. "Flots!"

"Flots?" Margie asked. "What's flots?"

"You know," Lou said. "FLOTS!"

"I think she means floats," the logger said. "Like pontoons."

The logger drew a couple of crude pictures on a paper napkin.

"There are two kinds of seaplanes," he explained. "One kind has two pontoons and looks like this. The other one is built like a boat with two floats coming down from the wings to balance it in the water."

Lou pointed to the one with the hull and the two "flots."

"That's the one," she said. "That's the one!"

"And you say it had red insignia?" the logger asked.

"*In-sig-nee-ah?*" she asked.

"Red dots?"

"Red dots—yes!"

"How big?"

"This big," she said, and made a circle with her arms above her head. "Great big."

– 269–

They all looked at her like she was drunk or crazy.

"Very low," Lou went on. "Little plane very very low. It fly right past in a hurry and then gone. Barely light, but I hear it and then see it. Jap plane!"

They gave her coffee and pie on the house. But they didn't believe her. She sounded the same as the day she'd reported her grandfather's face in the clouds. It was Whiskey Talk, and no doubt about it.

She went everywhere in town and told her story.

Nobody laughed at her, but they didn't believe her, either.

She was discounted. The flots and the dots could not be believed. Where could such an airplane have come from. Non-stop from Tokyo? No. No way.

Funny Louise.

Even now, I meet Romanian women and hum the melody from the lullaby and see if they recognize it and could maybe sing it to me, but they can't. If they ever could I would close my eyes and try to remember Lou's hands on my face and the kisses and the truest affection of my whole life up to that time. Those overflows. The kissy desserts.

The Survivors of the Jap-Sunk Tanker

I was in the right place at the right time.

It was after dinner and Matt McCormick and I had met to play until dark. We were near the ice house on the cliff road above the dock. It was late spring and there was a cloudbank on the horizon and the sun had just set in it.

There were no clouds anyplace else. No lightning. No thunder.

We heard a distant thud; a heavy bump sound.

It was followed, a minute later, by another one.

Bob Forty appeared and we told him about it. We couldn't describe it and he looked at us as if we'd been hearing things.

It was repeated. Twice. In a short interval.

"That's a heavy gun," he said. "A cannon. That's exactly what they sound like."

I had seen the framed picture of Bob in his World War One Army uniform with two medals under the glass. One was Christmassy with red and green stripes. The French gave it to him. The other was a rainbow of colors and he called it the Victory Medal. He had been in France, he said, and had heard plenty of cannons. And machine guns. And grenades.

"Look for the flashes," he said.

And all three of us looked at the horizon but didn't see anything. The bumping sounds continued and it got dark.

We heard the alarm from the Coast Guard station three miles away. It was the signal to man the boats.

The Coast Guardsmen had to run down hundreds of wooden steps to get to the covered boathouse where two large motorized rescue boats— twice as big as the fishing boats in the harbor; maybe 50 feet long—could be launched into the ocean by carriages on rails. Within a few minutes we could see and hear them heading toward the horizon.

I ran back to the house to tell my family about it. My father was still there, but my mother and sister were gone. My mother was in charge of the Red Cross Disaster Unit and had gone up to the high school where the supplies and blankets were stored. She had gotten the call from the Coast Guard. They told her that a tanker had been set afire by a Japanese submarine. The submarine had surfaced and shot at it with her deck gun. To save her torpedoes.

I visualized one of the polite Japanese men in black uniforms and little collars, one of the guys off the super-clean freighters years before, quietly giving the order to shoot the deck guns and set the tanker ablaze. There I was. On the edge of the war. Able to actually hear a part of it.

My father turned on the radio as if he actually expected to learn something about this incident. An hour or so passed and he said maybe we ought to go to the high school.

As we walked over, three big Coast Guard trucks went by. Seated in the back of them, under the canvas tops, were dozens of men, all as black as cormorants, huddled under blankets. Their eyes were round white dots on the dark faces and they looked like cartoon characters.

"They're covered with oil," my father commented.

Which they were.

We went to the high school gym where the disaster team had everything under control. Pans of kerosene and rags were there to clean the oil off the survivors. Dr. Baird supervised. Cots had been set up. Towels had been collected so the men could take showers in the locker rooms. Sheets and pillows and blankets had been found. Most of the town's pies had been collected. Coffee was brewing in a machine that made gallons at a time. Margie and Cliff were down at the cafe frying hamburgers as fast as they could.

The men were transformed into their old selves: blond men, red-headed men, brown-haired men—men whose freckles reappeared from under the oil. One by one they started to talk, but very quietly and only to one another. Then T.J. and Red brought a bunch of beer and kept it cold in washtubs full of ice, like at the 4th of July down on the beach or at the Sixes Grange Hall on Saturday nights. They stood there with openers and handed out the bottles to the men. Two town competitors were working together.

"For the War Effort," T.J. Collins said.

Then things got livelier.

The men opened up.

Hamburger juice and ketchup dripped down their chins, beer foamed up from the bottles, the gym got hot and steamy, and the men knew that they had made it. They had been pulled from the sea and were safe. They were with their countrymen.

The men smoked cigarettes and milled around in small groups reconstructing what had happened; where they were when the first shell hit, and what it was like in the water waiting to be picked up. And what a miracle it was that the ship sank without catching on fire. That they all would have died if the oil had burned.

With a few beers, it appeared, a disaster soon becomes an adventure—something that you successfully survive and can then talk about.

The ship's officers, five of them, were guests of the Commandant of the Coast Guard station in his big house above the town. He drove them to the gym where they drank some beer with the men and the Captain hushed everyone to tell them about the four men who were still missing and the three who had been taken to the hospital in Bandon. He said that buses coming down from Portland would take them out of town at ten o'clock the next morning and that he wished to say a few words beforehand—on the lawn in front of the Administration Building that faced down to the harbor. At "Oh-Nine-Hundred Hours," he said. Which meant nine o'clock to the rest of us.

The whole town was up there the next morning because it was one of the big events in the history of the place. They stood outside the main body of merchant seamen, silent and respectful.

Zoom Zumquist looked a little bleary, but he was standing up straight and had shaved and put on a clean shirt. So he was nothing we had to feel embarrassed about.

The Captain's theme was Victory. And not being vanquished. And that they had faced the enemy almost within sight of the homeland—which was just how close the war had come. Then he got angry and raised his voice and said something to the effect:

"In the shipyards in Oakland, California, this very day, they will turn out a Liberty Ship! A finished ship in only 24 hours! Think about it!"

(That was easy for me to think about. I knew that Don Doyle was down there in that very place.)

"The Japs couldn't have imagined such a thing when they started the war. Tankers take a little longer. And another thing! The new tankers are going to have 5-inch guns! And Navy gunnery crews! Not the pathetic little 40-mm that we had. No, sir! 5-inch guns."

Clapping from the crowd and the sailors.

"We'll go back to San Francisco and I've volunteered us to go right back aboard one of those ships and sail it out! Straight back to Seattle where we were bound for in the first place. And I'll tell you what I hope for! What I hope for with all my heart!"

And he made a big gesture seaward and said what we all hoped he'd say.

"I hope that bastard submarine stays on patrol out there. I hope the Catalinas don't find it and depth-charge it. Because I want it intact! I want to see that sonofabitch surface again, just like yesterday, and the little apes scamper out there to their deck gun. Only this time, . . . this time! . . . they'll be in for a little surprise. We'll nail it with a 5-incher! Amidships! *AND BLOW THE SON OF A BITCH OUT OF THE WATER!*"

A big cheer went up from the sailors and the townspeople.

And then more applause. And then another big cheer, like a bravo or an encore. We'd fix those guys!

Things settled down and the Captain said a few quiet words about the missing men and the sudden tragedy of it all. He concluded his short talk by saying: "Godspeed," which I realized much later (when I heard it over a troopship's P.A. system) was something Captains always say to men who must face danger. It is a "charm." It is the final word of the Captain's last message to you: "I wish each one of you good luck and Godspeed."

Which he said, and then the buses pulled up the hill and took them all to San Francisco. We waved back and forth with the sailors until the buses were out of sight; waved like true friends. Offshore, in water too deep and green to permit daylight, the *Larry Doheny* lay at the bottom of the sea, four of her men still aboard.

Attack Dogs

On November 7, 1942, the Coast Guard established a Beach Patrol unit and barracks at Port Orford and, with their dogs, combed the beaches and scaled cliffs on a day and night schedule. I remember the dogs, Alsatians mostly, which lived in white doghouses on the side of the hill near the high school. I could see them from the south side of my father's store. The dogs were trained to attack everybody in the world except their own handler. One of the Coast Guard guys reportedly told my dad: "My dog's ready to bite the ass right off the first Jap who thinks he can come ashore around here." That conjured up quite a picture for me at the time, the one of the Assless Jap. In my mind's eye this uniformed man was always standing, frequently near a fireplace mantle where he could put down his coffee cup. He would hold his plate of salad and other food as if attending a cocktail party buffet, smiling wistfully if anybody asked him: "Wouldn't you like to have a seat?" Being assless he could not, of course, sit down.

The Games

There were several games we played. Cowboys and Indians was one. Another favorite game was "Kick the Can," you remember, a glorified game of Hide-and-Seek (with elements of Tag). This entertainment was pursued at night when it was hard to see. A can was placed in a conspicuous area. The person who was "It" would try to defend the can (by touching anybody who approached it) and the other people would hide until the command was made to begin the game. At this time they would either come out of hiding (or be flushed out) and try to kick the can successfully in order to "Win."

Daytime Cowboys and Indians was quickly replaced by War. These were rudimentary games which depended on two teams, one team of which would hide, and the other team would flush them out.

The rules were pretty simple and consisted mostly of shouting:

"BANG—YOU'RE DEAD!"

At which time the kid in your sights would shout back:

"NO, I'M NOT! YOU MISSED ME!"

This would lead to the inevitable:

"I DID NOT!"

"YES, YOU DID!"

"*DID NOT!*"

"DID, TOO!"

"DIDN'T"

"DID!"

Infinity.

Richard Pugh decided to cure this situation by staging future battles with B-B guns. Even the stupidist kid among us (and there was no leading candidate for this honor, since each of us was stupid in his own area of specialization—one of my own being Transparent Lying) was fast to point out the danger of getting an eye put out. If B-B guns could kill birds, they could certainly put out an eye.

Here was Richard's Safety Suggestion:

"Don't shoot at anybody's head."

Richard had another great idea.

"We'll all take off our shirts. That way we'll know if we get hit."

You had to hand it to Richard when it came to logic. It was no wonder that he got sucked into walking into the ocean that time.

So we all reluctantly agreed to try it.

We took off our shirts and the Hiding Team went into the dense woods behind McCormicks' place to take up our positions. I was one of the hiders.

Richard led the attackers.

We waited in the woods for a long time. One of the dumb things that would happen once in awhile was that the Attacking Team would decide to go swimming or do something else. Just for the hell of it. To see how long the other team would wait it out.

We thought this was happening to us.

A very long time passed.

Two of our hiders were hidden up in trees, ready to bushwhack the attackers. They lost patience and came down.

At that moment, three of us were shot from behind!

Richard had led a successful encircling maneuver and ambushed us. They had advanced very carefully from the unexpected direction—slowly so as not to make any noise.

The three of us were hit from fairly close range.

We all screamed from the pain and astonishment!

Richard was right.

There was no way to shout: "YOU MISSED ME!"

I was marked with a big red welt on the back of my arm. Daryll Sauers (Dead Ted's cousin) had been hit in the back and was bleeding. Matt McCormick was hit in the neck. We turned around to face the attackers. Matt was hit again in the face. He crumpled to the ground with his hands over his face.

"HOLD IT!"

"STOP!"

"CEASE FIRE!"

Everybody was screaming at once.

The War was over. We had lost.

But, more urgently, Matt was on the ground holding both hands to his eyes.

There was blood.

We were all horror-stricken. The worst had happened.

"Oh, Shit!" somebody wailed.

It was Richard who found the courage to say:

"Okay, . . . let's take a look."

Matt seemed afraid to do anything but clutch his face. He was finally persuaded to move his hands away.

A B-B had caught him on the bridge of the nose and made a bloody furrow right up between his eyes. But that was it. His left eye was okay. So was his right. Great sighs of relief.

We trudged back to Matt's house to get some iodine and our shirts. On the way back, Matt dropped behind a little and shot Richard in the ass.

Richard yelped. It had stung him badly even through his pants and his underpants. The point was now clear to everybody. No more games in which people should be made to bleed as proof of winning.

Matt McCormick made the next major Weapons Breakthrough. Actually two of them.

He had been up to Silver Springs on his bicycle and found a whole bunch of popcorn bags that must have fallen off a truck. They were small bags, maybe seven inches high.

Once again, I happened to be on the Dunkirk side (the Losers) when Matt's technology was applied in combat.

As I've mentioned, the houses in town depended on firewood for cooking and heating. Wood fires means ashes—plenty of them, nice white fluffy ones. So it was Masterson's idea to load up the popcorn bags about half full, tamp them down real tight, and tape them up—then use them as hand grenades. Anybody who got ashes on him, either from a direct hit or a near miss, was declared out of the game. Once again, the "You-Missed-Me!" excuse could not be used since people were either marked or they were not.

Just as in real warfare, this technological advance drove a change in tactics. "Don't Bunch Up!" was an idea we didn't get from war movies; we learned it when four of us, the whole team, got wiped out with one well-hurled (or luckily thrown) "grenade."

High Ground became important in subsequent games. Fortification technology took a great leap forward. Caves high on the sides of dirt cliffs became popular because the defenders could merely drop grenades (later veritable "bombs" made with larger paper bags stolen from my dad's store). Our paper-bag ordnance was improved with the addition of finely ground flour to increase the marking power and the appearance of battle smoke.

The McCormick boys, Turd & Matt, astonished us all with the introduction of the World's Largest Portable Slingshot!

Some history is in order here. Lou Monescu moved her garage to a larger location north of town, into a building with a large metal roof. We would throw stones on the roof to make a racket. She would run out and raise hell, even with me. So we retreated into the woods well behind the garage where Matt McCormick discovered a (luckily) strategically placed myrtle tree with a crotch in a perfect position to attach a long piece of truck inner tube with which to then loft big clods of earth onto the roof. This caused a great deal of amusement because Monie couldn't tell where the clods were coming from, just that they made a terrific noise on the roof and caused her to run outside loudly ranting and swearing in her famous fashion but unable to find anybody.

So anyway, Matt and Turd got the idea of sawing a big limb out of the top of a tree and made a 6-foot-high slingshot, once again using an old truck inner tube for the rubber part and a piece of heavy canvas for the pocket. They practiced with it for quite a while to learn its ballistics and then volunteered to be on the "Losing" side in an attack against the almost-impregnable cave fort way up on a dirt cliff near Battle Rock.

The "Winning" team went up to the cave to load their bags of ashes and flour. I was down below with the two McCormick boys and Eddie Baker. Eddie and I immediately began to create an assembly line to load popcorn bags.

"Take it easy," Matt said. "We don't need many."

"What do you mean, we don't need many?" Eddie said. "We have to advance up the narrow path to the cave on a Suicide Mission if we're going to stand any chance at all!"

Eddie could get as serious as John Wayne in a war movie about this stuff.

"Forget it," Matt said. "We've got a new weapon."

"What is it?" Eddie asked.

"Yeah," I chimed in, "what is it?"

We could hear Richard's loud voice up at the cave. He was already calling us Chicken Shits and German Nazi Assholes who would be destroyed if we attacked.

"Come on, Turd," Matt said to his brother. And the two of them went up the bank to where they had hidden their tree limb in the tall grass earlier that morning.

They picked it up and carried it to the beach.

"SURRENDER!" Matt yelled to the boys in the fortification.

"BULLSHIT!" was the immediate response. And then laughter.

Two grenades were hurled from above and exploded in the driftwood.

It was a still day, so the grayish-white cloud hung in the air.

We were 15 or 20 feet out of range. Everybody knew the exact range of the strongest thrower, so we knew precisely where we were safe.

"*YOU ARE DOOMED!*" screamed Turd, who had heard this line in a recent horror movie and now said it a dozen times a day.

This drew another volley of grenades which had the effect of creating a smoke screen behind which we could erect the slingshot without being seen.

We created a hole in the ground and dropped the bottom of the slingshot in it. Matt and Turd had developed a brace made from another limb of the same myrtle tree. The brace went behind the slingshot to keep it from tipping backward when the rubber portion was pulled back. Eddie and I steadied the slingshot frame and brace while Matt and Turd loaded the weapon and pulled back on the strips of inner tube.

The air cleared and the four boys above looked down at the contraption, not knowing exactly what it was.

The first shot was fired.

THRUNG! it sounded like.

It was 20 yards too low and about the same distance to the right of the fort-cave on the cliff.

Jeers and cheers echoed down at us.

"STUPID!"

"WASTE OF TIME!"

Plus the usual:

"CHICKEN SHITS!"

"Okay," Matt said calmly, "let's try it again."

We reloaded and repositioned ourselves.

Another hefty THRUNG! and this time the grenade was lofted high in the air and well above the fort. The boys on the cliff couldn't see above very well and didn't know where it landed, but they had a sudden appreciation for the weapon and kept their mouths shut after they saw the bag zip above them.

We prepared the next round.

"*PREPARE TO DIE!*" Turd yelled. It was another line from the same movie.

Matt, the Aimer, fired again.

This time the grenade landed only five or six feet to the left of the cave.

"OKAY!" Matt screamed at us. "I'VE GOT THE RANGE. PREPARE FOR RAPID FIRE!"

He lobbed one straight into the cave. It caused a terrific commotion: screaming, coughing, choking, and noisy confusion.

"*AGAIN!*" Matt howled.

We had devastated them, but this wasn't enough for Matt. We had won, but the game hadn't gone on long enough for him.

He fired again.

"YOU ARE DOOMED!" Turd repeated as the grenade was still in flight.

Another direct hit!

"READY!" Matt again commanded.

He fired another round squarely into the cave.

The defenders were sputtering angrily for us to stop. They screamed the favorite cry of the Defeated:

"NO FAIR!"

The first two boys from the fortress came down the path. They were marked all over with ashes and flour. The other two stumbled around in the cloud of dust at the cave.

"READY!" Matt repeated, showing no mercy.

It was as if he was single-handedly making up for Pearl Harbor.

He missed and then called for another round.

He scored another hit and the two remaining boys cried their surrender.

It was an overwhelming victory and changed the face of battle in Port Orford forever. It was like the original invention of artillery that made mighty fortresses vulnerable.

The fort team gathered around the slingshot with great admiration.

They, of course, wanted us to take the cave and they would use the slingshot.

"What?" Matt said. "Are you crazy?"

An arms race never developed after the first use of this weapon. It would have made warfare too distant and impersonal.

We used the slingshot a couple of times to shoot ash-grenades at passing logging trucks, but Gene White (surprise surprise) confiscated the weapon and burned it in his stove.

The Invasion

Convoys began to be a feature of life starting in 1942. Olive green army trucks would drive past in long columns, heading south down Highway 101. We'd stand next to the highway and the drivers—soldiers in uniform—would wave.

One day a convoy came to town and stopped. This one had cannons—105mm and 155mm howitzers on rubber tires, towed behind trucks. There were jeeps with 50 cal. machine guns on mounts in the back. There were command cars and weapons carriers. Six-by's and four-by's. There were troops with helmets and packs on their backs.

These Army guys looked serious. They placed the howitzers on the bluffs. They put one of them right next to the ice house. On the steep slopes they prepared machine gun positions. Guys adjusted mortars on the road to the dock. Ammunition was unloaded from trucks.

Nobody could get an answer from them, not even Gene White.

It seemed to be one of those Military Secrets we'd heard about.

The townspeople invented their own story. There was going to be a Japanese invasion! That was the only logical answer.

Somehow the rumor got going that the Japanese had enormous submarines, Army submarines, with hundreds and hundreds of troops on them. Such subs could suddenly surface and the men would paddle ashore in rubber boats.

That was the story. The Japs would be along at any moment.

I remember that mid-afternoon picture.

The Army was deployed in its defensive positions all around the harbor.

The men of the town (plus Lou Monescu) had formed a second line of defense.

Gene was there with a 12-gauge shotgun cradled under his arm and his jacket pocket crammed with shells.

Bob Forty had a Springfield Ought-Six from his previous war.

Doc Pugh had an old Swedish Mauser that he was leaning against.

Dozens of other guys, fishermen and loggers, millhands and the town barber, were present with shotguns and large numbers of the region's favorite brush gun, the Winchester 30-30 carbine. Ammunition was re-distributed informally.

Lou Monescu wore an old six-shooter in a holster hooked on the belt of her pants. She wore a windbreaker with big pockets. She had a pint of whiskey in each of the pockets and took little nips from time to time. She would offer sips to the men next to her and they would quietly accept.

The Japs might get past the Army, but it didn't seem likely they would make it much farther than the old ice house. Lou and the men wouldn't permit it. They wouldn't tolerate it.

A young Army Captain made the rounds of the cliff, advising everybody to go home—that this was Army Business.

Gene White corrected him.

"This is Port Orford business. I'm Constable. I'm staying."

Other people said nothing, but refused to budge.

Bob Forty said:

"Where are you from, young man?"

"Wisconsin."

"Do you people shoot deer in Wisconsin?"

"Sure."

"Are there people in your home town who can shoot a rifle and hit a deer at two or three hundred yards?"

"Yes."

"Would you want them with you if the Germans were advancing on your home town? Or would you like to see them hiding in their houses?"

The Captain kept walking, trying valiantly to convince others to leave it to the Army—whatever it was.

Maybe this was something called Maneuvers or an Exercise. Whatever it might have been called, it was soon over.

The Army guys packed up and left without a trace. No submarines surfaced. No rubber boats appeared. No Japanese soldiers were stupid enough to try to come ashore.

The men shuffled around to return the borrowed ammunition. Guns were unloaded. Lou and the men drank the last of the whiskey. Gene's pickup rattled home.

The Invasion was over.

The Victors celebrated far into the night at Red's, the Pastime, and T.J.'s Bar & Grill. That's when Henri made his famous "Churchill" speech. Something like:

"I can tell you something! This! These Japanese are fools. They think we would not fight. But we would fight them past the taverns and garages, into the ditches. We would fight from behind trees. By the mill! Firing! Shooting! One by one we would kill them and they would say: 'Why are we not at home? Why have we come all this way to die?' We would fight these sons of bitches completely into the mountains and blow up every bridge. Every where. Not even a bicycle could go places and the Japs would be cut off for the bombers to kill them all. Bank on me when I say this. We would not give up!"

There was a lot of cheering and applause and the offer of more drinks than Henri needed, but he drank them anyway.

Short Memories

In writing a book about memories, you are apt to come up with subjects — 283 — that are very short. Following are significant memories that are only one paragraph long. Some are only one sentence long and you might wonder: why bother? I think it's in the interest of completeness and accuracy and for the benefit of future historians who might ask one another: "What was the biggest airplane to fly low over Port Orford in 1942, and could the children in the playground actually see the face of the pilot?" "When was the last May Pole dance?" "Did they fly kites or not in those days?" "Did kids slide down grassy slopes in Kotex boxes or not?" It is certainly not for me to decide what historians are going to wonder about two or three centuries from now.

May Poles. When I was in the first and second grades we had the very last Port Orford May Pole Dance on the school grounds. The girls held colored crepe-paper streamers and went in one direction around the pole and the boys held streamers and went in the other direction. The boys and the girls criss-crossed and the effect was to create a pattern on the pole. I didn't know why this was done and I thought it was stupid. It was one of the few times in my life that I thought something was really stupid and, sure enough, other people reached the same conclusion and they quit doing it.

Scrap Drives. When the war started there were a great many scrap drives. The government wanted aluminum pots and pans, copper, rubber, and junk of all kinds. At the height of one of the school scrap drives somebody donated a junker car. It was parked at the edge of the playground and a bunch of us kids decided to roll it over. We all pushed and a girl got her dress caught on a door handle and rolled over with the car. She screamed and disappeared. It was agonizingly frightening. She had merely been flipped to the other side, however, and the car didn't crush her and she wasn't hurt at all. She cried for a long time, however, and who could blame her?

Kites. The hill with the concrete letters spelling P O R T   O R F O R D was, in my opinion, the best place from which to fly kites in the entire world. I have the idea that box kites were invented when I was a kid because everybody was flying regular kites until suddenly box kites became all the rage. The trick was to see how many balls of string you could use in getting your kite as high as possible. Eventually you'd use too much and the string would break from all the tension and the kite would fly to Gold Beach or somewhere and you'd never see it again. Some people thought it was a great trick to write messages on pieces of paper they would hook on the kite string and then the message would travel up the string all the way to the kite. This made about as much sense to me as May Poles. A couple of grownups in town were avid kite-flyers and had big reels with handles to manage their string.

The Jig. The shortest memory of my entire childhood was of a kid who said he was Irish and danced what he called a jig. A jig. I had never heard this word before. I was walking down the boardwalk (no sidewalks in town, did I mention that?) to Pugh's drugstore and, about halfway down between Bennett's tall fence and the huge mud puddle, there suddenly appears this Irish kid who said the word, danced the dance, and I went on my way. No commentary. No questions. I stopped. I watched the jig. I kept going. And then this kid, who had only been in town a week, left town.

Chitum. This is a memory that may not be a memory at all but a hallucination experienced during a fever but I swear to God that I think I remember something about chitum bark being collected to make laxatives or some other kind of medicine out of. There was a tree that naturally shed its bark in sheets like heavy paper. You didn't hurt the tree when you stripped away this bark and put it in a burlap bag (gunny sack) and took it wherever you took it and got paid whatever you got paid for it. Maybe it was a dime a pound. (Old timers will now shake their heads and say: I vaguely remember that kid, Johnny. He made stuff up.)

Trick or Treat. On Halloween we did something that I now believe was invented by adults so that children could get into mischief without causing a lot of damage. In addition to begging for candy and putting it into paper bags, there was also the town practice of soaping windows. You'd wait until it got very late and quiet and then run around town marking windows with bars of soap. Ivory soap was best for this because it left a nice white mark on window glass. I remember being cautioned by my parents: "Now don't you go out there and soap anybody's windows, hear?" But, of course, all the children did and nothing was ever harmed. Merchants would go out the next morning with a bucket of water and clean off the windows. An annual rumor was spread to the effect that if Gene White ever caught you soaping somebody's window he'd stick your soap up your bottom. I never knew whether this was true, but I never took a full bar of soap, only a small piece, just in case.

One of the sad things about trick or treating was that a few poor people on the edge of town would have to keep their lights off and pretend not to be home because they didn't have anything to give the children who showed up in costumes.

Carving Jack O' Lanterns. Yes.

Biggest Airplane. A Boeing B-17 "Flying Fortress" made several low passes over the town at an altitude of only a few hundred feet. It was the first time any of us had ever seen a four-engined airplane. We ran into the school yard for one of the passes and it was possible to see the pilot and some of the crew members through plexiglass windows.

Kotex Boxes for Sliding Down Grassy Slopes. Yes. To be more precise, the big cardboard *cartons* that the boxes of Kotex came in. I thought the Amazing Cartoon gun was going to be a one-paragraph deal, but it turned out to be longer.

The Amazing Cartoon Gun

While we still lived in the house on the hill I received one of the best presents ever. I can't remember whether it was a birthday present or a Christmas present. All I know for sure is that I played with it only once and for just a few minutes and then it disappeared. It vanished.

I'll describe it for you as best I can.

It was a handgun and, if I recall correctly, it was silver colored and may have been made out of aluminum. It had one or more batteries in the handle and the side popped open and you inserted a little roll of film instead of caps. It was not a cap pistol and this pistol did not take pictures; it projected them through lenses in the barrel. It was a little pistol-shaped projector. On the film rolls were cartoons. The film was sprocketed (and was probably 8-mm, but might have been 16-mm) and when you pulled the trigger of the pistol you advanced the film one frame at a time. I remember pulling down the blind on the window of my room and projecting images on the wall. But only briefly. It was a most excellent toy and I looked forward to playing with it a lot.

I don't know what happened.

Maybe there was a party and a lot of confusion.

Maybe the present got thrown out with the wrappings.

Maybe some kid needed the toy a lot more than I did.

All I remember is that we searched the house for days and never found it.

If anybody out there has such a gun I wish you'd call me because I'd like to come over to your house and play with it for a few minutes.

Or maybe you'd sell it to me.

Yes, that'd be the ticket. Sell it to me. Then I could play with it as much as I like.

I'd play with it at night when I'm supposed to be sleeping.

I'd project cartoons on the ceiling and really enjoy myself.

This was one of the best toys in the world and I got screwed out of playing with it.

Do you understand what I mean?

I've had people ask me if maybe I invented the gun, like made the whole thing up. I tell them that I like to be thought of as a creative person, but I could never in a million years have invented such a wonderful toy when I was only seven or eight years old.

It was real.

It was not like the presumed goat. It was very real.

Going Back East

After the torpedoed-tanker incident, my mother was given the opportunity to go to Washington, D.C., to receive a commendation from the Red Cross for her part in the response and to attend further training in how to handle war-related disasters. It was agreed that I would go along on the trip and that we would leave in the summer. That was 1942 when I was just finishing the fifth grade.

I have already talked about one of my "problems," the one which adults defined as my inability to pay attention—and to focus on the subjects they wished me to focus on. I saw the difficulty in another light; I understood it as my reluctance to accept what was being dished out. They were trying to serve me the intellectual equivalent of liver and I was trying to ignore it. It smelled bad and it looked funny. I tried to hide it under the intellectual equivalent of my lettuce. Or, if I was actually forced to down it, I would vomit it back up. Nobody in town had ever witnessed this particular kind of rebellion and resistance to intellectual authority (which they determined, of course, to be resistance to their *moral* authority). What confused them so horribly was the fact that I was gaining intelligence despite the fact that I wasn't a part of the intelligence-generating apparatus, the school. Teachers were talking out of abstract books. I was talking to concrete adults. Nobody realized how much I was talking or to whom and about what. I was soaking it in. Pedants were trying to drill it in. The favorite technique of my parents was to shout at me, as if a piece of advice transmitted with sufficient volume would penetrate past my ears and into my brain.

My way to learn was beyond their capacity to teach. They wanted immediate comprehension. Actually, more than just want, they *needed* immediate comprehension. They needed you to know. And they would frequently use a stick to enforce this need of theirs. It was as if they were saying:

"I'm going to keep hitting you with this stick until I am certain you understand what I'm telling you; until I'm absolutely sure you remember."

My peers in grammar school, the girls especially, were very quick to learn how to handle adults and to parrot exactly what they wanted to hear. Their lives were serene. They did their homework and played back precisely what teachers and parents wanted to hear. They seldom got hit with sticks or slapped in the face. They conformed. They knuckled under. They kept their little noses clean. They didn't bitch about paprika.

I wandered through the world like my dog, Skippy. I was looking at things. And I was looking at them without the need to see a pattern or to determine that some things were more important than others. There can be a slight difference between *comprehending* (grasping meaning) and *apprehending* (to become conscious of, as through emotions or the senses). So I was, by this definition, an Apprehender, one who took things in and didn't file them. My mind was a messy attic instead of a library where everything was neatly filed under Reading, History, Arithmetic, and Writing.

T. J. did not have a syllabus for the course he unconsciously taught me about Being in the World or Living on the Street or whatever the name was of the practical stuff he tried to tell me—about keeping things in perspective and not going nuts. And Moran never tried to be a psychiatrist or a social worker on my behalf. He spent more time in our conversations asking me questions than he did making pronouncements. The first time I ever saw a man get tears in his eyes was when Moran asked me what I thought the difference was between learning things in school and learning things by walking around town. I told him that I was never glad in school—that there was nothing happy in their books.

It wasn't anything like walking along and finding something on the ground, or listening to somebody like Fletcher or Old Man Knapp suddenly and maybe accidentally unearth something of great interest from their memory. Learning is about discovery, not rote memorization. Some adults knew this and, luckily, they were my friends. The others who didn't were my enemies and were worth the effort to resist. I must say this: Crawford Smith has always been a sort of anchor in my life, an anchor that kept me from drifting too far away from things that mattered. He was also an example of a person who projects a kind of trust that is almost visible. Both he and T.J. had that quality and I have tried to emulate it and to seek it in others. I have sometimes found it. It's a combination of the fisherman's skill in not getting lost, and the bar & grill owner's ability to entertain people and retain some semblance of control. Those two guys would have made good management consultants. They provided leadership.

The point of all this is that Port Orford seemed to me to have a fantastic wealth of things to look at and think about. There was a great unexplored richness about the place. People were storehouses of special information and, if you were lucky enough, you might be present when they brought out a treasure for you to look at or hear about. So, when I had the opportunity to take a trip Back East, I simply wasn't ready for the complexity of it.

I have amnesia about most of it. It was too mind-boggling.

We took the train from Portland to Kansas City, Kansas. I remember only two events. The first was that the train was mostly filled with soldiers in uniform. There were a few marines and sailors, but most were soldiers; U.S. Army enlisted men. Somewhere in Idaho, our eastbound train was held up for an hour and I noticed a couple of westbound trains which were also waiting to proceed and they, too, were filled mostly with soldiers. I remember annoying my mother with the question:

"Why move soldiers from the east to the west and, at the same time, move other soldiers from the west to the east? Why not just leave them where they were? What's the difference?"

She snapped some nonsense about "because the Authorities know what they're doing, that's why. Do you suppose they'd do this without a *reason?*"

There it was: the reinforcement of the myth that everybody in authority has a reason and a purpose, both of which are lofty and unassailable.

The second memory is of going up a steep grade out of a copper-mining town that had a bunch of tailings. We seemed to be two hours just going up the hill and the town was always visible at the bottom. I am sure that this recollection is faulty but, since it is only one of two about that portion of the trip, I intend to preserve it.

Then there was Kansas City and Laura.

My father was married to somebody in Kansas before he married my mother. It had to have been in the early to mid Twenties. My father and his first wife had a daughter named Laura. I had seen a picture of Laura and knew that she was a beautiful young woman but I never had a sense of kinship. She was not my sister in the sense that my sister was my sister, even though my sister was my half-sister (just like Laura) since she was the offspring of my mother's first marriage to a guy named Johnson in San Diego or somewhere. But you know what I mean. If you live with somebody it's a whole lot different from just hearing about somebody.

We met Laura for lunch.

It was the only time I ever saw Laura, the only time in my life I ever talked to her. She was 19 or 20 and I was dazzled. She was gorgeous. Like a movie star. And this time I'm not kidding.

During my father's life he always complained that he never heard from Laura, but he never made the effort to establish and maintain a line of communication with her. She was very nice to me. By the time I was old enough to care about her, to be ready to pay attention, there was no way to track her down. I never knew her mother's name or where they lived.

When the song, "Laura" first came out, it reminded me of her. It always has. Listen to the lyrics some time. It was as if the song was about her.

Imagine a beautiful sister who was kind to you and that you liked but with whom you only had one meal in your whole life.

It is a fine memory, that lunch. Then we visited my grandfather Frank Quick's farm. I must first tell you that visiting my grandfather Frank in Kansas was as different from visiting my Grandmother in Portland as any two things could be different. If you went to my grandmother's house on a tree-lined street there was dim light and quiet. Cocoa bubbling in the kitchen could be heard throughout the small house. There would be photo albums to look at. There might be pleasant little outings to a museum. There would be pleasant conversations about subjects you had never dreamed of.

Grandpa Frank Quick

The first thing I remember seeing at my Kansas grandfather's place was the Chores List posted on the wall of the porch next to the kitchen. My name was on it. So was my mother's. She was even more surprised than I was.

It was as if the farm had fallen behind by at least a thousand tasks. I was designated to slop the hogs. A mother pig bit my ankle. I drove a tractor. I fell off a hay wagon, only I didn't break anything. I learned that pitchforks have three tines; hayforks, four; manure forks; five. I think. I gathered eggs from hens who wanted no such thing. I hammered nails in a major barn-refurbishment project. I swam in a muddy creek where a horsefly bit me repeatedly. I had never seen such a fly before. Huge. It hurt me. It angered me. The weather was intolerably hot and muggy. There was never such weather in Port Orford from where we had just come on a combination of hot buses and cold trains, mostly trains. On the coast of Oregon, nights cooled off, that was for sure. The Humboldt Current brought up cold water from somewhere, don't ask me where. The farm stayed hot from dusk to dawn and I remembered the minister's talk of demons who had to be held at bay. I felt their presence rising from the dirt and realized in the dark one night that the fly had been no accident.

We worked so hard it became funny. And when we left we wondered how they would ever possibly get along without us.

The trip continued.

The more I took in the less I could take in. The country was too big. I was on the train for days. In St. Louis, on the way to Chicago, we

– 291–

stayed in a hotel room which had no air conditioning and it was stifling. I could see a tower out the window and colored lights kept slowly changing on it. The next morning, very tired, I caught a glimpse of my mother, naked, in the bathroom. She immediately slammed the door. It was only the second time I had ever seen a naked adult. No, wait. The third. You had to count Laureen.

Rolling through Iowa I stayed up most of the night watching a lightning storm that never ended. It was one lightning strike after another.

It rained in Chicago. We had to go from one train station to another one and nearly missed our train to Philadelphia.

We got to Philadelphia and got a crowded train to Cape May, New Jersey, where we were going to stay with my Uncle George and Aunt Marianne. George was a Coast Guard engineering officer at the facility in Cape May. We had to stand up. There were no seats. My mother, misunderstanding her instructions, made us get off at Cape May Courthouse. It is not the same thing as Cape May. It was the wrong place to have gotten off. My mother was greatly irritated that we weren't met by George and Marianne. They weren't on the platform. George and Marianne were waiting for us in Cape May. They were irritated that we weren't on the train. I feared that we were lost. Now that I had a rough idea of how big the country really was, and how far away from Port Orford we were, it seemed like something worth worrying about. Nobody would ever be able to track us down in Cape May Courthouse, that much was for sure.

My mother, in her characteristic style, began a conversation with the Stationmaster in which she used statements about what she knew or thought she knew instead of questions about what she didn't.

"I thought Cape May was on the ocean!" she asserted.

"That's correct," said the Stationmaster.

"And I was told that Cape May was a reasonably sized city."

"It is," he said.

"Well, this place is out in the middle of nowhere!"

"You are right," he agreed.

"Well, where is everybody?"

Like she was Amelia Earhart and everybody *else* was lost.

The Stationmaster explained that we were in Cape May Courthouse, which was several towns away from Cape May. This was the stupidest thing my mother had ever heard, naming two towns very nearly the same thing. The Stationmaster didn't wish to defend the choice, it having been made probably two centuries before by some other people. He offered her one of two choices: either take a taxi to Cape May or wait two hours for the next train.

She decided on the taxi. While we waited for it next to the station, she indulged in some Westerner speculation about Easterners and came up with a conspiracy theory in which Cape May Courthouse was the bait in a trap to catch Westerners and make them pay cab fare to the place they were entitled to go to on the train in the first place. In her view of it, she, Ellen, had not made a mistake; no, she, Ellen, had been tricked! We had been duped into getting off the train where we had.

If that wasn't bad enough, she was really pissed off when she told the story to George and Marianne and they *laughed* at her. As if we were hicks and hayseeds. And that only tourists from far away and mental defectives got off the train at Cape May Courthouse instead of staying on until the end of the line at Cape May proper.

I remember only one paragraph's worth of stuff from the rest of the month in the East. It was July. Swimming in the ocean was wonderful and I did it every day. I found a friend and we'd go to the beach. There were amusement arcades at the beach and games to play for a dime. Oil from tankers sunk by German U-boats would wash onto the beach. Big Navy blimps would head to sea to seek the U-boats. The blimp engines sounded as if they were operating in deep barrels. Marianne drove us to Washington and we had a slight car accident in a Baltimore neighborhood where she'd gotten lost. It was lucky I'd had a talk about black people because we were in a community where everybody was black. Dark black. My mother and Aunt Marianne were scared. As if they were in danger. An elderly black man gave them directions and put his hand on my shoulder as he talked. They stared at his hand as if he was contaminating me. He was giving me assurance that he knew he would never be able to give the women. They were too far gone. I wasn't. He knew that I wasn't scared because I didn't know how or why to be and then he shook my hand and said that he had never met anybody from Oregon before and that it was a very high privilege, indeed.

I was confused when the two women would thenceforth talk about this "Close Call" we'd had in Baltimore.

Washington, D.C., is a blank except for a couple of monuments.

We went to New York and four things are still in focus. The dread fear of being on the top of the RCA Building. The wonderful grape drink I had at a sidewalk fruit-juice stand. It was so good that I asked if I could have another one, this time pineapple? Yes, my mother supposed, it was okay. I drank the second drink to the last drop and we then walked into a posh Madison Avenue jewelry store. I immediately became aware of the chemical reaction of the pineapple juice mixing with the grape juice and made it two steps toward the door so that I could throw up in the street. I threw up in the store instead. Nobody could possibly believe that a kid could vomit so much in such a short period of time. Nobody had ever seen that color of purple, lying there as it did in a pool on the gray carpet. I was too sick to be mortified. The mortification was left to my mother, Aunt Marianne, and Uncle George. It was something that T.J. Collins would have found very funny.

Another thing I remember was a Broadway comedy called *Hellzapoppin'* with two comics named Olson and Johnson. Johnson threw stuff at the audience from the stage. That, too, would have been right up T.J.'s alley.

I saw 5th Avenue up toward the park and realized that Moran had told the truth. The buildings were where he said they were. Only on a scale that I couldn't have believed. New York was on a scale that I couldn't have imagined. Central Park takes up only a portion of Manhattan. The Zoo takes up only a small portion of Central Park. All of Port Orford would have fit into a portion of the Zoo. All of downtown Portland could have fit into the bottom of Central Park. I suppose that's about when my mind went blank. It got overloaded; jammed up. I don't remember one inch of the journey back home, even though we took a different route so that we could see new scenery. I try and try to remember an image of anything and nothing's there and I can't see even a fragment. It's as if it never happened.

The value of the trip was immense. I was among a tiny fraction of the population of Port Orford who had ever been to a big city, especially one as far away as New York. It gave me some perspective. When President Roosevelt talked on the radio like the Country's Uncle, I knew how far away he was. We had driven past the White House, whether I recollected it or not. The President was a long way away; many days by train, all of those trains full of soldiers going from where they had been to the new place in the opposite direction.

A German spy standing next to the tracks in Kansas could have gotten a message to Berlin about the millions of G.I.s going from east to west and west to east every single day and correctly deduced that if the Authorities ever got organized, Germany was going to be in Deep Shit. Eventually, of course, the Authorities did and Germany was.

History as perceived and reported by Johnny B.

1943 and the End of the World

In 1943, we got back part of New Guinea, Guadalcanal, and the Solomons. Then Sitka and Kiska. Tripoli fell. Then resistance ended in North Africa. I took care of the necessary flags for awhile in memory of Grandpa Frank.

Here are other events which took place:

Soviet flags started advancing westward toward Germany.

U.S. flags started advancing northward in the Pacific.

A guy named Noble made a fortune with Life Savers (the Candy with the Hole) and purchased NBC's 16-year-old Blue Network with a check for $8 million. He turned it into ABC.

Some of the movies: *Sahara, Desert Victory, The Ox-Bow Incident, Madame Curie, For Whom the Bell Tolls, Watch on the Rhine,* and *Five Graves to Cairo.*

Some of the songs: "Murder, He Says," "Sunday, Monday, or Always," a bunch of stuff from the new Broadway musical Oklahoma (which included five songs by itself: "Surrey With the Fringe on the Top," "People Will Say We're in Love," "Kansas City," "I Cain't Say No," and "Pore Jud") plus "I Want to Be Happy," "Comin' in on a Wing and a Prayer," "Holiday for Strings," "Mairzy Doats," "They're Either Too Young Or Too Old," "Tico-Tico," "I'll Be Seeing You" (retreaded from earlier), "Pistol Packin' Mama," "Shoo-Shoo Baby," "You'll never Know (Just How Much I Love You)," and "Besame Mucho—Kiss Me Much."

(Some California kid said the word for "ass" in Spanish was "koola" so we'd go around singing what we thought was "Kiss My Ass" in Spanish. Another rare example of Port Orford humor.)

Radio? Abbott & Costello started (Camels), as did Bob Burns, the Arkansas Traveler (Lever Brothers), Danny Thomas (Chase & Sanborn), Abie's Irish Rose (Procter & Gamble), and Mr. & Mrs. North (Bristol Myers). We got interested for awhile in the National Barn Dance (Miles Laboratories–Alka Seltzer).

War Slogan: "Use it up, wear it out, make it do or do without!"

You couldn't find sneakers.

A Mexican volcano sprang up in some guy's corn field. Imagine that—a whole volcano.

Eight German spies landed at night from U-Boats lying off Long Island and Florida. They were caught and got the chair.

The Pentagon was completed, the world's largest office building. 6.5 million sq. ft. of floor space, 17 miles of hallways, and 7,748 windows. Meat rationing. So the service boys could get plenty of meat to eat.

Uncle Harvey dropped by on leave and told me in confidence that chipped beef on toast was called "Shit-On-a-Shingle" in the Army and—secondly—that everybody hated it except him. He loved making it and loved eating it. When it came my turn to be in the service, I was always the first guy in line for second helpings of S.O.S.

Cheese was rationed. Flour, fish, and canned goods were rationed.

During an appearance at the Paramount Theater in New York, thirty thousand of Frank Sinatra's fans went nuts and started a riot. 421 policemen, 20 policewomen, and 20 patrol cars responded. Talk about popular.

Oscar, the salesman from Heinz, told my dad that some lady hoarder in Portland filled her cellar with canned goods just before rationing started. A rainstorm flooded the cellar and washed all the labels off the cans! Ha. Ha. Ha.

Served her right.

The¨ B" Effect

From my earliest life I developed an idea I continue to refer to as "the Baker Effect," "B" for short.

I used to dislike Eddie Baker because he would trip me on the playground or jump off his end of the teeter-totter and let me crash to the ground, often hurting my testicles. Once I began the process of disliking Eddie it was very difficult to stop. Hatred works this way, it's just the way it is. There were a few brief interludes in which we were friends but, for the most part, we never were. In some way it is good to have an enemy as solid and dependable as Eddie. Someone you can so easily hate when the image of him is brought to mind.

One summer, Eddie discovered how to carve little wooden airplanes that looked like R.A.F. single-engine Spitfire fighters. Not only that, but he figured out how to produce perfect little propellers which he would mount on the front of the airplane with a pin. Since there is almost always a breeze blowing in Port Orford, Eddie could stand in one place holding an airplane and have the wind make the propeller go around. The model came alive. It looked real. Other kids wanted their own airplane and Eddie was happy to oblige. 50¢. Fifty cents! A fortune. But everybody agreed that it was worth it. I agreed, but I was not a qualified buyer. Only friends of Eddie were qualified buyers. I was a self-avowed enemy of Eddie. I had gone on record publicly that Eddie was an asshole.

Something had to be done. I suddenly disliked disliking Eddie. This is always the initial step in a major change of mind. One does not rush directly to liking the idea of liking. There are necessary transitions. There are staged changes. A groundwork needs to be laid. A new structure must be built. I had an idea for a beginning.

Back in the ancient Oregonian times of which I speak, there were actually three individual little bars of candy in a Three Musketeers package. So I walked up to Eddie and offered him one. It was a clear sign of a truce, the offer of a palaver. Eddie took the Musketeer and quickly took a bite out of it. He then asked:

"You want an airplane, don't you?"

"Yes, Eddie," I admitted, "I do."

Eddie's personality had changed by becoming an airplane magnate. He had learned directness, it appeared, and also grasped the idea of negotiating skills.

"It will cost you a dollar," he informed me.

"A dollar?"

"Yes. I don't like you. And you don't like me. So it will cost you a dollar."

There it was. Right out there on the table.

Directness.

I decided on the spot that it would be worth the additional investment not to have to put myself through the process of believing that I had to actually like Eddie, at least a little bit, in order to get my airplane. I also remembered the sign in Margie's cafe, the one that said: "We reserve the right to refuse service to anybody!" Eddie could, if he wanted to, refuse to sell me an airplane at any price.

"Okay," I asked. "When can I have it?"

"You have to pay first," Eddie said. "And then it will be about a week."

He acted like the president of Lockheed Aircraft, for crying out loud.

I told him I'd get the money.

But it took me several days to raise it. I rode my bicycle out to Eddie's house to deliver the cash. Eddie had built himself an airplane factory in the garage. He had a wing department and a fuselage department and a propeller department. Kids in Gold Beach had heard about Eddie's airplanes. Kids in Langlois were waiting to have their orders filled. I hung around and helped with some of the rough carving. Eddie's mom served some home-canned peaches that I have never forgotten. From that day forward I have never had any peaches better than those.

Eddie and I worked side by side and laughed. He delivered my airplane on schedule. It was a great airplane. But Eddie and I never became friends ever again. And that was that.

The Baker Effect is actually a "Rule" which says that you don't have to love people in order to get something you want from them.

But you knew that.

Just as you know that you don't have to invoke evil spirits to get what you want.

Final Thoughts of Fears

Fears?

A review.

Tonsils. That was the fright of my life up to 1943. Worse than the Japanese attcking Attu and Kiska.

Acting was second.

I remember two things about being in my first play, which was staged at the high school gym on the hill near the administration building.

First of all, when I complained about being scared my mother called me a Stoopnagle.

"Don't be a Stoopnagle," she would say when there were other people around and she didn't want to come right out and call me Stupid. I remember that very clearly as not being useful advice for one who had severe stage fright.

The second thing I remember was sitting in the woodshed on a chunk of wood turned on end looking at a new moon over the roof of the store and thinking:

"Don't ever let them talk you into something like this again. It is too frightening to think of being there in front of all those millions of people in the gym. Promise to never, never do this again!"

I got through the experience, however.

Being on a stage and showing off has a triple narcotic effect. First is the fear and then the realization of power and finally the satisfaction of applause when things go well. I became addicted to the drug, frightening as it was.

I would keep asking myself this on subsequent occasions: "Why are you doing this? Don't you remember the woodshed and the promise? What's the matter with you? Are you crazy? I know what it is! You actually are a Stoopnagle, aren't you?"

So I beat the acting fear.

I couldn't beat the nightmares.

I was respectful of the big waves on Agate Beach and of the power of their undertow sufficient to take a dead body to the Hawaiian Islands.

I was afraid of extremely high winds. But so was everybody else I talked to about it.

I was frightened at first, of the dead things that would be found on the beach from time to time. Fish, no matter what their size, weren't as astonishing as a dead sea lion. Sea lions had fur and human-looking eyes.

Their death was much larger than a fish's death.

I never quite shook my fright at finding a dead thing in the woods. Animals were supposed to run in the woods. They would run away and you would only see their hind ends. So it was a bad moment to stumble upon a dead deer in the woods. They were ordinarily so animate. I touched one such deer in a clearing one afternoon and my fright deepened because it was warm to the touch. It was probably the sun, now that I think about it. But I had the idea that it had just died and I had just missed its dying and I was glad that I hadn't been there for the creature's last breath and its eyes locked onto mine the way my eyes had appealed to the anesthetist when I was being held on the operating table at the Bandon hospital when I was absolutely certain that I was dying only I wasn't.

Being caught in a really terrible lie was bad. Bones were bad. Skeletons were worse.

I saw the blackened skeleton of what they said was a bear that got killed and burned in a forest fire. All things considered, it's a memory that I'd like to have skipped. Perk, when he was still called Perk, threw a dead snake into a fire we'd built and we went swimming and came back and its coiled bones were lying in the white ashes. Matt advised his brother to never do that again. It scared Matt as much as the deer had scared me. He didn't know that snakes are made with so many perfect bones. The McCormicks were Catholic and Matt looked up at the sky. After studying the bones and clenching his teeth Matt looked up toward God and probably asked forgiveness for his little brother.

Children were once sincerely sorry for some of the things they did. But that was a long time ago. Back when people feared death and only wished to die after they had grown terribly wrinkled and very, very old. Mrs. Leneive had once announced that she wished she could live forever but she succumbed. Death rode out of hiding in China or from behind the moon and carried her away.

Asthma rode in when I was 10. Although big in its implications, it is small and concise in memory, since every late-night attack was exactly the same. These attacks came at random and were sometimes weeks apart but in them I could not lie down and had to brace myself up on one elbow to be able to breathe. I would scrunch that way in the dark for two or three hours at a stretch, fearful that I would run out of air, wheezing and fighting for breath. I was given a prescription for some kind of pills but they didn't do anything. The attacks would have to run their course. They were the worst part of my life but were forgotten during the daylight. Thinking about the attacks was totally postponed until the reality of the next one at which time 100 percent of my attention was focused on it. Just moving air in; moving air in. It was as if nothing was exhaled because every breath had to be captured and nurtured and prolonged. They gave me a clock with a luminous dial so that I could log the minutes and chart the course.

These brushes with what I thought was death were darkly interesting and I learned something about concentration from them. It was nothing I could apply at the time. I would have to wait to use it much later in a ditch, again eyeball to eyeball with God in the dark, facing cowardice and trying to pull myself forward one inch at a time.

And I think I must have had the secret fear that I would never, in my whole life, ever hear my mother or father say they loved me. They never said they loved anybody, particularly one another. They never used the word out loud except when complimenting a picture in a magazine or, as in my father's particular case, to talk about corn bread.

My mother loved the color chartreuse for quite a long time. My father said he loved porterhouse steaks well done. My mother said she loved Chinese food, particularly from Hung Far Low's in Portland. (Honest to God, that was the name of the restaurant.) My mother's potato salad, according to my father, was the best to be found anywhere and he loved it and was crazy about it.

My mother would have loved to have owned a mink coat. She would have loved to have gone someplace fancy in a limousine. My father loved smoking Camels and my mother loved to look at wallpaper samples for a grand room in a grand house which she was never going to have except in her imagination.

Tombolos

That's the word I used earlier. Tombolo.

This is a magic word. It sounds like one, doesn't it?

A tombolo is a sand or gravel bar that connects one island to another, or to the mainland. So this story, too, is about connections.

The Jesus Place was a tombolo out to a rock. The roadway out to Mont St. Michel in Normandy probably started out as a natural tombolo.

I am fond of figurative tomobolos, such as the one that connects me back to Port Orford. Also, I've used make-believe tombolos to try to connect people to the truth. I have tried to bridge people to one another. And I sometimes attempt to link people to new islands of knowledge and experience beyond their ability to even imagine.

In retrospect, I should have spent my time understanding the bridges rather than the subjects bridged. I see now that I am more interested in relationships than knowledge. Ever since I was a little kid I don't think I've been smart enough to deal with real knowledge, but I can appear very smart because of my ability to see tombolo interconnections and make accurate predictions based upon more data or more possibilities than other people bothered to consider.

This is Tichenor-like Faking It. Or is it Skippythink? I don't know.

The other thing I've learned is that some tombolos wash away and disappear forever. I have waited, in some cases, like a cargo-cult native anticipating the impossible.

Other tombolos, like the roadway to Mont St. Michel, merely disappear at high tide. They're not gone forever. They come back at low tide and you can use them again. All you have to do is wait. The Jesus Place returns.

The picture at the front of this book shows me and my father on a tiny island in the Pacific. When the tide was in (and it was coming in in this picture) it was an island. When the tide was out, it was merely a rock on the sandy beach. There was never a tombolo. It was an island or it wasn't. It had water around it or it didn't. It was not two things at the same time.

This book is a tombolo from you to my island. A bridge that extends from me to you and then to the coastal town.

Be nimble, it urges you; be warned of the sneaker waves.

Be kissed.

Epilogue— Burial

I'm not a Tichenor. (Well, I'm only half a Tichenor.) I've got the nose, and I hurry up a lot, and there's no question that I've done a lot of Fool's-Hill things, but I've tried now and then to slow down and not let life pass by in a flash; to hang onto pieces of it and look at them in wonder; to pause by the sea; to smell an occasional blossom on a tree; to wonder how brightly colored tropical fish evolved; to hanker again for an electric train with lights in all the passenger cars; to stare at foreign money; the usual stuff.

I don't think I care much about the Tichenor Cemetery. I do and I don't. I feel like an outsider until I stop to realize that I am related to everybody there. Everybody. As a son, grandson, stepson, great-great-nephew, and so forth. Oh, what the hell, maybe I'd just have my ashes scattered in the general neighborhood; maybe just off the end of the cliff where I found the shells, where the smoke went up, where Fletcher leapt and the sun went down and where I would fly to elude my enemies.

But here's an idea. I could bury a piece of a chrome bumper and leave just a tiny patch showing. No. That wouldn't be very dignified. Tichenor spirits might be annoyed.

How about this, though? Maybe a teaspoon of stove ashes or a toenail could be put in a Baggy and buried over in the corner of the Tichenor Cemetery, marked with a small stone with a brass plaque that has been antiqued and made green to look ancient. It would say the one word:

Chief.

Then people who never knew about any of this would come upon it in the high grass and say.

"Hmmm. This must have been one of these people's dogs or cats. Maybe a parrot, even, what with that guy being a Sea Captain and everything."

They'll crowd around for a look.

At some point in the proceedings, visitors to the cemetery (maybe Californians) will say:

"Hey! I just felt something on my head. Maybe it's starting to sprinkle!"

Probably.

But I hope it's a seagull—maybe a lineal descendant of the one that nailed my old man.

But burial? I don't think so. I am buried here. This book is my plot. I am only figuratively at the edge of the Tichenor Cemetery in the corner out of everybody's way. Or right next to the holly tree out of the rain. Or symbolically in a fresh mound of black earth thrown up by a mole between my grandfather's and my mother's markers.

I am entombed in this book and will sit here in the dark until somebody opens the covers and then I'll spring back to life in my yellow Keds. The daylight or the lamplight will make the forests green again and the sea glisten and the foghorn sound. Frenchie's Dooz-Yem will backfire and I'll run down the street like the wind.

Finito

I got the word we were moving inland to Grants Pass when summer came. It was as if the world was about to disappear. I would be going to a different school in a different place. I would never have friends ever again. I would probably stop breathing if we moved.

That was on the one hand. On the other hand, I knew I had the experience of seeing the Washington Monument and the Statue of Liberty and had barfed in a fashionable Madison Avenue jewelry store. I had been to distant places. I had been past Davenport, Iowa. Way past it. I had been marooned at Cape May Courthouse. I could make it. I was kind of a Viking who had been to a new world and survived.

Our family left suddenly in the middle of the war, midsummer 1943. My memories are perfect up to that moment. Then they ended abruptly as if I'd passed away in my sleep.

I wasn't around when the town grew smaller and people died or changed into other people. I was like Barnie Winslow: I left in mid-sentence, mid-stroke. It was disruptive, our leaving. Like exiting the theater before the end of the movie. We didn't stick around for the finish.

But, precisely because of that abruptness, Crawford's voice will always boom from the dock. Lou will always drink whiskey and swear with the mechanics. Old Lady Betts will remain just as pleasant and knowledgeable as always. Gene White's pickup will rattle on and on across the decades, and the women at Red's will be ageless sleeping princesses waiting to be awakened by the right kiss.

Turd will be brave. Laureen will sleep smiling. Moran and Dr. Baird will understand.

My Shirley Temple mug will be pristine in the lost tree limb.

Margie's will be there with its rows of stools to spin on and chocolate cream pies and blackberry pies served a la mode. Cliff will be out back preparing a French dish that nobody in Curry County had ever heard of but was thrilled to try.

Thanks to this book, I can continue to live in Port Orford during the 30s and 40s. All things considered, I'd call it my real home in the sense Moran meant, because even with a sermonizing dad and an iceberg mom and all the other stuff, it's still where things are easy for me, where things are right.

THE END